CLASS OF 92

OUT OF OUR LEAGUE

Our journey back to the heart of the game

CLASS OF 92

OUT OF OUR LEAGUE

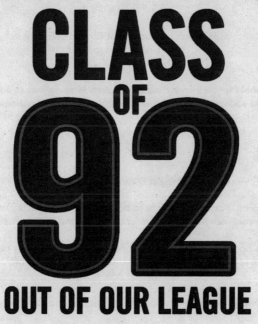

NICKY **BUTT**   PHIL **NEVILLE**   GARY **NEVILLE**   RYAN **GIGGS**   PAUL **SCHOLES**

with Rob Draper

BBC
BOOKS

3 5 7 9 10 8 6 4 2

BBC Books, an imprint of Ebury Publishing
20 Vauxhall Bridge Road,
London SW1V 2SA

BBC Books is part of the Penguin Random House group of companies
whose addresses can be found at global.penguinrandomhouse.com

 Penguin
Random House
UK

This book is published to accompany the television series entitled
Class of 92 first broadcast on BBC One in 2015. Class of 92 is an
Electric Ray production.

Executive producers: Meredith Chambers and Karl Warner

First published by BBC Books in 2016

www.penguin.co.uk

A CIP catalogue record for this book is available from the British Library

I found my love, by the gasworks' croft
Dreamed a dream, by the old canal
Kissed my girl, by the factory wall
Dirty Old Town, Dirty Old Town

'Dirty Old Town', Ewan MacColl

CONTENTS

PART 1

Gary:

It all came together on a train coming back from London. Ryan and I were talking about what we wanted to do after retirement. Ryan was still playing at the time in his last season. I'd been doing my media work for two years. We wanted to be involved with football but at times we despaired about the short-term nature of coaching or managing. We want to give something back to young people but, in my view, there's no point having a football academy if the kids haven't got anywhere to go when they're 16.

So it was during that conversation that we came up with the idea of buying a football club. It seemed outlandish but we were already involved in our hotel businesses with Peter Lim, so we could raise the finance. We started talking about Football League clubs and then wondered whether it might be better to start in the non-league and see if we could work our way into the Football League through the pyramid. Obviously we didn't know much about non-league football at that stage and I don't think we had appreciated quite how hard that would be.

Because of Ryan's connections in Salford he could quickly get us in contact with people at Salford City, and everything that has happened in the last two years at the club really started from that conversation we had on the Virgin Pendolino from Euston.

There have of course been some difficult periods and stressful moments. But I can honestly say that, other than time spent with my family, it's when I'm at Salford's ground, Moor Lane, leaning against the terrace bar at the far side of the ground watching the team, that I feel happiest and most complete. Apart from the fact there is an excitement about where we might be able to take the club, it is that feeling of re-connecting with football in its purest form.

In fact, the only time I ever felt, 'Why did we buy a football club?' was just before the contracts had been signed. It was March 2014 and Salford had a home game against Curzon Ashton. It was one of those lovely, sunny, spring afternoons. I was still full of optimism and energy at that stage and Ryan, Nicky, Paul and myself all went down to Moor Lane.

We had produced a document. I suppose you could call it almost like a project plan really, or a business plan. We all read the document, we all bought into it, we all invested the money into it and then went to watch the game.

And suddenly you realised that the reality didn't quite match up to the document! It was a million miles away to be honest. Everyone just kept saying to us, 'Do you realise just how difficult non-league football is?' We were like: 'Yeah, we know how difficult football is. It's tough, whether you're the owner, the manager, the players or anything.' But we didn't know.

That day I was stood behind the far goal with the lads, thinking, 'Shit! Lads, I'm not quite sure what we've got into here.' Salford got beat 2-0. They were obviously a bad team as they hadn't had a significant budget up to that point. They were still 12th in the league and Curzon were very good.

I remember thinking, 'Is this going to work? Are we really going to turn this club into something bigger?' There were 174 people there, though it felt like less. It was Moor Lane in its rawest form. You could hear a pin drop. You could hear every voice from everywhere and you're thinking, 'How are we going to get to the Football League? This is nowhere near.'

That was the only moment that I can remember thinking, 'Is this the right thing?' Once we'd got it and we started going down and we found our hill where we stand and we started to build a camaraderie with the people around us and the crowd started to grow and the team started to win and the players started to get more excited and the crowds went up to 200, 300, then you think, 'Oh, it's more people here now and it's more enjoyable.' Now attendance is up to 700 or 800 and we get 2,000 for certain games, and you're thinking, 'Right. Now you can see the potential of Salford.'

And that's what has always driven us. We wanted to be part of something for the long term. We wanted to be in charge, so that no owner or chief executive could say, 'That's you done, you're sacked.' And we wanted it to inspire and excite people, the community around us. But we also had an ambition of making the Football League, and we wanted to get there as quickly as possible. We planned to get there in eight to ten years, which was aggressive, to be honest. But that's what other clubs which have made similar journeys have achieved.

There is still plenty of work to be done. We're still a long way from the Football League. Just as importantly, we haven't yet set up our academy, but hope to do so in the next few years. Providing opportunities to young people, especially in the city of Salford, is a big part of why we've done this. When we bought the club, the initial idea came out of setting up an academy. I suppose, two years in, there is a regret that we've been so completely embroiled in first-team activity. That said, there is substantial work going on behind the scenes.

But despite all that, we have had what you might call an eventful and exhilarating couple of years. Most of the time, it's been enjoyable as well.

Most of the time.

1 MARCH 2016

DARLINGTON 3, SALFORD CITY 2

There is an unhealthy quietness in the dressing room. Heads are down and eyes are averting gazes. Joint team manager Anthony Johnson stands in the centre.

No-one speaks. Another ten, fifteen seconds pass and still silence. Then Johnson starts.

'The second fucking goal. When I do set pieces, where do I put you?'

A defender, Steve Howson, breaks the silence. 'One in front, one behind, one on the edge.'

'There you go. Do you understand a bit of accountability? Second ball, on the edge, the kid's come in and fucking scored . . . The third one. Talk to me about that.'

'It was my man. I thought the ball was gone,' says Evan Gumbs, another defender.

'That's accountability,' Johnson replies. 'My man, my man, my man. That's great. You've got big balls to come in and admit it. Does it change anything? It doesn't change nothing.'

It's been an awful night for Salford City. They are in a scramble to ensure they make the play-offs in the Evo-Stik Northern Premier League. Darlington are not just one of their main rivals; they have somehow become the most despised of opponents in the past two years since the two teams came up from the Evo-Stik First Division North together.

Johnson is hated here. He has been verbally abused by a teenage Darlington fan for large sections of the game and at the end another fan offered to fight him; he had to be pulled away. Just two weeks ago they played Darlington at home and were 3-1 up after 62 minutes; they lost 4-3. Tonight seemed better. Despite falling behind, they went 2-1 up after 83 minutes but they lost 3-2.

'I've said it before – and this isn't about belittling anybody by the way – and I mean this: have some fucking balls about you. Do you understand why I say you're mentally weak now? Has the penny dropped or not? Or do you still not agree with me? Come at me.'

'Agree,' says Howson.

'You agree that we're not strong enough? Anyone else or is it just Howson?'

Another voice from the far side of the dressing room appears to agree with a simple 'Yeah'.

'Webs?'

Johnson looks to Danny Webber, his most experienced player, ex-Manchester United with a full professional career behind him, a figure with status in this environment.

'As a collective, yeah,' he agrees.

'Not mentally strong enough. To get yourself back into the game like you did...Listen, second half we were dog shit. We didn't play as well as we did in the first half. But you grabbed yourself back into a game of football.

'They score the second goal and there's one thing that is going to happen. I turned to Bern,' he explains, referring to his co-manager Bernard Morley, 'and I said: "Bern. It's going to happen again." Not because of individual people holding their hands up. But because of the unit. The fucking unit. You ain't strong enough. You ain't strong enough to take instructions, you ain't strong enough to apply the instructions. You run around at times, boys, like fucking headless chickens.'

He turns to Howson again whom he will exonerate. 'Howson, you've had a worldy of a game by the way. You take some shit.'

Now he turns to the other central defender, Andy Dawson, who has come off with 14 minutes left due to a bruising injury.

'Daws. When you come off we fall to pieces. All fair enough, isn't it? Not because we've had to put Lynchey in there,' he says, referring to captain Chris Lynch. 'Fucking great game at right-back. Hally' – he looks at Steve O'Halloran – 'great game at left-back. You know what?', he continues turning his attention to goalkeeper Jay Lynch; 'Lynchey has made a couple of great punches, great saves. Defensively I can't ask for any more. I cannot ask for you to give me any more. But the rest of you boys ...'

The defence is being exonerated, so others feel threatened. Gary Stopforth, the midfielder, interjects, tentatively at first. 'We conceded three goals...' he points out.

Johnson is properly shouting now. 'You fucking have to defend, Gaz!'

'I know but we all defend...'

'Second balls!' shouts Johnson, still louder.

'...we defend as a team,' continues Gaz.

'It's a team thing...' agrees Johnson.

'Yeah but...' tries Gaz.

'Shut the fuck up!' he screams. 'If it's down to him, if it's down to him' – Johnson is pointing at Howson now, shouting even louder still – 'I come at him. If it's him, he takes the shit. It is a team thing. What I'm addressing here is that we've conceded three goals.

'They're the best side I've ever seen at pumping the ball and then recycling it. And I hate words like that. But picking the ball up and doing it again; setting it up, picking the ball up and doing it again. They're the best team I've seen at it. They're excellent at it. Whether you like it or not, they're good at it.

'But as a defensive unit, as a back fucking four' – Johnson is thumping his fist into the palm of his other hand now – 'we win every first ball. And the majority of second, to a point. But you switch off. All over, you switch off. Time and time again. They don't. We huffed and puffed. They don't fucking switch

10

off. Every time they got a free-kick deep in their own half, how many bodies did they send up? Nearly everyone, yeah?

'At 2-2 they were going for the win, weren't they? They got back in the game and got back for the win. When the ball came out and we cleared it on the first or second balls, it's come back on us, because we didn't get under the ball.

'It's happening too fucking often, boys, to keep wiping the slate clean and saying, "Let's go again. Let's go again. Let's go again."

'I'm not saying this because they've come from behind, but it's the same as two weeks ago when I've gone, "What has just happened?"

'And the only thing I'll say, and I ain't putting blame, it's when the subs come off, we fell to pieces. That can be my only explanation. I might be wrong. That's not because of the subs that went on. But because of the subs that came off, we fell to pieces. It's the only explanation, boys. It can be my only explanation to it.'

Johnson is now addressing the players who came on during the game. 'Are you given enough extra instructions when you go on? Are you given enough instructions by the players when you go on? "Go there, do this." You're not. You're fucking not. We do it. We do our bit,' he says, referring to himself and Morley.

'We can't keep coming in and saying, "Right. We'll put it right next time." Honest, boys. Once is fucking criminal. Not against these in general. To be winning 3-1 and to get beat in the last few minutes again and then to do it the second time,

11

the spotlight is now on me and him. And rightly so by the way. I take that. I've told you before I'll take that.

'Because I'll go out of here' – and here Johnson points to his loyal members of staff, coaches Glenn Moses and Craig Dootson, physio Val McCarthy and kit man Paul Rushton – 'and he'll blow smoke up my arse, and *he'll* blow smoke up my arse and *he'll* blow smoke up my arse and say: "Well, there's only so much you can do."

'It doesn't matter. That's our job. To make sure you lot apply what we train you and ask you to do. That's our job. The owners won't keep saying: "Unlucky, it's the lads. Unlucky." They won't. Once or twice, it's the lads. Three, four, five times it's fucking me and him.

'And they are right. Because we're trusting individuals and a team and it isn't working. I ain't questioning anybody's desire, your work rate or heart. I'm not questioning any of that, I'm not. I can see you're gutted. I can see people are hurting. And we've got two hours now on a coach together and it's going to be fucking awful. But this is me. I think that's come to an end now. Enough chances have been given. By the football club to us and down the ladder from us to you. Simple as. That simple.

'There's no question of what people are doing or not motivating or anything like that. It's not good enough. It's just not good enough. That is the bottom line of things. The fucking bottom line.

'I've told you before. People want to see you fail. Not you personally, not you personally, not you. But that badge you

12

wear, because of who the owners are. They want to see you fail. They want to beat you so fucking bad. And you haven't got the mental capacity, the mental strength, or the balls to stand up against it.'

No-one talks. It's another long, deeply uncomfortable silence.

'That's it. It's a long drive home. Let's get ready. I'm not going to stand here all night talking, boys. Unless you've got something to say yourselves. But I think I've covered it.'

***

It's just after midnight at Tebay Services, high on Shap Fell on the edge of the Lake District, and most of the team are unimpressed by the lack of fast-food outlets. 'This is when football is the worst,' says Gareth Seddon, the striker, who has only played 20 minutes at Darlington, coming on as a sub. He couldn't make a meaningful impression on the game.

Tebay Services is famous for its home-made, organic farm produce. Two ducks waddle across the entrance to the foyer. It's a proper working farm as well as a service station, though it's not receiving much love from Salford City FC after their last-minute 3-2 defeat at Darlington. There's still 85 miles to home. Salford City's season has been faltering for a while. Winning the title in the Evo-Stik Northern League Premier Division, which was the club's goal at the start of the season, is a long way off. Promotion to the National League North, the next tier of non-league football, is still possible if they can finish in the top five. Teams placed between second and fifth play off in a mini cup competition for one extra promotion place. Promotion is what is expected from the owners of the club, Gary Neville, Ryan Giggs, Phil Neville, Paul Scholes, Nicky Butt and Singaporean businessman Peter Lim.

On top of Shap Fell, the temperature is dropping below freezing as the players make their way across the forecourt to get their food. 'It's times like these you wonder why you're not retired,' says Seddon. It hasn't been a good night. They have only won five of their last 12 games and have lost five. They look as though they will slip out of the play-off places.

The defeat was bad enough. The dressing-room row was as fraught as it has been all season. Then, as the players board the coach, shovelling down slices of post-match lasagne provided by Darlington, there is the unkindest cut of all.

'Have you heard the bad news?' the coach driver, Ian Corrie, says. 'The A1 is shut. We'll have to go back home cross-country.' No-one has the energy to react verbally. An accident has closed the motorway home, so now the coach will snake across the Northumbria Hills to the Lake District and pick up the M6, turning a two-hour journey into a three-hour trek. Most of the players will be starting work before 9am the next day. They won't be home until 2am at the earliest.

On the coach the tap for boiling water isn't working either, so there's not even any tea or coffee to numb the pain. The inside lights are turned off. Outside, there is just the darkness of the Northumbria Hills. The coach is stuck behind an articulated lorry, not daring to pass on the single carriageway. The conversation is limited. The stereo, usually a loud feature of Salford City coach trips, is turned off.

A subdued conversation starts up between a couple of players. It is the standard post-match analysis. 'Why didn't we pick him up? Why didn't we finish that chance?' It's a long way to come to lose 3-2. The card game starts at the back of the coach. The coach crawls through Barnard Castle, a picturesque small town in Durham, delightful on a summer afternoon for tea; less so close to midnight with 157 miles to home. The first quiet laughs are heard from the card game. Kit man Paul Rushton brings up a couple of beers Johnson has ordered.

Tebay Services turns out better than expected. There was no Burger King or KFC but there were home-made beef pies and hummus, and falafel with a tomato-and-garlic-chutney sandwich from the farm shop. Back on the coach, the preconceived consensus that these services were 'shit' has been altered to take account of the quality of the food.

It's possible that any food would have done the trick, yet the change in mood is evident once the team have been fed. The conversations are louder now. It's past midnight but the steak pies seemed to have done the trick. No-one is trying to sleep. Instead most of the team is gathered round the table towards the back of the coach where Johnson, Gareth Seddon, Danny Webber and Jordan Hulme are sitting.

Webber has an online account on a roulette website. Many of the payers are pitching in, putting in money for one spin of the wheel on Webber's smart phone and Seddon is taking down who has bet on which number. The excitement is growing, anticipation heightened and spirits are good.

None of the numbers come up – groans all round and a discussion as to why they didn't just put it all on red. 'I just did what you said!' comes the reply. But everyone is smiling now. The abuse is good natured, no longer aggressive. Something has changed. The team has recovered its sense of identity over a spin of the wheel on a roulette wheel. It will still be 1.37am when the coach pulls up outside Old Trafford, where the players' cars are parked, but not many are sleeping. Instead Richie Allen is holding court with a monologue of his nights out on the back row of the coach and everyone is laughing. Most won't be home until 2.30am. Glenn Moses will get just a few hours sleep because he has a 5am start for work. Howson has texted his boss to say he will be in at 8am. No-one is getting much sleep tonight, but no-one minds as much now.

***

Gary:

I was offered the Valencia job by the club's owner Peter Lim at the end of November 2015. Peter's obviously a very successful global businessman who has backed us in our hotel ventures in Manchester and also become a co-owner of Salford City. He owns 50 per cent of the club. Valencia were going through quite a tough time and they wanted me to give it a go. Phil was already there as a coach, having joined in the summer before, so there was some logic to it. But I also had some family reasons to be here in Manchester. And I pointed out to Peter that I was running projects on his behalf in Manchester and it might prove something of a distraction! But in the end I felt it was an opportunity to which I couldn't say no. There was so much to learn. It was, in theory, only for six months. Who knows what it might develop into? So eventually I decided that I would go for it.

At the time I wasn't worried to be leaving Salford behind. In theory it should make no difference. We're not owners who run the club, day in, day out. I'd be in touch with the chairman Karen Baird and we'd speak regularly. I know people say I'm a control freak but I'm really not. It's the committee that was there when we took the club over, they run it. I only get involved in bigger decision or significant expenditure. We always knew when we bought the club there would be periods when a couple of us might have to step back and the others come to the fore. Because there are five of us, we have that flexibility. When one has a job which ties him down, another will ensure Salford is getting the right amount of attention. Still, football takes you unawares. I didn't expect to be in Valencia. When we first bought the club, Ryan probably didn't expect that he would be locked down for two years as assistant manager of Manchester United; Nicky the same, as United's Head of Academy. We probably never envisaged that Paul would be one of the most active in watching games and that Phil would disappear to Spain. There was a period last year for four months where there was just Scholesy on the ground.

But when I left the team in December they were going well. We had just had an amazing FA Cup game which had energised everyone at the club. And we were holding our own in the league. We knew from talking to people in non-league circles that it is very often the case that when you have a good cup run as a non-league team, your league form suffers. Very few teams manage a cup run and a promotion in the same season, for example. They have a big dip after they go out of the FA Cup, when all the excitement and the cameras have gone. So we were a little wary of that. When we first took over the club and when we first met our managers, Bernard and Anthony, we made it clear that the league was the priority. Cups were a bonus. But our goal was to get up and through the leagues and into the Football League. So the FA Cup run came as something of a pleasant surprise.

But we knew what might be coming. We knew the winter could be tough. And it was hard being in Valencia through January and February of 2016 and watching the defeats come in. We were in touch but, to be honest, I shut down most communication with people in the UK because Valencia required so much of my attention. Phil and I would be sat on the team bus in Spain following Salford games on Twitter. And though I never despaired, you did at times wonder whether we would make the play-offs. Every season the teams that finish between second and fifth go into a mini cup competition to decide who wins the second promotion place. And making those play-offs became our realistic goal for the season.

There was a particularly bad patch, a couple of weeks at the beginning of February. Funnily enough it was the time we had actually started winning some games at Valencia! But Salford played Darlington, who have become our main rivals, at Moor Lane. And despite being 3-1 up with 28 minutes to play, we lost 4-3. I understand the fall-out from that wasn't good in the dressing room. And then we went to Ilkeston, a team we should beat, and lost 2-1. It was then I began hearing that a rift was developing between the players and the managers. There were a couple of wins which seemed to steady things and then we had that match away at Darlington. When we went 2-1 up with seven minutes to play in such a big game, there was a sense that everything was turning around for the better. So to lose 3-2 was especially galling. And you could sense it the morning after.

***

On the morning after the Darlington defeat, Salford City club chairman Karen Baird is having breakfast when the phone call comes. It's Gary Neville, ringing from Valencia. There is an important issue to be discussed. It's not last night's result, however.

'Karen. Have you seen what Jordan's put on Twitter?'

Baird hasn't. It's 7am.

Jordan Hulme is the team's talented winger, 25 years old and outwardly full of confidence. The players have been especially annoyed with a Darlington journalist whom they perceive to be unnecessarily antagonistic. Hulme took the matter in hand, post match, via social media.

On the other end of the line, Gary Neville is continuing in his earnest fashion. 'It's not right, Karen,' he tells her.

After a five-minute conversation, Karen puts the phone down. Hulme is called; the tweet is deleted; an email is sent to the players instructing them on the dos and dont's of social media.

'I do get it,' says Baird later. 'They're representing Salford and everything's a story.' But Baird herself has some history in this department and had to delete her Twitter account earlier in the year. 'Gary told me off loads of times for putting things up. Between the stick I was getting from Darlington fans and Gary, I just thought it would be easier to come off it.'

Later, Baird is reflecting on Gary. 'We do fight. But we get on. I think because we get on we can have a row. He's the most intense person ever but I like him. He's dead passionate about

20

everything that he does. He cares as much about it as us, which is nice. And that's the shame, that he's gone to Valencia now. But I still have him on the phone or text messages all the time. It's funny him not being here. I suppose we did it before without him. Before we were making decisions for ourselves and now it's for him.'

Neville's phone calls tend to come before 7am. Texts can come in at 5.15am, sometimes earlier when he is an hour ahead on Spanish time. The older Neville brother has a need to be in control. His younger brother Phil and his twin sister Tracey were trying to organise their joint birthday party once. Gary didn't rate the restaurant they had chosen and suggested another. 'In the end,' Phil recalls, 'I said to Tracey, "We might as well go to the place he's suggesting. It will just make life easier."' Phil says this with a broad smile on his face. No-one knows Gary better.

'He's a control freak,' says his co-owner and close friend Paul Scholes. 'He's got to be knowing everything what's going on, who's doing this, who's doing that, what can you be doing. Whereas I just like going to watch the club, really.'

Baird, 45, is learning how to deal with Neville. 'But it's hard sometimes,' she says. 'Like trying to sign the players. I think Gary thinks: "We'll get the new players all signed up for next year." But we don't know what division we're going to be in so we can't get the players for next year.

'He'll say to me: "That player you want, which they wanted £20,000 for. He's coming to the end of his contract so we'll get him for £5,000 now." No, Gary. We won't. It's Salford.

21

Everyone wants more money. It's so difficult to do anything. It isn't just the Class of 92. This year is more difficult because of the FA Cup run and everyone has seen how much money we made. When the managers came in they said, "Karen, we could get people to play for us for £70 a week before. Now they want £500. It is mad."'

Baird runs an accountancy business. 'I have 150 staff working here and it's much easier than managing a football club. It is a lot harder and I think Gary is learning that. I'm sure Gary would normally say "Do this" and it would happen. I think I've learnt off them and they've learnt off us.'

She first met Gary Neville on Christmas Eve 2013. Rhodri Giggs, Ryan's brother, used to be manager at Salford City, which meant Giggs, who grew up in Pendlebury, a district of Salford, knew the club president Dave Russell. Giggs approached Russell to tell him that he was interested in investing in the club; Russell told Giggs that he would have to speak to Baird, the new chairman.

'So Gary phoned me and we ended up meeting him on Christmas Eve in George's Restaurant in Salford.

***

Ryan:

In my last season of playing for Manchester United, in 2013–14, Gary and I were having a lot of conversations about football. We were reflecting on the fickleness of the business.

The only ones in football who get to choose whether to stay somewhere for the long term are the owners.

Gary was working for Sky Sports as an analyst, having retired in 2011. But if you're coaching or managing, it is always short term and you're always at the whim of an owner. We had spoken about setting up an academy for young players from the Greater Manchester area to give them some of the opportunities we had had. We had been to London for a business meeting and on the train back, Gary said: 'Look, I don't know how long you're going to go on for, but this idea of doing an academy and doing something for young people in the local area isn't enough. Everyone wants to do that when they've finished playing football. But soccer skills courses are like babysitting services for the rich. Academies don't work unless you've got somewhere for them to go on to.' So as we were talking we came up with the idea of buying or taking over a local football club, but one that's quite low down and growing it from its roots, to give people a chance. And then to set up an academy alongside it for local people and local players.

We wanted something that we could more or less guarantee we would still be doing in 25 years' time. And that's how it started really. Then we got right down to the details and looking at where we could do this? We talked about clubs at a higher level and even League Two, but I mentioned Salford as a possibility, though at that stage we didn't have a clue about it. I knew a couple of the people on the committee at the club and I've known Dave Russell, the president, for years. My brother, Rhodri, had played there and coached there for a bit.

We made a phone call on the train and got to speak to Dave, and we met him at the ground. Dave told us that Karen had taken over as chairman and that's how we ended up meeting her in the restaurant I co-own, George's, on Christmas Eve in 2013. Salford seemed ideal because of the ties the five of us have to the area. Gary and Phil grew up in Bury, Paul in Middleton and Nicky in Gorton, but we had all trained at United's old training ground, The Cliff, in Salford.

***

When Baird met Giggs and Gary Neville, she was still relatively new to her job. She had only taken over a year before in the summer of 2012 when the board had elected her chairman. 'The way the Class of 92 put it originally, I read it that they'd come in and take over and we'd all go,' she recalls. 'And that would be it. And I thought: "Oh. I'm enjoying it now." I'd only been doing it a year or so and I didn't feel ready to give it up. But you have to do what is best for the club. It was a bit of a shock really.'

Baird had only become properly involved in the club 18 months before the meeting with Giggs and Neville. She knew the former chairman, Darren Quick, who drank, like her, at

The Barton Arms in Salford, as did the current president Dave Russell, who was president when Baird took over. The club had fallen behind in their accounts and the pair knew Baird ran an accountancy business. She got them up to date and before she knew it she was the club treasurer. Only then did she realise what she had taken on.

'I was sat there at the committee meeting and there was twenty men sat there in their fifties just talking all over each other, arguing and talking, and I thought: "I must be mad!" In October 2012 I joined and Darren decided in January that he was stepping down at the end of the season, because of his work commitments. All of them at some point asked me if I would do it, I imagine because no one else wanted the responsibility and because I just made decisions and got on with things.

'At one of the meetings I was at, there was an issue over 20 stolen footballs and there was two hours of "What are we going to do?" And I was just like: "Can we just pay for the balls and move on?"'

***

Ryan:

Looking from the outside, Karen probably didn't know what to expect from us. But the last thing we wanted to do was make lots of changes. Having spoken to her and having seen how the club was being run we were pleasantly surprised. The club was actually making money, which was just unbelievable for a non-league football club. So Karen was doing a great job and we could see how passionate she was about the club and how she enjoyed it. It was perfect for us because obviously we were willing to give her more tools and she can use our experience with football. But also we need to use the experience of the committee and managers in non-league football, because we have none.

One of the main things for us was to build trust with the committee. I would imagine, when we're coming in, the thought would have been: 'What are they going do with us? What are they going do to our club?' And we had to say: 'Look, our intention in the first couple of years is that we're just going let it run. We will improve the team budget. We will put some money in. We will try to improve the image of the club and the fan base, just through awareness. But we won't be doing an awful lot.'

The club committee are all volunteers. We don't pay them anything. They're incredible and it's *their* club. They *do* run that club. There are things we have to get used to which are alien to us, for example, the turnover of players. Players will just move for the money, so if someone offers £20 more a game, they go. It's totally understandable when all deals are so short term. We needed to adapt to that. And obviously for us, being a footballer was our main job. We were dedicated to it. Most of these lads, it's not their main form of income. It's just an extra way of earning some money, so it wasn't their priority really. Some lads would book holidays for when we'd got a game or pre-season, or they didn't want to go to training, so we just had to get our head round that.

That said, I think we have adapted quite quickly. We're not stupid and we realised that it can't be like a professional club. Lads are coming straight from work, sometimes they can't make training because of traffic or they've got a job somewhere else and they can't afford to lose those jobs, so you have to just try and adapt as best you can whilst moving the club in the right direction. By no means do we put up with anything we think is unreasonably lax, but also we need to be a bit understanding as well. It's not the Premier League.

Instead of just throwing money at it we've tried to bring little bits of professionalism around the edges. Things like making sure there are good physios always around. Even the kit can make a difference; you feel a million dollars in a good kit. We also have the partnership with the University of Salford media department for filming games so they can be analysed. So we're giving the club a bit of that professional vibe. It's not so much changing everything straightaway; it's about evolving and changing the mentality a little bit so that it becomes: 'Every game we need to win.'

What's important to us is that we improve the team, that we move up the league and we improve the facilities for the fans, for the people who come and watch the games.

It's important that we set up an academy and that we grow our own players. It's important that we try to make the club sustainable, so we have to try and commercialise it in some way. We have to improve the fan base and try and get local people to support Salford. If we can get just over 5 per cent of the population of Salford to come to watch us in the next ten years, that would be around 15,000. That's our aim. Can we get five per cent of Salford to support us? We're not going to beg them, though. Ultimately we believe that if we provide good facilities and exciting football, we keep ticket prices low – it's still £7 and £1 for a junior – they will come and hopefully we'll get good crowds. After the FA Cup ties, the area was buzzing. I had people come up to me who wouldn't know me and they would be talking about Salford; or people who didn't know about football and they were really interested in Salford City and wanted to ask me more.

***

Baird is the only woman on the board of Salford City but she's no feminist. 'Not at all!' she says, apparently offended. 'I'd say I'm probably the opposite. I just get on with it. I don't think: "I'm a woman." It doesn't even cross my mind.

'I think people can make an issue of it, can't they? It's like these meetings for women in business. I'm just like "get on with it".

'When I first started in accountancy, I was the only one in audit in Warrington. I've always been surrounded by men, at work and everything.'

Baird remembers trying to drum up support for the club when she took over as chairman. Attendances would hover around the 100 mark; 150 on a good day. She traipsed around Salford delivering fliers to 3,000 homes. It made no difference. Attendances remained stubbornly low. At Christmas, once promotion was ruled out, the club tended to let the best players go, because they couldn't afford them. 'It's just a circle of surviving and the committee were getting older. The fact that someone would come in and take all that off you and you've not got the issue of how we are going to pay the wages this week.'

Since the Class of 92 took over, Baird has been their main go–between. 'The Class of 92 haven't come in with their size nines. We're still here doing everything that we did. Everything is the same and people have seen that. They've not come in and ridden roughshod over everything. And there is not one single club which would have turned this deal away.' The most controversial change they made for their first season, 2014–15, was to change the shirt colours from traditional tangerine to red, as they played in at Manchester United. But Baird insists most fans ultimately were able to rationalise the switch.

'What if I had said to the fans: "There are some investors who have come in and they wanted to change the colour but we turned them away and they've gone and set up with Trafford down the road, are you happy with that?" You can't have it all ways, can you?'

The club has changed, though. They never had a social media policy for the players before the takeover.

***

Phil:

We were in such a strong position early on in the 2015–2016 season, and then we went through a sticky patch. You're constantly looking at the table, figuring out, 'Right, can we make it, can we go up? Are we now just settling in the play-offs?' It was definitely a nervous time. There were some tough times. I don't know if it was the knock-on from the FA Cup, but there were a few games where we were in the lead and ended up losing. If you're on the other side of that, when you keep losing games when you've got to win them, it's hard. When you're winning, you always believe that you will, and it's not a nice feeling when it's the other way round. When you're 2-1 up, at the back of your mind you're thinking, they scored, they might score again, and your confidence can be really fragile. When you get bad results you do doubt yourself, as a manager, as a coach. But you just have to work hard to get through those sticky moments.

You have to recognise when you're not doing well and what you're going to do about it, not only the managers but the owners as well. That's when they need our support. You have to trust the managers, like the managers trust the players. It's not easy, especially when you've had a bad run of games. You want to do something but sometimes the answer is not to do anything at all and just let them get on with it. You hire managers because they can do the job, and you have to trust them. You can help them but more often than not you can't do a lot. You just hope they'll get the results, and things will turn around.

8 MARCH 2016

SALFORD CITY 2, WORKINGTON 2
HALF-TIME

'We've got to learn from it.'

This should have been easy. Salford were 2-0 up after 13 minutes and looking comfortable against Workington, another rival for the play-off places. But they've contrived to come in at half-time 2-2. Captain Chris Lynch has just burst through the door into the Portakabin. The rest of the team are quiet, a little ashamed possibly, and settle down in their seats in the makeshift dressing room.

'Apologies for the second goal,' comes a voice.

'Two goals again!' says Lynch, to no-one in particular.

No-one else speaks.

Bernard Morley stands at the entrance to the dressing room.

'Everybody alright, yeah?' he says.

Then he starts.

'Tuesday night games, boys, playing against your Workingtons, against your Darlingtons, and you go 2-0 up after 15 minutes, the game plan off to a T. Off to a T. They didn't look like they wanted to be here, did they? Change of formation, and they kill us. It's down to individual errors. It's alright pointing the finger at him' – he is looking at left-back Steve O'Halloran – 'for giving a stupid fucking foul away, but we still should defend that.'

Now he turns to midfielder Luke Clark. 'It's alright for him going and getting caught on the half-turn in his own box and giving the ball away. We still should deal with that.'

The volume is rising now.

'Do you know what, it's a fucking circus! People have a go at us and they score. I don't feel sorry for you, I don't. We scored two shitty goals, didn't we? They'll be sat in there saying: "Two shit goals they scored." It were. Doesn't matter how you score 'em. They were shitty but they weren't errors.

'He's right,' he says, referring to Chris Lynch's exasperation as he came in, 'We don't learn. We don't fucking learn. And it's all over the pitch, by the way, it's not just defensively. It's all over the pitch.'

He turns to forward Jordan Hulme. 'Jordan: five, ten times you've had grass in front of you. But you're just not on the same wavelength that you were Saturday. It's one good game and one bad game.'

He now speaks to John Johnston, the winger. 'JJ. You were the star on Saturday. We wanted to give you the ball every time. Tonight you're sulking. You're sulking. People are giving you information and you're going, "Fuck it". What's up with you? If you don't agree with it, leave it until half-time, we'll address it. If we hear someone passing you information that isn't right, we'll fuck them. Not you. But the information is right what we're giving you.'

'But you told me where to stand ...' starts Johnson.

'Not on that occasion! Not on that occasion where Gaz passed you information. You didn't take it on board. Stop nit picking!

'And it is shit. Because our concentration levels slip again. They're not a good side, are they? They're not a great side. It's not like: "Fuck me, second against third, the passing's great." Four shit goals. Four goals and he's banging his head against the fucking wall and so I am because you're thinking: "2-0 up. If we can just replicate what we did Saturday we're laughing here." We just don't learn. We just don't fucking learn.'

He stops. No-one speaks so Morley starts again.

'Forget the two goals. I'm watching what we're doing off the ball. One or two just do things and think: "Right. Jonno's said I've done well or Bernard texted me at home and said 'Well done'." And it's as if you think, "Fuck that. I'm going to go and fuck it up." That's what we think. Because what I watch out there, it's like: "Wow, has he really just done that?"

'Clarky, that's not acceptable but that's him.' He's referring to Clark losing the ball on the edge of the area attempting an elaborate turn, which would have looked exquisite had it come off. 'And you know it's not acceptable, that, but then what you do, Luke, you go and do that and then five minutes later you do it again.'

He turns away from Clark to address the team now. 'You have to give him the information and say, "Clukey…"'

He means Clarky but he is talking so quickly in his anger that the names Luke and Clarky have become jumbled. No-one laughs. Morley corrects himself.

'You have to tell him: "Clarky: do that again, mate, and we'll fuck you." He's done it once. Don't go and do it again. I know he doesn't need a bollocking because he knows he's fucked up. But then he goes and does it again. Tell him. That's what's costing us points.

'The second goal. We're diving in. Stick, just mark your fucking man, get your arm across him, but we're not, we're sliding, going to ground. We don't learn. Ten games to go, we don't fucking learn. He said it last week, he'll say it today and he'll say it next week. Just do the basics what we're asking you to do. It's as simple as that. And if you don't win then, we can't turn round and say: "Well, he hasn't done that and he hasn't done that." We got beat by a better side.

'But we're not. We're giving them a head start every week. Every fucking week. Don't make it difficult for yourselves. We're a good side with a good bench. Yeah? Get your fucking heads up.'

Morley leaves the dressing room and walks outside. He's too frustrated to stay. But this isn't over. Anthony Johnson steps up to have his say.

'I get to a point, Lynchey,' he says to Chris Lynch, 'where I understand why you stop talking to them. I understand, me. I do. Whether I accept it or not is a different matter. But when I shouted at you on Saturday to relax. What did you do?'

He's looking at central defender, Steve Howson.

'What did you do on Saturday when I shouted "relax"? Lashed at him. Remember it?'

'SO FUCKING ROLL ON THREE DAYS,' Johnson is screaming now at Howson. 'You're right in front of me tonight and what am I shouting?'

There is a pause. 'Relax?' suggests Howson.

'No, no I didn't,' says Johnson. There is confusion. Howson is unsure to what he is referring.

'I said, "Stay on your feet!" Did I say that? You: dive in, and he rolls you. Running back to your own goal and I shout the same thing again: "Steven. Stay on your feet! Stay on your feet!" He's running towards the corner flag. "Stay on your feet." What do you do? Because you don't listen. So come at me with it, whatever the fuck you want, pal, you don't listen.'

He hasn't finished on Howson. 'Never going to tell you "Well played" ever again. Never. Got absolutely bitched off the lad who scored the first header.' Howson looks genuinely hurt.

'Who was stood next to you when that ball crossed the line? There was two players stood there, not marking him?'

'Me,' says Evan Gumbs.

'What are you doing? WHAT THE FUCK ARE YOU DOING?' Johnson is shouting as loud as he can now. 'ANSWER ME NOW! I'M ASKING YOU A QUESTION!

'I didn't read the seconds.' Gumbs means the second ball, after the initial cross is cleared.

'YOU WEREN'T MARKING. Because you do this.' Johnson mimics a player watching the ball, eyes in the sky, a basic defending error. 'You watch the fucking ball because you're gormless. The kid wins the first header, so he's out of the game, he's gone with it as well. The kid's just stood still watching gormless twats.

'You don't learn. You think: "Ah well, Jonno said 'Well played, back four' last Tuesday when we got beat and he had an argument with Gaz. And he rang on Monday, whenever it was, and said 'Well played.'" And you all switch off because you think you're better than you are.

'It's alright. I can put up with a lot of shit. Not that. Mark a set piece. Two-nil up. And you think, "Ah, it doesn't matter. Not going to go in to challenge, even though he scored I don't know how many goals last few games; let him win the header." It's alright Bern saying, "They're shit, them." Do you want to know what they're saying about us? We're fucking crap.'

Outside you can hear the faint sound of 'Heaven Knows I'm Miserable Now' by The Smiths playing on the tannoy for half-time entertainment.

'We're all waiting for him to throw a ball in the net.' He's talking about the team's reliance on striker James Poole to score wonder goals. 'Do you know how fucking embarrassing that is?'

Johnson moves on to the second goal they conceded, from their own throw-in, something which should never really happen to a well-coached team.

'When the fuck have we taken a throw-in 30 yards from goal and given it in-field. Ever. Tell me when. Because if we have, tell me: "Jonno, we do it all the time." Do we or not?'

A few mumble the requisite answer in the negative.

Johnson turns to Gary Stopforth. 'And you're fucking encouraging him!'

Stopforth objects: 'When?'

'On that goal, I heard you say to him, "Good lad". So don't say you didn't. Because I turned to Bern and said, "Shut the fuck up!"'

Another player interjects on behalf of Stopforth. 'He said, "It's gone. Good lad."' It turns out Stopforth had meant to encourage the player, O'Halloran, who had taken the inadvisable throw-in, rather than criticise the mistake.

Johnson pulls back. 'Okay, okay. But after it's happened did you say, "Don't ever do that again?" Did you say that again?'

'No, because . . .' starts Stopforth.

Johnson interrupts. 'Because afterwards he took another throw-in the bottom end and we did the exact same thing.'

Stopforth comes back: 'I told the full-backs not to throw it in.'

Johnson climbs down. 'Did you? I apologise. If you've said to your full-back. Sorry, Gary. Soz, Gaz. You're right if you have. But my fucking point is no one listens.

'You have all just nodded your head and said: "Yeah, he said that." Nobody listens. You don't listen to me. No-one listens to him. No-one listens to him. So what is the fucking point! That's where we're at. Get out of jail cards. Third place come to town, we're 2-0 up from a fucking throw-in and a corner. Great corner by the way, boys, great corners.'

Johnson is now talking about Salford's goals, but even they are unimpressive, both of them soft ones to concede by Workington. 'No-one's gone up there and beasted it. The keeper's just flapped them in. It's not like anyone has made fuck all apart from a set piece and a throw-in. It's embarrassing. And when I say it's embarrassing, if we're coming in here 2-0 up and we've played shit, I'm buzzing my bollocks off, aren't I? Saying: "Fucking hell, boys, the game plan worked."

'What's embarrassing is how you allow them to do what they've done. They haven't been in the game. Their No. 9 doesn't want to get involved in the game. He stands offside on the keeper's kicks and as the game approaches goes bang and tries to put you off, so half the time you've got no one to mark next to him.

'That's all they want. Second balls drop, they pick them up because they're on the front foot. They're on the front foot, picking second balls up. And even then they're not hurting you. They're just gaining fucking ground. Where we look dangerous

The main stand at Moor Lane, built in the 1920s by the Manchester Rugby Union Club.

The Salford City 2015-16 squad with the owners having dropped in for training (© Gareth Lyons)

The owners at their club.

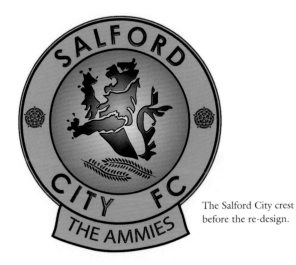

The Salford City crest before the re-design.

The current Salford City FC crest with some young fans.

Paul Scholes joins in training in the first year of ownership, 2014-15 (© Gareth Lyons)

Captain Chris Lynch in the Portakabin dressing room at Moor Lane in 2014-15, with Danny Webber and Gareth Seddon in the background.

Gareth Seddon attends a training session.

Gary Stopforth, a trainee at Blackburn Rovers, and a stalwart for Johnson and Morley.

(© Gareth Lyons)

Bernard Morley and Anthony Johnson take charge of their first Salford game at Bamber Bridge in January, 2015. (© Gareth Lyons)

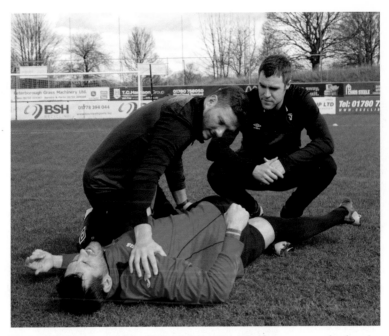

Physios Val McCarthy and Steve Phillips helping Gareth Seddon warm up, who doesn't seem to fully appreciate their efforts. (© Gareth Lyons)

Gary and Phil pose for photos on match day.

Gary Neville, with Paul (above) and Phil (right), in his favourite spot, the terrace barrier in the far corner of Moor Lane. (© Howard Walker)

Paul and Gary share a joke with fans against Spennymoor Town in April 2015. (© Howard Walker)

is, when that happens, we've gone bang into Pooley and got on the half-turn.

'But, Jordan, your passing. I don't know what's up with it, mate? You're sliding balls in between full-back and centre-half when he's stood square to you. Why not just give it him to his feet? Why not? Tell me why you don't give it to his feet? What did you see?'

Hulme starts to argue his case. 'I've seen him set off so I . . .'

'Well he might have set off but he can win the ball when he stood next to you,' Johnson interrupts. 'He's ten yards away.'

'Once he's set off I've got to do that, haven't I?' says Hulme.

'Why?' counters Johnson. 'Just play the ball a yard in front of his run. Yes or no, is that not what you're taught when you're young? Pass in front of somebody. Pass the ball to your fucking mate. Because that's the way we get through. He's fucking killing the left-back, killing him. But we're not picking second balls up on the edge of the box.

'It's a horrendous game of end-to-end shitty football that no one's got control of, on either side. And the times we do try to do something we get punished because the game is condensed within 15 yards of fucking space.

'There seems to be an issue with passing to people tonight. Just give it to your fucking pal. If you give it him and he can't be arsed to move, like you said, Jords, and he gets bogged down, then we'll fuck him and say, "Why didn't you make your run?" But we're statues.

'Get the ball into Josh, into the spaces in front of him. Let's get the ball out fucking wide. Isolate them. Pick up second balls.'

He turns to his central midfielders, Clark and Stopforth. 'Clarky, Gaz. Can you play forwards on the front foot, into the forwards' feet, so you can get it back and then go out wide? Stay switched on. Don't look into space when I'm talking – be like that in the game and we'll get punished. Yeah? Come on, boys. Come on, boys. Fucking raise it!'

***

The second half has gone better. Danny Webber comes on. Chris Lynch completes a hat-trick as Workington hopelessly fail to deal with a long throw.

Johnson relaxes a little, stood a few yards away from the bench. But he's worried about the referee. 'How can we only be given one foul in sixty minutes?' He needn't worry. Shortly afterwards the referee awards Salford an extremely dubious penalty for an alleged hand ball. Richie Allen converts it. Webber then scores to complete a 5-3 win.

The team troop off to applause. Fans congregate at the fenced-off area by the entrance to the dressing room and Stopforth applauds and thanks them. The players make their way to the dressing room, but goalkeeper Jay Lynch isn't happy.

'Every fucking free-kick, everyone drops into space and I can't come to claim the ball,' he complains. 'I can deal with those if you stay up.'

Howson, a defender who is one of the culprits, objects. 'Come through us!'

'Yeah, but every time you're killing my space!'

'But you can just come through us,' repeats Howson.

'What and flap at it because you're all on my toes!' He's referring to the Workington's goalkeeper's unimpressive performance.

'But you're better than him,' says Howson. 'You can do it coming through a couple of boys.'

It is threatening to damage the post-match atmosphere. Tunji Moses, a sub, has to remind them that they have won the game.

Johnson takes control. 'Spot on, Tunji. That is all it's about. You just beat third in the league, 5-3. That's all it's about. And it is frustrating because the goals we conceded are dogshit. But let's have it right, boys. We had a good goal with Richie and Webs, but we won't score four like that again, as well. So you can look at it both ways, can't you? We have had two massive results there. Massive, in two days. You can't ask for anything more than that. Eight goals against third and fifth. Well done.'

'What about Clukey's performance?' shouts a player.

Johnson dissolves into giggles at this. It was co-manager Morley who jumbled up Luke Clark's name at half-time in his anger and called him 'Clukey'. But the half-time aggression is gone.

'Who called him Clukey?'

'Bern at half-time,' comes the reply.

Stopforth is laughing. Johnson has the giggles. Clark is smiling sheepishly. Morley is shaking his head and laughing. Kit man Paul Rushton has the heartiest laugh, Jordan Hulme the most expressive. Everyone is the dressing room has a broad smile.

'Clukey!' repeats Johnson tittering. 'Clukey!'

***

Nicky:

You always go through bad patches at certain times of the year and we had that bad patch in February 2016. We seemed to be doing OK but then we suddenly started losing and drawing games against teams we would expect to beat. Because of my job with the academy at Manchester United, I can't often be at games. But I always check the results on the phone and obviously there are some teams you expect to beat and you don't check the phone as regularly because you're not as worried. But all of a sudden we were finding that we had lost or drawn those matches, which was coming as something of a shock.

We still had massive confidence in Jonno and Bernard and that they would get there eventually. I think the biggest problem was that the goals dried up. We needed to get the goal scorers going again. We had a few injuries as well which didn't help, but it's the lack of goals which hurts you. It's a killer because if you're not scoring, you've always got a chance of being beat cheaply.

The more impatient members of the ownership committee maybe wanted to go out and buy more players and maybe I was one of those! But you do have to stick with what you know, do right by the lads who got you there and back them up with maybe one or two signings, which is what we did.

Sometimes you can look back at difficult periods in a season and with hindsight it's easy to say you just need to keep calm. But it's not like that at the time. You have all sorts going through your mind as an individual, as owners and as a committee. You think you want to change it somehow and the first thing which normally happens in football is that you change the manager. That wasn't an option for us. We knew we had two guys in charge who were passionate and talented. We knew they could get results; we knew they could generate a team spirit which gets you a long way. They had proven that. And if you sacked people every two minutes you don't get that team spirit and you don't get that continuity.

So you then look at bringing in players and if you support the manager, you have to support what they want. We had that conversation and I think Karen spoke to the mangers and told them that they need to start getting results. It is a results business. But we grew up with Sir Alex Ferguson and our core beliefs focus on continuity and patience. And I think that will repay you in the end. The managers sit down with us and the committee at various points in the season and discuss what we need to get to the next step. If we back them, they can do their job.

As a player I've been through many periods where it's just not happening for you. The shout we always had among ourselves at United was: 'Get back to basics.' You get your head down, get your passes in, get your short passes in, don't try anything too spectacular, and you steadily get your confidence back. And when you've got your confidence back, that's when you start to do things off the cuff. The ball-playing midfielders get their passes through to the strikers; the strikers start to finish instinctively; the defenders start to read the opposition balls. Then the game becomes a lot easier and you don't have to think too much. But to get to that point, you start by doing the bog standard things: stick to your team shapes, play your normal game plan. And when it all starts to click, then you can build from that base. If you get your base right, worse-case scenario you get draws; but the best-case scenario is that you get wins and eventually that does start to happen.

But these periods happen at any club at some point in the season. It's different as an owner, of course, because you feel more responsibility. At times you do have that feeling: 'Why have we got into this?' I had a bad moment last season, before Jonno and Bernard came, when we went up to Kendall Town in the autumn of 2014. Scholesy and I went up there to the Lake District to watch. It was a cow-field of a pitch, we lost 6-0, we had two sent off and the referee was terrible. I was thinking: 'You put all this time and effort in, as well as the finance, and you have no control over things like the ref or the pitch.' Of course you have some control over the managers you pick and the players you bring in. But you can feel a bit powerless at times.

At that time we were still getting used to non-league life. In the Premier League you know wherever you play, you're going to play on a decent pitch. It's literally a level playing field, and it can't be an excuse for a bad result. And the referee is a full-time referee and even though we complain about mistakes in the Premier League, the refs are, of course, very professional and very good. But at this level you're relying on guys doing the job part-time, who have been working all week and might be knackered. And clubs haven't got funding to get the pitches perfect so if there's a bad spell of weather, it does affect them. That's just life in non-league football and it can cost you.

Kendall was when I had my worst moment of: 'What are we getting into here?' Because we can't really control much of it. But there was a degree of pride there which keeps you going. If you get involved with something and you commit to something and makes promises, you want to see it through.

***

When they tell you to bring a change of clothes with you to court for sentencing, it means you're probably going to be sent to prison. Bernard Morley is streetwise enough to know that.

So he was prepared for what he assumed was coming. Dressed in a suit to stand in the dock, he had been advised by his barrister to bring a track-suit or something more suitable for a prison van. Morley was mentally adjusting to leaving home, partner Jema and young son Tomas and daughter Halle-Mae. The police had done him a deal. Plead guilty to lesser charges of Section 47 Assault and prison would be unlikely. But now it seemed as though his trust had been misplaced. The charge carries a five-year maximum sentence.

It had started in a bar. It had been a long day's drinking but the atmosphere was convivial enough. Some older men then came into the bar and Morley engaged them in conversation. 'Wow, you're the double of my granddad!' he told one of them. Immediately Morley was aware of spittle in his face.

'Disgusting, isn't it?' recalls Morley.

Morley punched him and the man struck back. Friends on either side immediately weighed in. 'That fight then led to another fight and then we're talking about a 50-, 60-man brawl.' Glasses were smashed and Morley's antagonist was cut in the head. The police did me a deal and said, listen, if you plead to X, Y and Z we'll make sure you don't go to prison.

'And then, purely based on the fact that I was trying to split it up, the judge took my side and said: "As bad as what we've seen..."' His voice trails off. 'It's all on the CCTV so I never instigated it. If I'd have instigated it I'd have gone to prison.'

In his heart, though, he probably knows he is fortunate. The scars over his eyes tell you that this wasn't one a one-off. 'I was a boy. It's just who I was; not that I've ever been a thug. I had to do a lot of community service. I've been electronically tagged. Just being in the wrong place at the wrong time and, I think, sometimes men come at me. I'm not gonna sit here and say I'm an angel because I'm not. I never will be. But boys are boys, aren't they? Up till you're about the age of 27, 28, and then you actually start to think: "Well, this is not good, this." I can honestly say it's never been drug-related. Never. On my kids' lives. I've never touched a drug. But drink is a demon. In this day and age, unfortunately, fighting seems to be the in thing and taking drugs and stabbings. Management in football was what got me out of all that. It really did, because you sort of go down one road or the other. It was either Jema and football or it was prison and being a thug. Jema's been put through the mill a little bit and loyalty can only go so far, can't it?'

Morley and Anthony Johnson have known each other since they were teenage youth trainees at Bury Football Club. Both were ultimately rejected, deemed not good enough for the professional game, but they kept in touch as they worked their way through various non-league clubs. 'We've been in trouble together, years ago when we were on nights out and we have that instinct to protect each other,' said Morley. 'So we've got that, which I'm not saying's the right thing to do. But we've got each other's backs, on and off the pitch. I trust him with my family. I trust him with my kids. I trust him with my wife. And, irrelevant to football, if I ever needed 'owt, I could ring him up and say: "Listen, Jonno, can I lend this off you or can you do this?" And he knows me.'

Morley was an excellent non-league player, a play-making midfielder. Johnson will happily concede that his friend was the better footballer. Morley played for two years in the USA in the league just below Major League Soccer, which is where former England captain Steven Gerrard now plays for LA Galaxy.

When he returned to England he played for Rossendale United in Conference North, two divisions below the professional game, but his career was cut short at Brigg Town in Lincolnshire at the age of 22. 'I'll never forget it. Basically someone just give me a hospital ball...' He means the kind of poor pass from a team-mate that leaves you straining to reach the ball with an opponent closing down on you. 'I should never have gone in for it but, me being me...as I've gone to stretch out with my left leg the opponent has just come in with his foot and he's just hit me there on my standing leg and my knee snapped out. I don't think it was malicious, because he didn't go off the ground or 'owt. It was just non-league: wanting to get a kick at you, that sort of thing.

'It was a double fracture to my right patella and to my tibula and fibula, so it was thought that I'd never play again. But I didn't think that would be it, because obviously my mentality was that I was gonna get right, no matter. I had a bone graft, which my body rejected, so I had to have an operation. The rods that they fitted weren't fitted right, so they had to come out, and then I had to have a knee brace. It took nearly three years, and then I had septic arthritis I and then I got MRSA. I got it really bad so, physically, I was gone. I got back playing but I had to step down a couple of levels because of the injury, which was hard. But then I obviously started playing with Jonno at Clitheroe and I sort of got back to what I was, but not as fit.'

He fell out with the manager at Clitheroe and ended up at Ramsbottom, where he knew the chairman Harry Williams, in the North West Counties league, five levels below the professional game. At the age of 25, he had fallen from the cusp of the professional game to a league well down the football pyramid where most players are on pin money, around £50 a week. But as the best player he found himself the most influential personality in the dressing room. 'I'd played for the chairman, Harry, as a kid so he had begged me to come to play. He said: "We can't pay you what Clitheroe are paying you but we'll meet you halfway. Come and see the season out." Then, as I got there, you just sort of like, not take over the changing room, because I've never been like that. But the respect that you've got in the game, the fans liked me, and what not …

'So I rang Jonno and I said, "Listen make, would you ever contemplate taking over at Rammy as their manager?" And he laughed and said, "Are you serious?" I went: "Yeah, why not? Just think of the players we can get, the lads that we know that are fed up of travelling about. We'll make it work." And he said, "Right, let's go and see Harry then." So we went down straight after work.'

Williams, in his sixties, was busying planting daffodils on the banks behind one of the goals at the ground. He looked suspiciously at Morley and Johnson. 'What are you two mongrels doing here?'

'We want the manager's job!'

Williams started laughing and said: 'Are you stupid? You're 25 years old.' But Morley and Johnson were both fed up with travelling to eke out non-league careers. Ramsbottom is a few miles from Johnson's home, five or six from Radcliffe, the town south-west of Bury where Morley lived. So Morley persisted: 'This will be our own baby, this; this'll be us as managers taking the club through the leagues.'

It didn't seem terribly plausible. Not only did these two young men have a reputation for brawling, Ramsbottom is a club which attracted around 80 spectators for its home games and which had finished 18th in the North West Counties League the year before. The ground is one of the most picturesque in Britain, nestling among the Lancashire hills with the East Lancashire Heritage Railway running behind the far goal. Players taking penalties can be distracted by the tooting of a 1930s steam train. It's pretty but it isn't Old Trafford; or even Moor Lane. Until recently there was only the pavilion and a couple of cowshed-like buildings to protect the handful of supporters from the rain. It is a better level than parks football but it is only just removed from the Sunday morning triers.

'Don't be stupid,' said the chairman and got on with his gardening.

A week later, mulling the idea over, Williams sounded out the Ramsbottom committee. They agreed: it was a stupid idea. But on the last day of Ramsbottom's season, when they lost 6-3, Johnson had come to watch Morley. When Morley came out of the shower and joined him in the bar, Johnson was grinning. The chairman, Williams, said: 'Do you want a beer, boss?'

Morley was confused and looked at Johnson. 'What's he going on about?'

Johnson said: 'He's given us the job.'

Morley and Johnson spent the summer of 2011 excitedly planning. Their confidence was unbounded. They begged friends of friends to play, dragging them down to a level of football well below their abilities. Their weekly budget to spend was £1,000. A top player might get £100 a week; most would get less than £50. But they believed they could win promotion to the Evo Stik League; they dreamt they might one day even reach the far-off Nirvana of the Evo-Stik Northern Premier League.

They lost their first game 5-0 and had to apologise to the fans. But by the end of the season they were fourth, a club record. The next season they won 30 consecutive games and were promoted to the Evo Stik League First Division North, and Johnson and Morley were the North West Counties Managers of the Year. They thrived at the higher level, finishing sixth, just missing out on the play-off positions. A year later they made it to the play-offs. The team top of the league gains automatic promotion to the higher division and the teams finishing second to fifth play each other in a mini cup competition to decide who will win the second promotion spot.

In the 2014 semi-finals, Ramsbottom played Darlington, which had been a fully professional football league club just four years previously but had fallen on hard times. Darlington didn't appreciate the young, upstart managers with loud mouths and aggressive manners. When Ramsbottom beat them 2-0, a mini pitch invasion ensued, with Darlington fans turning on Morley and Johnson. Punches were thrown as the managers were bundled back into the dressing room. The animosity would follow them to Salford. But in the play-off final that year, Ramsbottom beat Bamber Bridge. Morley and Johnson had taken the club from a level just above parks football into the Evo-Stik League Premier Division, just three leagues below the professional game. Crowds had almost trebled from the handful of 80 locals who had previously gathered at the rudimentary ground.

People were beginning to take note of the club with the bizarre combination of two young managers in their early thirties with a penchant for conflict. In the crowd watching that play-off final was Karen Baird, who had made a mental note of whom she would like her next managers to be.

***

Gary:

We didn't actually appoint Bernard and Jonno. It was Karen who introduced them to us and made the decision. I went to meet with them, as did Scholesy and Phil, but the reality is, it wasn't our recommendation. We had never heard of them, we didn't do any due diligence on them. We trusted Karen and the committee to make that decision and to get it right.

They had a reputation before they came. They'd knocked out one of our lads on the touchline in a cup game about four weeks before we actually brought them in as managers. We knew they bordered on aggressive on match days, that they could sort of sometimes flip over the edge. They had a disciplinary record that wasn't great in terms of their teams, but that didn't bother us because I've played a lot of players in my time who lived on the edge, who got sent off, and who trod that fine line between passion and aggression. Modern football fans want more passion, but then when someone misjudges that and goes over the edge, they're a lunatic and they want them banned for ten games of a season or kicking out the club. There's a fine line and I think that I've always understood that fine line and respected it and that's where I am with those two. I think they're on the edge and that, to me, is a good thing.

They created something that I've not seen in a football dressing room. In the early days of United when the six of us broke through, I would say our dressing room was special, up to around 1999–2000. In those days, we'd go out for a drink on Tuesday nights in the Living Room. We'd be singing together, baring our souls to each other. Everyone knew everything about everybody. The spirit they have in the dressing room at Salford, I've not seen in football, other than those few years at United. I see pictures on Twitter and I think: 'Oh my God! What are they doing?' But we stay out of it. It's not our dressing room. It's *their* dressing room and we don't get involved in what they do.

All I see is the end result, which is a team that dies on the pitch for them every single time I watch them play, barring one or two games, in two years. Even now they've added experienced ones to the team, they buy into their method of creating that spirit and camaraderie. And I suppose if you look back to managers in the 1970s, 80s, 90s, there was a lot less about tactics. It was more about team spirit, camaraderie, togetherness, harmony on the pitch, fighting for each other. We have a 70s or 80s culture at Salford of fight, spirit, guts – one that I think every modern manager would like to have back, but it's different now in modern football. They have created something special and I admire them. I envy them, having been a manager myself for four months at Valencia. When I look at the dressing room they've got there and how together they are, I think: 'Bloody Hell!'

Usually the impact of a long FA cup run has devastating consequences. Teams that do well in the cup can't sustain it in the league. We wanted managers to represent Salford, the club, us, and they do because they've worked the absolute maximum. You feel like every defeat kills them. I would love nothing more than for these managers to stay with us and take us through to the Football League. Obviously we inherited a manager in Phil Power when we came here and after seven months we sacked him, as we didn't feel he was the right fit at the time for the club, and we then had this reputation of sacking managers. But we're not people who will sack managers just like that. We just won't. We will stand by them and do the right thing. Obviously sometimes you have to make a change, but our idea would be to stand behind managers. It would be great to see these two managers go up the leagues, but the challenges are obvious.

When we first took over the club, Karen and I spent probably seven or eight days touring clubs who'd made similar journeys. So we'd been to see AFC Wimbledon, Fleetwood, Morecombe, Fylde and FC United. We asked them about everything: facilities, team improvement, coaches. And every single one of them said that they felt that you basically appointed the best manager you could at whatever level you were in, be it in the North West Counties League, the Evo-Stik League or the National League.

And they all felt that managers tend to have two good years and then a plateau. Often they didn't have the expertise in the leagues above them. They would often go through a couple of leagues with promotions and then they'd start to struggle.

Andrew Pilley, the owner at Fleetwood, who are now in League One, the third tier of the professional game, said that his favourite times were in the Evo-Stik League because the atmosphere and camaraderie was amazing. It almost becomes more political the higher up you go. He felt that back then it was 200 or so people who were just having a good time.

I can see that now and I realise it might never be as good for us owning a football club as it has been in this last probably 18 months because it's been brilliant. It's been fantastic. But when you move up you've just got to be ruthless, change the manager and move on if you want to keep progressing. I want these two to improve their knowledge as they move up and obviously they've bucked the two-year trend already, by going from North West Counties League with Ramsbottom to where they are now in five years. So I'm hopeful, but most of the clubs which have gone through the divisions, apart from FC United, who kept the same manager, have had to change managers every two to three years.

I've not changed what I think about managers and stability because of my experience in Valencia. It comes down to: 'Are they doing a good job? Are they working hard? Are they passionate about the club?' Not always: 'Are they getting results.' We didn't expect them to win a promotion every season. But if we had finished tenth with the budget that we've given, I'd have been saying: 'We're going backwards.' Progression is the important thing. If it's not happening you have to consider whether there are circumstances as to why they finished seventh – did they have six injuries all at once? So it's never perfect. But I've always said a manager needs a couple of years to bed himself in before you make a judgement. I'm not talking about giving a manager 26 years! I think two years, two and a half years is about right. If you've given them two or three transfer windows and you've given them a pre-season and there's no sign of progression I would say then you've got a bit of a problem.

***

Ryan:

We didn't know a lot about Jonno and Bernard beforehand. We did know that they had been successful at Ramsbottom and had two promotions on the trot. We knew that obviously they were good at their job, but you don't get joint managers very often. We did wonder: 'How does that work?' But we quickly saw what they were all about. They knew their football. They were aggressive. They wanted to bring in players that they knew and they trusted, which we were quite happy with. And quite quickly they had an effect on the team. It's not always easy coming in in the middle of the season. But they quickly got the lads to agree with them, so that was really the key to the promotion in 2014–15.

You get the feeling that they do live for football. Obviously, I'll never be in that position where you have a job as well as football. After leaving school, it's what I did every day. But you get a feeling with Bernard and Jonno, even though they have got jobs, it's a huge passion of theirs and they want to be successful. They're young and they're ambitious and that's why we like them because, like I said, they want to take the club right to the top and we will be interested in surrounding the club with people who are like us: people who want to be successful, who want to take it seriously, who want to be professional, who want to be the best.

People talk about them and they do talk about their aggression. There's no point in hiding behind it. It's there. They're aggressive characters and that's how they work. But underneath that they know about the football as well. So as long as they're using the aggression in the right way there's nothing wrong with that. You have different personalities in football. You have quiet people, you have aggressive people who are in your face, which obviously they are, and it's about being yourself, about being who you are to get the best out of you and then get the best out of the players.

They're very in your face, they're aggressive, they tell you what they're thinking, they don't beat around the bush. You play like your managers, don't you? Your team should be broadly what your manager's like. And they're great motivators.

***

'I live for the weekend,' says Morley. 'I don't just mean football. You build your weekend from the Thursday onwards. You're like: "Friday this, Saturday that and then Sunday."

'Friday nights we always go out for meal with Jema and the two kids.' Morley is father to Tomas, 13, and Halle-Mae, four. 'Halle-Mae is in that mindset now where she knows every Friday we go for a Chinese. Saturdays are brilliant. I like to have a bit of lie-in and then go for a good long run. Away games are good because you're out the house quicker, if you know what I mean. You're up at nine, you're out at 10, whereas for home games, you're sort of hanging about. If TGI's opened a bit earlier we'd probably get there early.' TGI Fridays in Prestwich, just off the M60, is like a second office for Morley and Johnson, a place where they meet before games to eat, talk, discuss and pick teams.

Morley's weekend routine at present includes church. He and Jema were married at St Mary's Church in 2015 and his wife converted to Catholicism, partly because of the wedding to Morley, who is from a Catholic family. Morley, though, is a reluctant attendee. 'You've got to be dedicated to get up at half 10 every morning to go to church for an hour and a half. Church is boring. These churchgoers, I respect them for doing what they do but it's just not for me and I feel like I have to drag myself to go, but when I'm there I'll join in and I'll do whatever's got to be done. I'll take part, but it's a relief every Sunday come 12 o'clock and you know it's finished. Jema she feels like she owes the priest something because of how much hard work he's done.

'I don't know what to believe, because there's believing it and understanding it. I don't actually understand the extent of what I have to believe. In general, when I go to church I don't disbelieve what they're doing. I don't think millions of people would believe in something that I shouldn't, so if millions believe in it, why shouldn't I? I'm all about balance. I don't see why I shouldn't, but I don't understand why I should. If I went to church a lot more, I'd probably understand why I should.'

Morley met his wife in Sol Viva night club in Bury when he was 19. 'Jema wanted to be with me there and then sort of the next day but I'd just come back from playing football in America and my plans were to go back. And I was a boy at 19. I was just doing what boys do. Then she sort of gave me an ultimatum 18 months down the line and said, "It's either now or never." Because I would just sort of be going back to hers and it's just not fair, is it? I know that I would never use a girl, but it was easier for me just to be friends with benefits, if you know what I mean, which is not right. But she obviously gets to the stage where she thinks: "Right, well it's that or nothing. You either commit to me or you don't." So she texted me saying, "That's it. It's now or never." To be fair, it was an ultimatum.'

Marriage seems to be a celebration and acknowledgement of 14 years of building a relationship, sometimes against the odds. 'No-one ever pushes to do anything. I'm a man. I'm not gonna be pushed by anyone. But I've put her through a lot of shit, fighting and police and courts, I've put her through so much shit in her life, she deserves for me to commit to this, which is the only thing she probably wants me to commit to. I want to make her complete.'

Defeats or poor performances, though, weigh heavily on Morley's weekend. Another blow comes over the Easter weekend with a 0-0 draw against relegation threatened Whitby Town. There was a torrential downpour during the game and conditions were atrocious; but so were Salford. Usually Morley will have a beer with Johnson after the game, but that Saturday he and Johnson, along with their assistant coaches Glenn Moses and Craig Dootson and kit man Paul Rushton, sat in the tiny Portakabin next to the changing rooms.

'We were just trying to get to the bottom of why we're in this position. Why we're relying on other sides to get us into these play-offs.' Morley was particularly down. He felt the team, which has for this level excellent back-up, was letting them down. 'I said to Jonno: "I'm done with making excuses for everybody."

It was then that Moses, normally reserved but always positive, uttered the unthinkable. 'Even if we make these play-offs, I'm not sure that we'll win them.'

Morley was shocked. 'That hurt, because this is a man who is one hundred per cent convinced how good we are. Glenn loves it. And he's not sure. And that Saturday I got to the point where I told the lads that I'd had enough. I told them that I can't wait for this season to be over. And that's not just because I'm not getting my own way, it's because there's been too many sort of hindrances and lads getting injured and excuses.'

Morley was unforgiving in his post-match analysis. 'Jesus Christ, boys, we're 22 men in this changing room and such and such has got a sore groin, such and such has got a sore back. Seven years as a player and ten years at this level of football, I've never seen 'owt like it. You get the best treatment and the best resources in whatever you want and all of a sudden you start to hear players saying, "Well this is sore, that's sore."

'Sides used to think Salford City were a scalp because of the ability in the changing room. Not any more. We're a scalp because of that badge and who owns it. You lads have let that happen. Teams aren't coming to Salford City and fearing what a good side we are. They were six months ago and they were three months ago. But now anyone's thinking they can come and beat us. You've let that happen. You boys have let that happen. Jonno and I continue to do what we're doing. We've not been complacent in terms of training and the way we set up. We're not asking you to play a formation we've not played all season or individuals or whatever.'

No-one really responds. The heads simply sink lower; eye contacted is avoided. Later Morley says privately: 'You're wanting someone to say, "Listen, this is what I think it was today." But they don't. They just sit there and you think, "Come on, lads. We're meant to be a team of leaders here."'

Morley is worried that some of the players that are on good contracts for this level are losing their hunger; the owners have backed the managers to get the players they wanted and now those players are not delivering. He feels the pressure of that scrutiny.

'It's not just a step up, it's been a massive jump from Ramsbottom,' says Morley. 'We seem to have cut a bit out and just gone straight to the top, where you've gone from impressing a chairman that's been in the game 50 years at Ramsbottom and who was a pensioner, to five elite footballers who questionably could be two or three of the best managers that England will see in the future. They have looked after me and Jonno last year but I can't stress enough to the players how it's all about winning and forgetting who your owners are when you put that shirt on. It's about yourself, your self-preservation.'

In the supporters' bar after the Whitby Town game, Howson approaches him. 'You alright, gaffer?' Morley wasn't. 'You shouldn't really take your feelings to heart but you can't help it. I'm a human being. Should I be alright? Then you get a text message off your wife: "How are you?" And you go home and it just ruins everything. And anyone that says you can go home and not take football home with you, they're wrong. Because your body goes on shutdown. I go into mourning. I go into mourning when we get beat or we draw on Saturdays. I get home. I've got my daughter climbing all over me and my little lad is saying, "Can we play football?" And you say, "No, Tomas, and I don't want to play on the computer." I won't say I'm getting used to it but I'm starting to adapt because I have to adapt. You've got to. It's not fair. And if I've got a future in the game at a better level I have to accept that. Nobody accepts getting beat but you have to accept you're gonna get beat.

'We were meant to go on an Easter egg hunt that Sunday. And I made an excuse that it was gonna rain. I knew it was gonna rain. so it weren't an excuse, but Halley was buzzing. She's four, and she's like: "Come on, Dad, come on, all the eggs are gonna be gone!" But we get to the front door and there's massive rainclouds and it's a bit of a relief for me because it's an effort to go.

'And it's not fair. My kids love doing things, but they know that my football is a hindrance. They know that. They know that it, not comes first, but they know that if Dad's got football, we're non-existent and I get that. They respect that. It's how important it is to me. They love seeing me on telly during the FA Cup ties. They thought that were great. Halley was three at the time, going into school saying: "My dad's this and my dad's that." And the teacher says: "Your daughter speaks so highly of you." She hasn't got a clue about what a manager is but she knows that she's seen her dad on telly and she's seen Jonno and she's seen her Nana. Whereas Tomas is telling everybody that I'm mates with Gary Neville and Scholesy. I'm like: "No, they're not my mates. They're just associates."

'We ended up going to a local pub that Sunday with a couple of other partners with their kids, so the kids were playing outside, wet through and Jema's sort of happy. She had a lager shandy. It's weird this, but because you start talking about something else apart from football with your mates, because you're having a beer, it sort of blanks the football out just for a short while. And then a local will come up and go: "Oh, bad result yesterday, Bernard." So it doesn't ever go away. It doesn't. And it ruins my weekend. Even when we've won comfortably but we haven't played as well as we wanted them to.

'It drains you. And you pick up coughs and earache which you never usually would because you over-think things. You take it to bed with you, you wake up with it and just think that it's gonna be tough to make these play-offs whereas right through I would have put my mortgage on it, minimum, that we'd have been in the play-offs. I would have put my mortgage on it and that's not because I'm over-confident or arrogant, it's because I believe that if I was a player playing against this set of lads I'd be thinking, "Wow, what a team these are. These are a good side. These'll win our league." And it hasn't come to that for whatever reason, whether it be the FA Cup run and everybody wanting to beat us, whether it be the owners, whatever it is it's happened. So even on Sunday I'm still on shutdown. I'm still morbid.

'I can't stress to you how much it means to us, and it did at Rammy. It's not just because it's Salford and who the owners are, it's just our own. My lad's 13 now and he's at that age where he starts to be deflated that dad's in a mood again and dad won't play the computer with me. And I know that. I know he thinks that, but he'll understand when he gets older that whatever I sort of put my mind to I want to do well and I want to win, and I really hope I try and put that towards him and I always say to him, he knows how important football is to both of us and he's just got to learn this year that I have to sort of share my emotions and balance them, but a little bit better than what I do.'

***

Phil:

I love what the managers do, their independence. We've got a quite good scouting system for Salford. Our structure's quite good for a team at that level. We want reports from the scouts on players, games, systems, set pieces, everything. And we'll say to the managers, these are all your reports, make sure you check them. And they'll be: 'Thanks for that.' And just put them to one side. And

I love it, because they won't be railroaded. This is our way and this is the way we're doing it. This is the way we get success and part of me admires them, because you can be snowed under reading reports at a club in the seventh tier of the game and thinking, 'Fucking hell, what do I do with this?' They say: 'Yeah, good, yeah, you go and watch that game, you go and scout that game. You go and scout that player.' We will come back and say: 'This player's good, maybe we should sign him.' And they'll be going, 'No, I want *this* player.' 'Yeah, but we had four reports, brilliant reports on this one.' And they'll say, 'Bad egg. Bad knee. We want *this* player. Put him in this dressing room, he'll be like a bomb going off, he'll be brilliant.' They're right. They're so determined in what they do and focused. *We* have to learn that, at this level, we aren't the experts. We are learning from them.

I know they're old school and make the team run at times. It happened to us. We disrespected Alex Ferguson one day in training and he sent us for a five-mile run round the university. Right round the university, day before a game. We were doing boxes. That's when there are two groups in two separate boxes close to each other, doing an exercise of short passing to improve your touch. Me, Gary, Scholesy, Butty, Ryan, David Beckham would all be in one group. We were first-team players by then. We kept putting the ball into the box next to us, which was the manager's. And he went: 'You do that again, you're running round the university!' It was just an off-the-cuff comment.

Brian Kidd used to take our boxes and then, two seconds later, he just rolled a ball into their box and the manager was: 'Right, you lot! Round the university!' And we did, right round the university, honestly. The day before a Premier League game. We were in our late teens, early twenties, first-team players, and he's made us do a five-mile cross country the day before a game. Once when we were in the youth team, we lost an FA Youth Cup game on a Tuesday night in Bradford. Eric Harrison, our coach, got us in at seven o'clock the next morning, took us up to the training ground. There's a big, steep hill nearby. We did an hour running up and down the hill – seven o'clock in the morning. It wasn't a gentle warm-down session. We had lost the Youth Cup. He was teaching us that the Youth Cup was important.

You watch Atletico Madrid now. They play a game, and the day after they train. They go out and train! Not hard, but they train. They're training their mind. You're not tired. Go out training. Sports science has obviously progressed a lot. I know it's important. But there's a reason why we were all able to play for so long in the Premier League. Scholesy's knee had completely gone, he kept going. Gary's ankle had completely gone, he kept going. It's not a coincidence. It's not sports science that kept them going. It's the drive. It's what was put inside you between 16 years old to 20 years old, when you were hurting.

***

Tink. Tink. Tink. It's like a gentle melody playing outside, slightly muffled, as Anthony Johnson remembers it. *Tink. Tink. Tink.*

There is a musicality to its repetitiveness. *Tink. Tink. Tink.*

'You don't think anything of it,' says Johnson.

It is only when the commanding officer shouts 'Right, lads, your turn' and you emerge from the armoured personnel carrier that you realise the gentle melody is the noise of bottles smashing against your vehicle.

Johnson was 18 years old, two years out of school in Tottington, a small town in Greater Manchester between Ramsbottom and Bury. Now, armed with a rifle, baton and a riot shield, he was thrust into the middle of a sectarian riot in Ardoyne in north Belfast.

'I remember the back doors flinging open and we just jumped out the back and there's a car turned over on fire. I'll never forget that car, the flames and black smoke, the first thing I saw. And you're jumping out thinking: "Right, okay." There's people fighting, there's rocks being thrown, there's the Royal Ulster Constabulary being attacked. And this is 11 o'clock in the morning.'

Johnson, 7th Parachute Regiment RHA, had done his training in Norfolk and in some ways that was worse than the actual riots. 'I got beat up more in training than I ever did in Northern Ireland,' he says. But, of course, in training there's fear but no real danger. 'Training isn't real. You know it's not real. When you jump out of somewhere into the real world you remember every single detail of things.'

Johnson was on rubber bullet duty. His job was to fire warning shots above the mob if it became unmanageable. It would have made him an obvious target. The bullets, supposedly used for crowd control, were responsible for 17 deaths over the time of the Troubles in Northern Ireland.

He had watched the TV footage from 1988 of Corporals David Wood and Derek Howes being dragged from their car and executed by an IRA mob when their car had strayed into a funeral cortege. As he moved to within range of the Catholic side of the riot, he was grabbed. 'They're pulling you out and you're thinking: "Once I'm in there...well, you've seen all the videos of what happens when you go in the wrong area, like the two lads, at the funeral; and they shoot them. We watched all that. All that's part of your briefing. So that's going through your mind. You'd have your shield but all the time when I was on a wall, you'd have your baton and people pulling at you. And I'm an 18-year-old kid. I'm a 15-stone man now. But then I was the same height, six foot, but probably 11 stone.'

After a few hours, it would be time to rest. Johnson would be back in the APV (armoured patrol vehicle), with 15 other squaddies, and ordered to get some sleep. All the time you could hear that gentle melody playing. *Tink. Tink. Tink.*

'There'd be a bench on either side of the vehicle and you'd sit down there and try to sleep. But you're not sleeping really. Then they'd come in and say, "Right, your turn." You get out and then your armoured vehicle would be a different colour because of paint and firebombs and other stuff. And you'd think,

"What's going on here?" I remember once we'd pushed the rioters back and they'd stopped throwing things at one another and I got talking to a kid. I don't class myself as being religious, but I come from a Church of England family and we was on the Catholic side and this kid was a Liverpool fan. And we were just talking in general and I've got my rifle in front of me because you took turns at being on 'stag', which was being on guard. And then you would just be talking. Just talking to normal lads. I was always at the Catholic side of the street, for whatever reason. I don't know why. I never found out why, but I was always on that side. It was normal, talking about everything you can think of. They were great people. But they were fighting over nothing. Why?

'Then the sun would start going down and people would be coming home from work and they'd start to congregate: hundreds and hundreds of people on a street. On a street that was probably ten metres wide, terraced houses on both ends, and they'd start to congregate and that's when it started to go off. It started to go off, royal. So then we would form a wall of shields; your shields would interlock with one another.'

It was September 2001. The Northern Ireland Peace Agreement to bring the Troubles to an end had been signed two and a half years prior to that. Johnson was there ostensibly to protect Catholic schoolgirls who were attempting to reach their school, Holy Cross, which was situated a few hundred metres away in Glenbryn, an area almost wholly populated by

Protestants. Because of the tensions in the area, the Royal Ulster Constabulary, the police force of the time, were required to walk them to school, with the army as back-up.

In December 2000, two men in the area had been shot dead, the first a Protestant and the other a Catholic, killed in retaliation. The Protestant community had said that they felt threatened by the presence of the Catholic parents walking through Glenbryn and had blockaded the road to school. The girls, aged from five to 11, needed an armed escort as residents from Glenbryn lined up to hurl insults and missiles at them and their parents as they walked to school. Every day for two months the same procession would take place, with police and soldiers removing or preventing any blockade and lining the route so the girls could make their way to school past the threatening protesters. As the dispute escalated, television crews from everywhere would descend on the housing estate in north Belfast to beam the extraordinary daily ritual right around the world. To outsiders it evoked images of white parents attempting to prevent black children attend schools in 1950s Alabama.

'I would be walking down the road with these kids and my shield,' recalls Johnson. 'And I remember a coffee jar bomb being thrown. It could have nails, glass, an explosive device, whatever. You could hear the noise of it breaking. Bang! It hit an officer at the front. On the arm, I think, but I can't remember what happened to him so I'd be exaggerating if I tried to tell you, because it was up at the front. But it went mad.

'It's a case of getting the injured bloke out of there; obviously the RUC sort all that out. But you have to protect the girls as well. And as all that's going on, the fighting's getting close. So you form a human tunnel. There's probably 50 of you, 50 RUC officers, 200 protestors. Bearing in mind this is all at half seven in the morning and these kids are going to school. I don't know what they had for their breakfast over there.'

One day the TV crews from around the world disappeared: it was 11 September 2001, and all eyes turned to New York. It was the same month England played Germany in a World Cup qualifier, which was shortly before Johnson was deployed to the Ardoyne. On that day, Johnson was in Loughall. 'It was a beautiful, beautiful place. I was in this armoured Range Rover and I had a transmitter radio. We're all in there, probably about five of us, in the back, and we couldn't get any commentary from the game, except every time a goal was scored you heard the radio crackled louder with the noise of the commentator and crowd. We couldn't hear the words but the crackling is getting louder and it's going off all the time. And I'm thinking: "England are getting hammered here!"' England won 5-1; Gary Neville and Paul Scholes were in the team.

Later in his tour he was deployed to Aughnacloy, in County Tyrone, on the border with the Republic of Ireland. He was the first point on road blocks, stopping cars and checking for IRA suspects. 'It was known as bandit country, being so close to the border. I was trained to stop a vehicle, pull them over and then we had a card that we had to read off to tell the driver what to do. It was a rolling roadblock.

'So I'm in the middle of the road and I stop this car. I've got my man on the other side of the road with his rifle. We've got one behind and you have another, your officer, who was a lieutenant, on the radio, ready. So I asked for the details and she stunk of beer, this girl in a car full of women. Stunk of beer. Wouldn't give me her details, wouldn't tell me anything, just wouldn't work with me. So I said: "Get out of the car." As I'm doing this my boss, who is watching, is on the radio to me and he's gone, "Let her go." I've gone, "No, I won't let her go." And I said: "Get the cattle traps out," which is spikes they throw across the road so they can't go anywhere. And my commanding officer is going, "Jonno, let her go now."

'Turns out the woman was an important republican. And then she spat at me. I remember a woman behind her, she was leathered, spitting at me. The republican woman looked at me and said, "You're in big trouble." Window goes up. Off they go. We were part of a different regiment over there and the next morning the senior officer came down to our barracks. He said to me, "You need to come up to the office." There was a command control room. So I went in there and I had to make a statement of what happened. And I weren't allowed out the base for my own safety for two weeks.

'There's a place called Lisburn in Northern Ireland and you go there for a day out, on the beer, do whatever you want, a bit of shopping, and I weren't allowed to go. I was fucking fuming. I'd been there for like three, four months. I was ready to go and I was fucking fuming that I weren't allowed to go out. But I look back at things and I think what people go through and I think: "You know what? You haven't got a clue how certain people have lived their life." Those kids I spoke to over there during those riots. You walk a mile in some of their shoes, with what they've had to put up with. A country that's part of us! Walk a mile in their shoes before you sit here and fucking moan about immaterial things. It bugs me, because I saw it at a young age and I think it's stuck with me all the way through.'

Johnson did four years in the army. He'd joined three months after leaving school at 16 and the reality of army life was beginning to sink in. 'Do you remember the adverts? "Join the Army, see the world." And it was like that at first, but then there was Northern Ireland. So I came out. Not because of that. It wasn't that I'd seen enough. More that I struggle with bullshit. I struggle with monotonous things that I don't think make sense.'

He trained for his HGV licence and worked servicing armoured trucks. 'I loved it, loved the job. That's wat I did during the day, servicing the oil filters. And you'd clean a wagon three times in a day. I used to think: "Why?" They'd say, "Well, because it's discipline." No it's not. I'll clean it when it's dirty and I'll change something when it needs changing but you're wasting my fucking time. Don't waste my time. It's all to do with breaking you down and building you up. I got all that. I get it. I understand it all, but I didn't like putting up with the bullshit side of things.'

The army did change him, though – and, he believes, saved him. His parents were divorcing at the time. He remembers the date: 'Sven-Göran Eriksson's first game in charge against Spain and Chris Powell played left-back.' He has measured out his life in football fixtures. 'It was at Villa Park. I got the phone call from my mum and that's when it happened. 2001 – February, perhaps? Am I right?' (He is.) 'And it turned my world upside down.'

Johnson is the oldest of three children. His mum was 17 when she had him, and his dad 18. His brother and sister followed soon after. They lived in a two-bed council flat in Tottington and then in a council house. 'We never went without anything but times were tough. My mum worked five days a week at the hospital. My dad, I never saw him; he was at work. Now he's my best mate, but he worked six days a week, 12-hour days. He'd come home from work, get me in the car, take me to football training, five nights a week for the different teams I used to play for. My brother and my sister went without everything. They didn't play for any teams, didn't do any hobbies and not because my parents wanted to push me, but because my hobby was so demanding. My football. And I was pretty good at it. My parents did everything around me. I always remember as a kid my mum and dad rowing and I might hear my mum say, "It's not always about him." And she didn't mean it in a bad way.

'My dad would say to me: "Do you know what we do for you?" And I didn't have a clue what they did for me at the time. I didn't have a clue. So we were that tight a group of a family, and you get to 16, 17 and my mum and dad are only in their early thirties and my dad left my mum. He was having an affair. He's married the woman he was with now and they've got a daughter and it nearly killed my mum. It nearly killed her. And for whatever reason, I still don't know to this day, I didn't side with my dad but I felt sorry for him. My dad cheated on my mum and I felt sorry for him and it broke my heart. I was lucky in a way that I went Northern Ireland because if I'd have stayed at home there'd have been trouble. Trouble at home. I'd have got myself into something, because I'd look for a reason, a way out for aggression.

'At the same time that year I got done twice for drink-driving in the space of a week. So I used everything as my excuse, everything, but there's no excuses for what I was doing. Loads of kids nowadays see their parents split up, unfortunately, but at that time I'd never lost a grandparent, I'd never had any trauma in my life and that was the first time in my life where something catastrophic happened to me. Then I went to Northern Ireland. By the time I came back from Northern Ireland I was different. I was a man. I accepted it. I'd accepted what it was. My mum eventually met her husband who she's been with since. They've got a daughter together. Both of them are really happy and everything's great. It's hard to put into words what it is, but it was the most traumatic thing I'd ever gone through in my life.'

Johnson had joined the army straight from Elton High School, in Bury, which coincidentally is where Gary and Phil Neville had also been. Johnson was always the best footballer at the school – Phil Neville had left the year he joined – and was captain of the school team. But he left without qualifications and at 16 he was released from his traineeship from Bury Football Club, deemed not good enough.

'I hated school. I hated it,' he says. 'I always felt like the teachers looked down, as if to say, "You're not gonna be good enough at football to make a living out of things."' He still keeps his childhood school books in a drawer at his home. 'I still have them, where the teachers would write each thing down. I look at some of the stuff they wrote about me. They talk to you all personal, like they know you. And they're just judging you on that lesson. I've still got it all in my kitchen drawer and I read it just to look back at what people said about me. To prove them wrong. What I believed at the time was that they didn't give you anything new at school. They were teaching things that didn't matter in real life. That's how I saw it at school, and all I wanted to do was play football at Bury.

There were two teachers he remembers fondly. 'There was one who was my form teacher, Mr Denham, but he was also a PE teacher and he understood. He was only there for two years, my first two years of school, and when he left, he mentored me. I remember being ill in hospital. I had pneumonia when I was 11, 12 years old, and he came to hospital. It always sticks with me that; that a school teacher came to hospital to see how I was. He was the manager of the town team as well. And he looked after me. He was only a youngish bloke. He was only like in his mid twenties at the time and then he went and I lost a lot of interest after that.

'I had another form teacher, Miss Stone, who would have been in her late twenties when I was 14, 15, and she just let me be who I was. She must have thought, if I let him be who he is, he won't disrupt anything, and she was brilliant with me. I remember her writing: "If he applied himself the way he does in PE and in football, he'd be a genius" and I loved that, because it was my choice not to be like that in maths and science. I'd made that decision to be like that.'

Like Morley, he has been in court and in trouble with the police for brawling. 'I've got a few scars on my head. I've been arrested a couple of times with Bernard, in fact. Just fighting. Aggressive, loutish, thuggish; everything you want to call us, that people think we are. That's what we was, but we were 19, 20-year-old lads. It's not what most people did, but in the estates we were from, that's what lads do in them estates now. It was just one of them things.'

Morley and Johnson were arrested together for an affray in Deansgate, Manchester, in their early twenties when still non-league players. 'We'd been in a pub. They used to have punching machines in pubs and you'd punch them as hard as you can. The irony of it all is we weren't even involved. We were stood near it and there's two groups going after it and one took something against me. I've turned back and he's hit me with a glass round the side of my head.' He still bears the scar. 'Bernard smacked him, knocked him spark out. We ended up outside and at Deansgate Locks and there was about five of us and we ended up fighting 20, 25 lads. But you're in a confined space and they're just throwing chairs at each other and punches. There was blood everywhere. And because of the side of the bridge we were on, they all retreated into the bar and we were on the street when the police turned up. And they've got you on camera doing what you're doing. It was nothing different to what happens every Saturday night, which is a shame that it happens. It took two years to go through court. We pleaded guilty and they dropped it to affray. So they had us in the dock and we'd have got two years and were about to get sent down. But the judge was lenient with us and we got probation. That happened three months before we got the Ramsbottom job. Since we've started managing, since May 2009, we've never been in trouble with the law.'

In team talks Johnson is the more forceful of the Salford City co-managers. Bernard Morley can be aggressive when necessary, but Johnson is the fiercer of the two. 'I suppose, when the shit hits the fan in a situation, he is a lot calmer than me,' he concedes. Johnson can also be calm and encouraging and his players are extraordinarily loyal. But if he's angry at a performance the intensity of the verbal attack is extraordinary. He says that against Workington at home, when the team had conceded two terrible goals after being two-nil up, a particularly ferocious onslaught, was the most angry he had been.

'That. Fucking hell. That's the worst I've been since I've been at Salford. I knew we'd win that game. But before the half-time whistle went, I was doing my team talk in my mind; who I'm gonna get, who I'm gonna drill, who I'm gonna get personal with. Because it was individuals again who switched off because we were 2-0 up. So I'm planning it and planning it and planning it, what I'm gonna say. Then when you come in, everything you've planned doesn't come out how you want it to come. But how we work, Bern will always speak first. It calms me.

'I get that we look thuggish. I get it. I accept it as well, because it's not a lie. That's how we are in the changing room, sometimes, but most of the time when you're winning games it's not like that. Danny Webber was on the radio and he was asked about me and Bern, how we are, and he says, "Do you know what? We have a good time, we have a great time." He said that it's a brilliant group. And I love that, because I don't need to be told by anyone how good we are or what we're doing. That gave me a lot of satisfaction, as people might think that's how you manage a changing room (through shouting), but people actually enjoy being in that changing room.

'The one thing, our biggest main thing, is the spirit. I don't mean team spirit on the pitch but I mean in general so when someone comes into our camp, whether it be a physio or a new player, they instantly feel part of what we are. People might look at it from the outside and go, "I can't believe you do that." Once that door closes after a game I don't want some lad sitting on his own thinking, "I've fucked up for everybody else." We're all in it together. So I'm the first to crack up on the way back and start smiling. I'll do my analysing the day after, two days after, three days after, not on the coach on the way back. I want everyone to be happy, so they think: "Right, well at least the gaffer's knows it's gone." Realistically it hasn't, but we'll deal with that in our own time, away from the lads. But we want them to, not be happy that we've been beat, but we want them to be happy in each other's company.'

Like his parents, Johnson met his partner, Kayla, young. 'She was a year older than me and I was playing semi-pro football, so she's never known anything different than me being at football.' They have three children: Lewis, who is 11, Isobella, four, and Zach, two. 'Kayla doesn't watch the football. She's a Manchester United fan and used to watch them with her dad but she doesn't come to football with me. Bern will come with his kids and they'll go out and play, but I don't think I could cope with that.'

Johnson worries about his work–life balance. He drives a truck for a living and a typical day will start at 4am and end 12 hours later. If it's a training night, on Tuesday or Thursday, he will spend ten minutes with his family before heading out to training. He'll get home at 10pm and everyone will be in bed.

'Kayla understands why I do it and how much. She understands when we win how happy it makes me, and that makes her happy. So I'm so lucky to have that.'

There are some fringe benefits to the early start. 'I could be up at 3.30am sometimes, sometimes at 6.30am. But that's my best time. At half three in the morning on the M62 or the A1 going up to the North East, thinking, because there's nothing else. I turn the radio off. No texts. There's nothing and your mind is thinking: tick-tock, tick-tock, tick-tock. Everything's so clear then! The clarity of absolutely everything in your life or whatever you want to think about at that point, it's the best time. It's the best time.'

But he is concerned about the effect that losing games has on his family. At Moor Lane, after a defeat, Morley, Johnson, kit man Paul Rushton and assistants Glenn Moses and Craig Dootson will cram into their tiny Portakabin room and analyse what went wrong. 'We went to Ilkeston, got beat 2-1 and we were just shit. Our arrogance stunk. We turned up and we thought we were better than them. When we lost at Darlington, I take it personal because I go over everything: have we done something wrong? What did we do? Should we have changed that? So you go over everything before you've even gone off the pitch and into the changing room. So not only are you delivering a post-match team talk but you're also analysing your own decision-making.

'I can't cope with losing and Kayla knows that. So when we lose she knows how to deal with me. I'm very lucky to have a woman who understands what it means to me. Because, rightly or wrongly – and it is wrongly – all this is to the detriment of my family, to my wife and kids. When I took over at Rammy with Bern in 2009, Lewis was only three. They've never known anything of me other than managing. That's all they've ever known. And the one thing that I regret is that my dad gave up everything for me. I've got brothers and sisters and he give up everything. He used to take me everywhere, all over the world, on tours and to Bury and trials and places, and what I'm actually doing is the opposite to what my dad did for me. I miss out on my kids because of this.'

He worries he might over-obsess on Salford and on football in general. 'I focus that much on it that it drains me. It makes me ill at times. Constantly push, push, push, push, push. I reckon I get a cold every two weeks. I come out in cold sores, ulcers, mouth ulcers now. Stress. But I keep it in. I keep it all inside. For my family, my children. That's the big thing, going home to my kids. When I've won, I'll open my phone up straight after the game or whenever and Kayla will say, "Brilliant, well done, darling." Because she knows I'll come home and, it sounds awful, but when we've won I'm the best dad in the world and brilliant.

When we lose I go into mourning. It's the only way I can describe it. I go into mourning and there's a lot of pretend. I pretend a lot of things and I hate that, having to pretend, even though it's with my family: pretend I'm alright. And I come out in ulcers and all sorts. Then when we win again ...'

When they win and he is sat in the Portakabin it is the feeling he enjoys most of all.

'I cannot explain the buzz of winning. Winning a game. Winning a league. I don't enjoy the football. I don't enjoy the week, the build-up, all that. But when we win, to me it's like England winning the World Cup. I sit back in that little room and I go, "Phooo!"' he breathes out deeply, contented. 'That feeling lasts for 12, maybe 24 hours and then it's the next one. There's no enjoyment with it. But I love it. I can't over-emphasise the feeling I get from winning.

Even when he's driving his truck, his mind is on the football. 'It's like a volcano. I'm constantly reading up on things. I'm looking at how we can improve, and I'm so lucky that there's two of us managers because how people do it on their own is beyond me. Because of the area we were sort of brought up in and the way I am, I've always pushed. Like I said, I despised being at school, but I enjoyed the camaraderie part of it. Loved it. I was daft as a brush with the lads, loved it, but I always felt I was better than what I was doing. I've always thought I've got a point to prove.'

***

Paul:

I don't find elite football as interesting to watch any more, especially in England. You hear about people saying English football's the best football there is around. I think Spain's by far the best league. Germany has better teams. In Italy probably the strength in depth isn't great. They talk about Italy being a bad league but I don't think English people look at it. They say it's boring. No chance. The Juventus team would beat most teams in this league. They came up to Manchester City and beat them easy. But we have this interpretation of the Italian league that it's rubbish. They only try to defend. No chance.

The Spanish league's the best by far if you're judging on the European competitions. In the quarter-finals of the Champions League and the Europa League in 2015–16, they had six of the 16 teams. Nearly half of them. The Premier League had just two.

There needs to be a real step up in quality in England. Other than Sergio Agüero, Kevin De Bruyne and David Silva, we don't have the best players. All the best players are in other countries.

The best players are in Spain or at Bayern Munich and Juventus. We're linked with big players – Gareth Bale is a top player – but we don't get them now. Not any more. You never see a Lionel Messi coming over here, you never see a Neymar in the Premier League.

I probably do enjoy watching Salford more. I don't know if it's as much that I don't like the hassle of going to the game, getting in, sitting in traffic. Going to Salford's, I park up behind the goal and get out of my car. But I genuinely get more enjoyment from watching even my son's team, Royton Town. It's like a men's team, but he's 16. He started playing a few games for them last season. I went to watch him once, it was 5-4. It's just entertainment. There's some good players, really good players, but it's not always the best for quality. In the Premier League in last two years, have I really seen a game of high quality? A game that I've thought: 'Wow!' It's difficult to think of any.

Then I think of games abroad that I've watched: Real Madrid–Barcelona, Bayern Munich–Borussia Dortmund, proper games of football. I can't imagine Real Madrid players, Barcelona players, watching our games and being as excited as we are to watch a Real Madrid–Barcelona game or a Bayern Munich–Dortmund game or Juventus–Roma, something like that. Now 10 years ago, in those days, other than Real Madrid...I don't think Bayern Munich were particularly special. Juventus were good, don't get me wrong, but I think English teams were probably on a par with them.

It's all about money and sponsorship in England these days rather than football, rather than entertainment. And I don't think that's just from the top teams either. I think it goes right down through the league. I know there is pressure on managers, but styles of play become so negative because managers are frightened of losing their jobs. If you lose three or four games on the trot obviously you're under big pressure and you're sacked and that makes them think: 'Right, do we need results or do we need to find a way of playing to entertain people?' It's rubbish. It spoils English football.

I'd probably be sacked after five games if I was a manager, wouldn't I? I really don't know if I'll ever manage. I've done my UEFA B licence. I haven't done the A licence. I will get it done. But I'm just wondering, is it worth it? I haven't had any major offers. I had one offer from Oldham a couple of years ago. But you have to start somewhere; if you get your coaching badge you start doing a youth team, doing something first, and if you like it then you take it from there, I suppose. I haven't done it enough to like it or not like it really. I think if I really got into it, I could enjoy it. But I wouldn't be one who'd be worried about losing his job for not playing the right way. I suppose you never know, though. But if you're doing it the way that you think it should be, if people are paying to watch, I'd want to entertain.

The money's the most important thing these days about football because owners, the majority of them, are just interested in making money for their football club. They don't care what they see on a Saturday afternoon on the pitch. They're purely businessmen, whereas at Barcelona you have a balance between business and football. Obviously they have to make money for the club's sake, but it's a club that is a co-operative owned by the fans, not by one businessman or a group of individuals. So they want to make it pay, but making as much money as they can isn't the primary objective. It's entertainment. Winning the Champions League, winning the best prizes. That's why they have the best players. And why clubs like that are the best teams.

PART 2

PART 2

Gary:

When I think of my childhood, I don't remember anything else other than sport, whether it be cricket at Greenmount cricket club, queuing up to watch United, playing for my Saturday and Sunday team, or watching my mum and dad play netball and cricket and rounders. We were a family obsessed with sport. Saturday afternoon was going to Old Trafford, queuing up and going to the game with my dad. You don't realise how special it is when it's happening. I used to get in the car and go to Old Trafford, drive over Barton Bridge and actually, to me, that's what's special about football. It used to be really important in father-son relationships, and now that more women are going to games, it is in father-daughter relationships or mother-son relationships.

My dad died in August 2015, having just arrived in Australia to watch my sister, Tracey, coach the England netball team at the World Cup. We went over to Australia and we couldn't get the body back for three weeks, so we carried on doing things in the time before his funeral. Because what else do you do? Obviously we were upset at the time and still are. You still have those moments now. I can be sat in a hotel room and they will come. I suppose everybody's the same when you lose a parent. You don't want to take their name off the favourites list. They're still there. You don't want to delete that number. It's there. It always will be. You have that minute and then you move on again.

For my mum it's probably very different. It will be a longer process. But for us, we have to move on and we had to move on immediately. We carried on watching Salford. He was 42 years old when he had his first heart attack, and you knew that it was going to come in the next five, 10 or 12 years.

My dad had been involved in a football club for 25 years. He had seen the ups and downs and knew about being beholden to fans, and knew that you never please everyone and that it's a money pit. That was his concern, I think when we bought Salford. But he loved coming in that first year with us and we used to go to away games. I used to travel with him. I remember going to Ossett, to Brighouse with him and I wish I was still going to games with him now. I'm not sentimental and I don't talk about it, but going back to Salford does feel like going back to old football, like you do with your dad when you're younger. It feels like when you used to drive in your car, you got there, you queued up, you paid, there was a pie and peas. It just felt it was old football again. I watch Premier League football every week, but those were probably some of the most enjoyable experiences of watching football I'd had for a long time.

It was the first time probably that I'd travelled to a game with my dad since I was a kid, because after I was always travelling with United or I was travelling to Premier League games. He always was there. He always came down. In fact it got to the point where he started to choose to come down over going to Old Trafford! And he began to go to games that we weren't at. To be honest with you, it's the way we are as a group. You've got Scholesy bringing his son, and you bring your dad and Scholes would bring his father-in-law, and Giggsy brings his mates, Butty brings his son and Phil brings his son. We've always been quite close and you always felt as though there was a little bit of a family element to it. We always stood over there on the far side of the pitch. We didn't dominate the directors' box. We came into the board room sometimes at half-time for a drink, but we just migrated over to that far side and we all stood on that hill and you'd have a laugh with a few of the fans around. I just hope it doesn't change too dramatically as things progress, that we always have that fun of what we've experienced in the last two years.

We're obviously looking at the potential of new grounds at the moment and what we're going to do in terms of Moor Lane. And one of the things that I've insisted we look at is a family zone. Not a family stand, where you just get a cheaper ticket and sit there. It's a zone. It's an area where kids can play football. There are activities, so parents can stand there and have a drink but they can watch their kids do stuff. I want there to be a place where people can always go behind one of the stands and think that their kids can run around. I love it on match days when you look behind that right-hand goal where we stand and you've got a five-a-side game going on with all the kids that have turned up for the day. That's my childhood. Going to watch my dad play cricket or my mum play hockey, netball or rounders. For me, the idea of kids playing sport whilst there's sport going on, that is community. At the age of six or seven, I didn't want to watch every single game of cricket. I didn't want to watch football. I wanted to go and play, myself. That's how it should be.

***

Ryan:

I remember when I was about 19, playing for Manchester United, and was at the Hacienda one night, when that club was at its peak. And there was some hard lads from Salford in there. They came over to me and said: 'You're not from Manchester. Don't forget that. You're from Salford.' It soon got drilled into you if you didn't already know anyway. 'Don't ever say in interviews that you're from Manchester. You're from Salford.' Because it's part of the Greater Manchester area, people don't realise it's a city in its own right with a population of 220,000, which is as big as Swansea, bigger than Portsmouth and similar to Wolverhampton. It is one of the biggest cities in the UK without a professional football club.

I moved here when I was seven years old. My father Danny Wilson played rugby union for Cardiff, one of the best sides in Wales. Rugby union was an amateur sport then and Swinton, which was a professional club in Salford, signed him in 1980. I didn't want to move. I was seven years old, living in Cardiff and I was really close to my grandparents.

But I soon adapted. For three or four years I used to go home and away to watch Swinton on a Sunday afternoon. If it was away you'd obviously go to the likes of Batley and Dewsbury. They're only an hour and a half away, so we used to always go. I went to nearly every game for three or four years. I played rugby for Salford and played for Langworthy. But football was always my first love.

At the bottom of my road where I grew up there are some fields called Rabbit Hills, near the old Agecroft Colliery, where a lot of Sunday League and rugby teams play. It's about half a mile from Moor Lane, Salford's ground. I started playing kickabout games there when I was seven or eight. In fact I never played for a team until I was around 10 years old and that was my primary school, Grosvenor Road. Even then it was all a bit unstructured. You just had to work out your own problems, and sometimes it could be frustrating because you come up against other teams who were well drilled, and when that happened, you had to solve the problem yourself. I wasn't getting told what to do really; I was getting told to just play. At that age you don't recognise if you're good or not. I was in the team, so I was okay. But I've one team photo from primary school and I'm holding the ball, so I think I was captain. I must have been doing something okay, something right.

One afternoon the milkman, Dennis Schofield, was driving his float past Grosvenor Road and he stopped to watch a game. He's seen me running down the wing and score a goal and he's asked one of the teachers: 'Who's this lad here? Is he playing with any team?' My mum was there so he's introduced himself and as I came off the pitch I could see him talking with her. And mum just said, 'This man has just asked if you'll go down and play for a Sunday league team called Deans Youth. He'll pick you up, he'll take you.' That was it. So that was my first team. And my best mate now, Stuart Grimshaw – Grimmy – I met when I played my first game for Deans. He went on to play for Salford City.

You look after each other in Salford. It has that community feel. Deans wasn't just a football club for me. I used to train and just stay there all night in the youth club. What else was I going to do? Go home and do nothing. Many of the lads would do that. Mind you, I also had to stay because Dennis used to give me a lift home. He would manage loads of teams and if I was first to finish and he was still coaching, I had to wait for him. He used to give me and a couple of other lads a lift home.

After I had played a few games Dennis explained that he was a Manchester City scout and that he'd like me to come down. 'But I'm a United fan,' I said. I wasn't at all sure. He told me not to worry about that; that it would give me a chance to play against all the best players, with better facilities, and that I should do it. There were three of us who went down from Deans and we were all United fans. I was about 11 years old and suddenly you're at Platt Lane, you're on the astroturf and under the floodlights, and you're given nice kit. And you get to play football. So I loved it, despite being a United fan. But you soon realise you have to step up a level, which was great for me. I don't want to seem arrogant, but it was quite easy playing for my primary school, playing for Deans, and suddenly it's a bit of a wake-up call that actually you're not the best and there are a lot of good players.

I was at Moorside Secondary School and football and rugby league took over. I would play football and rugby on a Saturday; and football and rugby on a Sunday. So that was my whole weekend. I enjoyed the physicality of rugby. Both at my school and at my club, Langworthy, I was the best. But then I played for Salford and we'd play against the likes of Wigan and St Helens and you realised that, actually, you're not the best. I went for trials at Robin Park in Wigan for Lancashire and there were players miles better than me. But I was picked for one game, against Cumbria in Barrow. I was about 14. I think that might have been my last game of rugby, because I signed for Manchester United soon after.

I was always aware of Salford City when I was growing up, but the first time I would have gone to watch is when my mates and my brother, Rhodri, played for them. So when Gary and I first spoke about it, they went, do you know anyone? I said, yeah, I know Dave. So I asked a friend, Tony Camilleri to get Dave's number and set up a meeting.

***

SALFORD

Artist Laurence Stephen Lowry was, like Ryan Giggs, an initially reluctant inhabitant of Salford. His family moved to Station Road in Pendlebury when he was in his early twenties out of financial necessity. But, like Giggs, he also grew to love it.

Salford provided the inspiration for some of his most famous landscape paintings, his artistic career starting in an era when cotton mills and chimney stacks still dominated the landscape. Football featured in his work as well. 'Going to the Match', now owned by the Professional Footballers' Association and on loan at the Lowry Gallery on the redeveloped Salford Quays, remains one of his iconic works. It shows a crowd gathering for a game at Burnden Park, Bolton, with the game itself in the background, a secondary feature. It was the people who interested Lowry.

Salford has all the typical features of a modern British city. There are five-star hotels by what used to be thriving docks and are now BBC studios and elegant waterside flats for the gilded property-owning classes. Then there are the tower blocks of the Salford Precinct, where TV documentaries are made about the drugs trade and gang shootings. Further north are the suburbs, lavishly green in the summer, with trees and plants in bloom, and large houses for professional classes. In Worsley Village, where Ryan Giggs lives and owns a restaurant, the cottages and canal boats give it a quaint, almost rural feel.

And in the city centre, where the architecture of the 1960s dominates, the rush of progress is most evident. Where once there was a cattle market on Cross Lane, which only closed in 1931, there is now a busy road with housing and tower blocks. Broad Street, which a century ago was an elegant boulevard at the heart of the commercial centre, is now overwhelmed by the A6 dual carriageway and overlooked by tower blocks.

Dave Russell, Salford City's club president, has lived through many of these changes. For more than forty years he has run a car bodyworks business in the centre of the city where he was born. He looks younger than his 71 years, with a full head of silver hair. He is invariably smartly dressed and always engaging and the city's biggest advocate. He has been married to his wife Jean, whom he met at Clarendon Secondary Modern School in Salford, for 51 years, and they have two children, five grandchildren and three great grandchildren.

Where the new-build houses and tower blocks now dominate, were once the classic two-up, two-down houses of the kind Dave grew up in, and made famous by *Coronation*

Street. In the late 1950s, many of those homes in the centre of town were demolished and the residents relocated to Kersal and moved into the new tower blocks. Yet there was no wistfulness about a lost sense of community from his old home. 'We had a bathroom in the new flats,' he said. 'So it's hard to complain, isn't it?' Previously the tin bath had sufficed. 'And the whole community was moving with you. Everyone went. It was like being on your holidays permanently. The golf course was there. That was our Wembley for football, you see. The local playing fields were down the road. It was the great times of your life. People in Salford are the friendliest people you'll ever come across. Everybody who comes down here enjoys it and just mixes in. There's some really good lads, nice people.'

There are only hints now of that Salford transformed by the industrial revolution. The cotton mills were already closing down in the 1930s, due to competition from Japan, though that process accelerated rapidly in the 1960s. There was even a coal mine, the Agecroft Colliery, near where Ryan Giggs played his first football, which was prominent in the miners' strike of 1984 and which only closed in 1991.

Salford was transformed by industry. The population of 12,000 in 1812 had risen to 70,244 by 1842 and to 220,000, close to its current population, by the end of the nineteenth century. During that time Friedrich Engels moved to Weaste in Salford, sent there by his father, who was a mill owner in Germany, in an attempt to calm his radical opinions. He would meet in Salford pubs with

Karl Marx, who travelled up from his London home, and discuss ideas for *The Communist Manifesto*. His experience living among working people in Salford only made him more radical. 'The working people live, almost all of them, in wretched, damp, filthy cottages…the streets which surround them are usually in the most miserable and filthy condition,' he wrote in *The Condition of the Working Class in England* in 1848.

There are echoes of that industrial past in Salford's most significant cultural landmarks. Walter Greenwood's novel *Love on the Dole* was set in Hanky Park, the housing estate demolished to make way for the precinct. The people of Salford were promised the 'finest shopping precinct in Europe'. By the time it was finished in 1971, the council had run out of money and could only deliver a fraction of the original plan. *A Taste of Honey*, written in 1958 by Salford resident Shelagh Delaney and set in the city, was at the spearhead of the new wave of kitchen sink drama in the late 1950s. It was folk singer, dramatist and Communist party activist Ewan MacColl, father to Kirsty, though, who delivered perhaps the definitive word on the city. His song 'Dirty Old Town', written in 1948, is a homage to post-war Salford, referencing the gasworks by the precinct, the factories and the docks.

They play 'Dirty Old Town' before every Salford match, but Dave Russell doesn't like it. 'It's not a dirty old town,' he says. 'I love it.' And it is true MacColl had an ambivalent relationship with Salford. His second wife, Peggy Seeger, would perform the song with him and told the *Salford*

Star, 'I don't think Dirty Old Town is necessarily negative. It's the same feeling that Ewan had towards Salford all his life, love and hate; that it was a place which was living and breathing, it had a pulse. He was frightened of Salford. He was frightened that he would never get out of the poverty of his childhood, and the exploitation. To him it represented what the whole industrial revolution did to people. We visited his street several times. He didn't like going back. He felt kind of guilty that he'd escaped the bad parts of it. But when we did go back the conversations with friends and acquaintances who hadn't left were something to be heard, talking about all the people they knew, and he came alive in a very strange way to me.'

MacColl's original performance of the song is more like a lament than a celebration. It was most famously covered by The Pogues, in a much more upbeat, lively version, which Seeger says MacColl disliked, saying they never understood the loneliness of the song. It is The Pogues' version, however, which they play at Moor Lane.

The Salford Docks, referenced in the song and which are now the home to the Lowry Gallery, shopping centres, up-market flats and hotels, was also once a thriving industrial centre, exporting cotton and importing goods from around the world upon completion of the Manchester Ship Canal in 1894. Trafford Road, with its 38 pubs, became known as the 'Barbary Coast', not after the West African coastline but the notorious San Francisco red-light area. More than five thousand men worked in the docks at its peak, but by the late 1970s they were obsolete, the canal no longer navigable to the new giant container ships. The docks eventually closed in 1982. The old entrance is now a Chiquito Mexican Restaurant and, in honour of Lowry, there's a Matchstick Man pub. The site of the old dockers' social club is a Shell Garage and a 24-hour shop.

***

About the time the docks closed, Frank McCauley, a stalwart of the Salford City committee, remembers the Wilson family moving into Beverley Road on the edge of Swinton. 'The rugby league club owned the house at the top of Beverley Road and so the family moved in there,' he says. 'Ryan lived at the top of our street, at the top of the road. Him and his brother Rhodri would be outside kicking a ball around at the top of the street.'

McCauley, who is from Strabane in County Tyrone, came to Salford as a teacher in 1974, having planned on staying a year. He met his wife Christina soon after and has stayed ever since. Tall, angular and bearded, he is 64 and the meticulous keeper of records at the club, the details man. As a French teacher and head of year at St Lawrence Roman Catholic High School he was a committee member with the City of Salford Schools Football Association, so had an early view of Giggs's talents. 'I told loads of people at the time, I would willingly have paid money to go and watch Ryan Giggs play football at 15 years of age,' said McCauley. 'I was involved with Salford schools and in 1989 Ryan Wilson, as he then was, was in the Salford under-15 team which made the English Schools Trophy Final when he also went on to play for England Boys. There were a couple of good lads in the Salford Boys team: George Switzer, who went on to United as well and actually made the reserve team before any of the Class of 92 did. Ben Thornley, who went on to play for United, was a year younger. George and Ben both ended up playing at Moor Lane. But Ryan was the best young boy I've ever seen.'

Russell also recalls the excitement surrounding Ryan's father switching to rugby league. 'I used to watch his dad play for Swinton. They used to play on a Sunday afternoon at half past three. His dad was a fantastic rugby player. That's where he gets his pace from, Ryan. His dad was quick. They were a good side and his dad was one of the star lads there.'

Giggs has never moved out of the city. Russell, who has known him since he was a player at Deans, says that has been important to local people. 'Life's about who you're with, not where you are. And he's got a circle of friends here. His mum lives local. Everything's there, isn't it? Why move to Hale Barns and you see somebody once a fortnight when you can see them every day? Ryan is just one of the lads. He's still Salford. He's never moved to other pastures. He's had chances to go to Real Madrid and he's still stayed at Old Trafford. He's kept his roots, hasn't he? Though he has got the best house in Salford.'

***

Ryan:

I'm not going to lie. I did think about moving to Hale or Alderley Edge, because at a younger age you think that's the thing to do. But Salford was where all my friends are. Why would you be stuck over there? All you would have are your team-mates, who are not necessarily your best mates. So what was the point? All my best friends are from Salford. Kelvin Gregory I've known since I was seven. When I moved, his house was literally opposite as you come out of the primary school. Even though he's a few years older than me I knew him since then. We only became good friends when I was 18 or 19. He went on to play for Salford as well. I got to know Tony Camilleri through Kelvin really and just being around the area. Camma played for loads of non-league clubs, including Salford. So all my three best mates played for Salford and I would come down and watch whenever I could. And then there is Grimmy, who I met that day at Deans.

The four of us have all been fortunate enough to do reasonably well. Stuart and Kelvin went to university. Kelvin's a solicitor who runs his own company. Grimmy owns his own company selling nuts and bolts, but industrial sized ones for submarines and stuff like that. Camma didn't go to uni but he's a workaholic. His dad had a café, a butty shop. He was peeling potatoes at like 12, 13. He would be up every day at four o'clock in the morning. He started as a window cleaner with a little Astra van and he played for Dave when he was coach at Salford. But now he runs a contract cleaning company for hotels in Manchester and London. We never had much money as kids, but you didn't feel like you were poor. You just worked hard and got on with it. And football was an escape for me.

* * *

Manchester United was once a club in the heart of Salford. All around are the memories. The Lower Broughton Playing Fields are where Salford Schools played their games, and where Ryan Giggs represented the city. Down the Lower Broughton Road and next to the River Irwell, which snakes through the city, is The Cliff, where, until 2001, the first team used to train. On Saturdays, you used to be able to wander down and watch the A team play, a mixtures of reserves, youth team players and injured first-team players. A mosaic of Duncan Edwards adorns the front entrance of the training ground and it is still used by United for their community work. The sense of history is almost palpable. The Busby Babes trained here; Best, Charlton and Law; Cantona.

Right next door, on the Lower Broughton Road, are the run of modest semi-detached houses where out-of-town youth team players such as David Beckham and Mark Hughes lived in digs. It's only 50 yards from the training ground entrance, so there was no excuse for ever being late. This is where Beckham, the Nevilles, Scholes, Giggs and Butt had to perform cleaning duties in the morning during their apprenticeships. Before that, they would be down here on Thursday nights playing in the aircraft-hangar-like indoor pitch, which is still used for United community projects.

Once the cleaning jobs were done, they would be driven round in a minibus to the Littleton Road training ground, where the youth team played. Around the corner is the Lower Kersal Social Club, which is run by Tony Bardsley, father to Phil, the former United and current Stoke City player. He was about as local as you could get. Players now drive out to the wide open rural spaces of Carrington, a village on the edge of Greater Manchester which looks more like rolling Lancashire countryside.

***

Gary:

Salford is massive part of United's history. I mean, The Cliff training ground, that place is almost like a shrine to us. I went there at 10 years old. That was like a second home. We were gutted to leave that place in 2001. We left, just after we had won the Treble, because everybody was so tight, but the club outgrew The Cliff and it's a shame it couldn't stay in Salford. Salford was United's heartland. To be honest with you, the more I look back at our time at The Cliff, the more I think Carrington, while a fantastic facility, is a soulless venue. It's taken the training facility away from the community, whereas actually I think the reality is that it could maybe have stayed within the community. Manchester City have built their training ground in Beswick, which is where their heartland is. That's not a criticism of United. Clubs now need 50 or 60 acres, and to get that in Salford would be near impossible. To get the actual level of facilities that United would require for their academy, their teams, the medical facilities, the sports science, the pitches, is just an incredible ask, and there probably wasn't that sort of land available in the heart of Salford. It's a shame but that's the reality.

We believe in Salford as a city, we genuinely do: the people, the place, the spirit of the city. Tell a person from Salford they're from Manchester and you'll soon be put right. I love Manchester. I love Manchester city centre but I also think Salford's got something special about it. It's very raw. I think that people are very resilient in their defence of their city. They have this determination. You wouldn't take the piss out of anybody in Salford. They'll pull you back down to earth. Anybody who's done good from Salford that gets carried away, they'll pull them back. That's the feeling you get. 'Don't forget your roots.'

***

They've been playing sport at Moor Lane since the seventeenth century. In fact it is believed to be the oldest sports ground which has been in continuous use in the North of England. 'There's a print that goes back to the middle 1600s when this was the original Manchester racecourse,' says Frank McCauley. 'This was all open moor and so the print shows a straight coming, coming straight down and there were annual horse meetings on here. Then there was all sorts: archery, athletics, and the first northern tennis championship was played on here in the late nineteenth century. Then there was a hockey club on it. Then Manchester Rugby Union Club came on just after the First World War. They constructed the stand in the 1920s. They stayed here till the mid 60s and in fact there's a photograph showing an England possibles against an England probables rugby union international trial on this actual pitch in 1938. So they had Manchester rugby and international players playing for them.

'Then their main support base moved to south Manchester. So they moved and an amateur rugby league side, Langworthy, came on for a few seasons, then it lay dormant. Salford came on in 1978, but the dressing rooms were in under the stand. There were no floodlights, there was nothing at all. The pitch was probably about either side upwards of five yards longer, and wider because they still used the old rugby-size pitch. The back of the stand was actually open at that time, so the players themselves built the walls, plumbed it all in, put the electrics in – they did it all themselves. There was a little tea bar where the club chairman Harold Brearly used to sell the pies. Harold helped found the club as Salford Central in 1940. You might not always agree with him, but he was the mainstay of the club for 60 years, until his death in 2008. He did everything: player, manager, secretary chairman and president. In later years, he would enjoy watching Kabaddi, the Indian game, on TV while he served the pies.'

It was in 1984 that McCauley was asked to become Salford club secretary, having done the admin for a local amateur side. He remembers the first AGM he attended in the Brearly's front room and the balance sheet which read: 'Income – nil; expenditure – nil.' At that stage Salford were still known as Salford Amateurs – and their nickname, the Ammies, persists.

'The club began as Salford Central in 1940 and then they became Salford Amateurs,' says McCauley. 'Salford Amateurs were a really successful amateur side and for about five years in the late 70s they were the top amateur side in Lancashire, winning the Lancashire Cup and the Manchester League. But the Manchester League was a self-contained league which didn't go anywhere, so when they wanted to move into the non-league pyramid they moved into the Cheshire League and that coincided with the demise of a really good side. So when I came they had just joined the North West Counties League, which then had three divisions and is the league just below what is now the Evo-Stik League.

'But nobody got paid in those days at all and sometimes a lad got a game because he had a car for an away game. A lot of the good Salford lads at the time didn't come up here and play because they were better off financially playing elsewhere. Even at that level in those days at North West Counties level, there were plenty of clubs paying expenses to draw better players.

'At the end of the 80s Harold got Dave Russell involved, and it was really through Dave's involvement that the club became semi-professional and then we just dropped the amateurs nametag as well. The club was competing as Salford FC, and then Dave had the idea of getting interest from the council and asked whether we could we take on the City name because you need approval from the council to do that. So they allowed us to have City in it. But it was through Dave's endeavours that the floodlights went up and we got the first little bar that we had. And we started paying expenses to players, so that was at the end of the 1980s. And really we more or less had the same committee then as now. We have been together for 30 years.

'Through all the years, there was always a great bond. There was always a great camaraderie between us, and loads of arguments, loads of fallouts, keys thrown across the bar. "That's me fucking finished." You wander off and you walk out. Over the years, we've had massive differences of opinion about how things might be done and this, that and the other, but we were always able to come back again. We never lost anybody in that respect.

'That was always part of the massive enjoyment for me. The football was one thing and I love the football, but it was an opportunity to get to know people outside of the sphere I was working in – teaching. My wife always says to me: "You know more people in Salford than I do and I'm born and bred in

Salford." And it is true. That was always a core thing here – we socialised together, we always had a laugh, we had a good craic and so on.

'You go to some clubs at this level and the people in the committee room at half-time or the board room are not workers. They're there in their blazers and their badges and the ties and so on because they're ultimately responsible for the running of the club but they're not doing the turnstiles, they're not doing the pitch, whereas at Salford City, when you go into that committee room at half-time, the Salford blokes in there, they're the committee men, they're all doing jobs. We go to some grounds and it's, "You can't go in the boardroom unless you've got a shirt and tie and this, that and the other." It's not the way we do things.'

Dave Russell had played for good amateur teams and become involved as assistant manager at Chorley, who were then in the Northern Premier League, what is now the Evo-Stik League. 'I was asked to get involved and, if you're going to do something, when you've been involved at the highest standard, you want those facilities, don't you? And you want to attract better players? So I thought, "Let's see what we can do to get in the Northern Premier League."'

According to McCauley, Russell is the man who had the initial vision that Salford could grow into something bigger. 'Dave is a Salford man through and through. And we always had this thing that Salford was the biggest city in England without a professional football club, and everybody was a United supporter or a City supporter or Salford rugby supporter, and he put lots of effort in to try to raise that profile.'

At that time, Brearly become President and Dove Taylor, a former player, was chairman. After the death of Brearly, Ged Carter, still a committee member today, was acting chairman before Darren Quick, who had played for the club, took over. 'Darren was chairman for about seven years but being chairman of a non-league side in the North West Counties is a difficult position to carry out, because you're the one that people look to, to be bringing the big money in, the sponsor.'

That said, under Quick's stewardship with Russell as president the club finally made it into the Evo-Stik League first division in 2008, four levels below the professional game. It didn't go well. They went through four managers that season. 'I think we had six points at Christmas,' says Russell. 'Eight weeks later we'd only got another two points. Then we signed a centre-forward called Steve Foster from Fleetwood. It was a real risk as he was on good money.'

Foster's first game was at Lancaster. No-one was impressed. It looked like Russell's money had been wasted. The manager was about to take him off when he scored. That day, Foster scored all five in a 5-3 win.

'We took off from there,' continues Russell, 'but on last day of the season, back end of April, we went to Garforth in Leeds and we had to win to stay up and Rossendale had to lose. They were drawing 0-0 at half-time. We were getting beat at half-time. We won 5-2 and they got beat 3-0 and we stayed up. That was the best moment for me at the club because we were dead and buried at the end of February. It takes a lifetime to get into that league, and to drop out of it would have been soul-destroying.

'I think we ended up with 38 points, which was an absolute miracle after everything, and that still ranks as our biggest achievement. That was better than the FA Cup run this season. The great escape we call it. That was our signature tune for quite a while. After that we kept in it and then we were just middle of the road then – 11th, 12th, 13th in the league till the lads came along. I think the worst we finished was 16th. But it's a hard league, you know what I mean, and if you're not paying the till you don't get the best players, do you?'

At this stage Quick was tiring of the chairmanship. 'To get sponsors to come in and to raise some money to get a wage bill going, you can only do it so long, because it becomes a drain on your personal finances and on your time,' says McCauley. 'If you're in business it becomes a drain on your business and your time is being taken away, and that was what was happening with Darren, so he decided he wanted to step down. Because Darren knew Karen Baird. She started coming to a couple of games and then Darren suggested she would be good for the committee. That summer, in 2013, when Darren was stepping down, there was no-one else that wanted to take on the mantle and she was asked and she said she'd do it and then in December the phone call came through.'

***

Ryan:

You hear stories like that about Garforth and staying up and it makes you appreciate the people, like Dave, who were there before us; they're what make this club. Without them there wouldn't be a club, so we're not going to trample all over the heart of the club. Like Dave said, we think this is progress. You have to progress in life. Also you've got to keep the traditions. Sometimes it's difficult. Sometimes it's hard because people have different views. We would never have got rid of the committee. That would have been alien to us. It's not that there are never disagreements. You'll have disagreements, but as long as we're all pushing in the right direction and we want the right thing for the club, we're a team. That's all we want.

But the committee are the club. We've believed in them the last couple of years. There's committee members, there's supporters, there's people around the club who've loved the club for 20, 30, 40 years, so we have to recognise that. We have to honour that and feel comfortable with that. That's how we work. We've had the same with United and we're not arrogant. We're not saying they know everything. I think we know about the football. We recognise that the fans, the people around the club who have been there a long time need to be around the club and need to still have an impact on the team because they're important.

And the club is important. Football takes you away to a place where you can forget about your troubles; you can forget about any stresses. I'm not saying that throughout 90 minutes you're not stressed; you are. And there's highs and there's lows, but it takes you away. It's an escapism, whether that be at the very top or at non-league level. That's why football is loved throughout the world. It would be the same at non-league level or Champions League level. Salford supporters are no different. They love to come to a place where they can enjoy it. They can escape their worries and their stresses. They enjoy it, because that's what it's all about. It's about coming along to the club and enjoying it and creating relationships.

The reason we bought into Salford is the five of us are always looking for challenges but we also recognise the profession that we're in. It can be short-term. You can be in and out of a job in no time and we wanted something where we knew that we would be in it for the long haul. Something we had control over. You don't have control when you're a coach or a manager or a player, someone else is in control. Then you're a number. We wanted this to be for the next 20, 30, 40 years. We've got a short-term plan: obviously we want to get to the Football League as quickly as possible. But we have a long-term plan as well, where we have something to look forward to in 20 years' time. In our environment as coaches, and before that as players, you couldn't do that because it could end at any time. At Salford you can commit and you can control your own destiny.

***

Barbara Gaskill has been serving food to Salford fans for a quarter of a century. She was born in Manchester, in Crumpsall Hospital. Other than that brief moment, though, she has lived in Salford for all of her 56 years. Husband, Terry, 57, was born there and likewise has lived there all his life. They have lived all around the city, from Lower Broughton, to Swinton, to Walkden, raising their two children.

Gaskill, known to all as Babs, works as a seamstress for Burberry but is being made redundant as the company relocates its operation to Castleford. She is typically sanguine about it. 'Something'll come up,' she says. 'I'll think of something. At one time you could walk out of one job straight into another machining, but it's all gone now. China and places like that. I don't understand how they can do it so cheap. But they can. They do everything cheap, don't they?'

She's always liked football and 'as a teenager' would meet up with friends at the Salford Dockers' Club before watching Manchester United games from the Stretford End. Her husband Terry, a machine operator at a steel firm, Arcelor Mittal, also likes football but theirs is a mixed marriage. He stopped going to watch Manchester City at the end of the 1970s. 'It wasn't just the money,' he says. 'It was the hassle of getting there. You used to have a bus from Salford precinct what they put on, a special bus to take you straight to Maine Road, and they stopped it. So then it was like getting the bus to Manchester and a bus from Manchester to Maine Road, so I thought, "Just go to Moor Lane."' That was 27 years ago.

Their children, Kelly and Mark, are now 38 and 36 and have each conferred grandparent status on Terry and Barbara, but when they were younger Terry would walk them up to Moor Lane. 'I went for probably seven or eight games,' Terry recalls, 'and then they asked me if I fancied coming on the committee and helping out. I wasn't sure at first.' Then, a year into his time on the committee, the two women who ran the catering van, Norma and Marlene, decided to pack it in and Barbara was asked to take over. 'It was just a portable caravan thing,' remembers Barbara. 'We had the bar in it. We had the food thing in it. We had the chairs, didn't we? That got burnt down, that one. We put the wheelie bin next to it and the kids set fire to it.'

A new kitchen was built, next to the bar area, with a hatch out of which to serve. 'I just had an oven and microwave. And I'd keep the pies in the oven, microwave and we had a tea urn thing.' And Gaskill would happily serve her meat pie, mash and peas topped with gravy if required.

During the 1980s, when Dave Russell became involved in the club, it was a simpler time, before semi-professionalism entered the game. 'I remember the players would get £10 a game and they spent all that behind the bar,' says Barbara. 'They all did. None of them took any money home.' No-one seems more committed to the club than Barbara. She has toiled at the café and attended endless committee meetings.

Ironically, though, given her commitment to Salford's cause, Barbara rarely watches a game. 'I understand a bit of it,' she says. 'But I've not actually seen a full game. When it's pre-season and all that, I'll go on the coach to the ones in Wales. I'll go to a few of the friendlies. Just have a day out and watch.' But for league games, she will be in her kitchen.

On a matchday the Gaskills will be down the ground at 11.30am. Neither is paid. (No-one on the committee is.) 'We have to get all the pies prepared,' says Terry. 'I get the posts out, put them together and then Jimmy Birtwhistle, who's on the committee, will turn up and he'll help me lift them in. There's always something to do. I have a bit of a moan. Then I'm on the Nevile Road turnstile. I moan on the gate a lot. It's a bit hard on that gate. You get people wanting to come in for nothing. It's only seven quid and you'll still get people now wanting to come in for nothing or saying: "Such a person's left me a ticket." You're getting big crowds now and they won't move from that turnstile. It's hard work. It's getting quite a problem. People have got aggressive when you won't let them in. Sometimes they try to jump over the turnstile. Before, when we didn't get big crowds, I knew everyone by name as you'd come in. We used to hope for Mossley – that was the big crowd years ago. We were like: "Can't wait to play Mossley and we'll get a big crowd, get a few bob in the club." That would be about 150.'

'Years ago,' Barbara concurs, 'when you'd get a hundred people or something like that, you thought, "Whoa, we've got a good crowd!"'

The first the committee members knew of what was coming was when Karen Baird contacted them in 2014. 'She said there was a meeting and that they had important news,' recalls

Barbara. The offer from the Class of 92 was announced and discussed. 'At first we thought they just wanted to put some money in,' says Terry. 'We didn't know they wanted to take the club over. That's the impression we got. We went to a meeting at the ground and almost everyone agreed to it because we were going nowhere. Dave Russell was great at getting money but he was going to his friends all the time. Then we got called to another meeting at Karen's office, it's only round the corner, and Gary Neville walked in. I didn't expect him to be there. I thought it was just Karen, because Karen had had a meeting with them and I thought Karen was just going to relay what they'd said at the meeting.'

Barbara remembers her first impressions clearly: 'He came walking in, didn't he? Sitting around the table and just chatting and explaining why they wanted to take over. When you first meet them you think obviously, with who they are, they might be a bit, you know? But they're just down to earth people the same as us, aren't they? They've got money and all that. They still had to work for it, hadn't they? And we all sat round the table and he told us what was going to go off.'

***

Ryan:

Babs is a typical Salford character who says it how it is. She loves her job. Babs is our kind of person who, together with other characters around the club, make the club tick. There are people like that at Manchester United. People who have worked at The Cliff and now at Carrington for years. These are the people that make football clubs. These are the people who you have around the game but never go onto a pitch on a Saturday. Behind the scenes there are people who are the essence, who are the heartbeat of the club and Babs is one of them.

***

Initially it all seemed exciting. The 14-person committee approved the deal with only a small minority arguing against. But quickly into the first season Barbara felt she was being marginalised. 'The original thing was they said my kitchen was too small because they wanted pie warmers and all this, that and the other. So we had a meeting and Gary Neville had the idea to put on a burger van instead of my kitchen. So I said, "Yeah, alright, where's the burger van going to go? What happens when we leave it at night?"' She had already lost one kitchen to teenagers with a fondness for fire. 'He wanted a big American diner. Well, Karen looked into it and it turns out they cost around £20,000. And she told Gary, "They're a bit expensive." And then they were going to put it right over the other side of the pitch.'

Barbara has always served her pies on the near side of the pitch, next to the main stand, where the bar area is and where the vast majority of the crowd stand. Although the Nevilles, Scholes, Giggs and Butt prefer the far corner when they attend, few others do. Barbara was adamant: 'I just said, "No, I'm not going up there." And then I said, "There's a patch of land there what you've not built on yet. You said it was for the bar store room. Why can't I just have a kitchen built there? Just put the kitchen on." Then all of a sudden Karen texted me to say: "Gary said, yeah, you can have the kitchen built. So that was it. Then when I saw it there were a couple of things wrong. The sink's not in the right place but it works. It works, doesn't it?'

The whole kitchen-sink drama wasn't over even after Barbara was safely ensconced in her new facilities. The FA Cup second-round game against Notts County brought a visit from the Salford City health inspectors. Because paperwork hadn't been attended to and the risk of E coli hadn't been properly documented, Barbara would receive only a one-star rating. It meant she passed but only just. Worse was to follow. The *Mirror* used the Freedom of Information Act to publish the inspection report, saying the café had been 'slammed by health inspectors'. The story was picked up by all the local papers. 'That's what annoyed me,' said Barbara. 'I'd done it all those years, obviously, I've never killed anybody, never poisoned anyone, and then as soon as they come in the papers get hold of it, you get a one star. It wasn't that it was dirty but the paperwork wasn't done and the sink wasn't in and things like that which I'd already told them about. One of the papers said: "Give Gary Neville a yellow card." I went absolutely mad. I've never done paperwork before. But Gary got a girl who works at the Hotel Football and she came here and went through the paperwork. And as soon as they got that, it went straight to five star, that little café. But they never put that in the paper, did they?'

Despite the initial issues with Gary over the site of the kitchen, both Barbara and Terry remain supportive of the takeover. 'They've been good,' says Terry. 'I was a City fan, but they have been good with us. When we won the league last season we had a free night at their hotel, Hotel Football. We had a meal at George's, which is Ryan's restaurant. So all the committee went to that George's and had a meal and a few drinks. And when we went to pay, Gary had already phoned up and paid it. And we went to London for a pre-season friendly against Hampton last season. We got the train all of us, all the committee. And I couldn't believe the hotel they put us up in. It was beautiful. We had a sit-down meal at the hotel.'

It wasn't all plain sailing with the fans, though. There was suspicion among many when the Class of 92 first took over the team, and when Peter Lim, the Singaporean businessman, was announced as an investor just a few months later, there was another wave of discontent. 'I think that upset a few people. We lost a few supporters because of that,' says Terry.

'I think that was because they changed the colours and the badge,' Barbara interjects. 'But we'd all looked at it and agreed on it or didn't agree on it. We told them, didn't we? The fans had a meeting with Gary. He sits in the middle of the floor and he says, "Right, this is what we've discussed." And they tell us they're changing the badge, changing the colours. They tell us first and then they told the fans. I mean, some of the fans were right against it.'

There had been several different team colours over the years – but never red. 'We've played in tangerine, a yellow kit; we played in green; we played in blue; we played in white,' says Terry. 'We've always had different colours, haven't we? But the main one probably has been tangerine and that's upset a lot of people. Some of them were Manchester City fans. One couple were season-ticket holders at City and at Salford. They never come now. Another friend, who works at the tax office, he never came again. He used to do articles in the programme, he's old-school. If you're going to go up, you go up, with the same sort of money as every other club in that league. And he never agreed with putting money in. Others didn't like the change of the colour but they still come and they still want to support.'

The previous badge had been a lion taken from Salford's ornate yet rather traditional crest, but the newly-designed badge, wasn't greeted with universal enthusiasm. 'One of the fans said it looked like *The Lion King*,' says Terry. He said, "You'd better make sure that's not copyright for *The Lion King*." But Gary keeps them all informed. Obviously when he's been over in Spain he hasn't, but when he's over here he has a meeting. He invites the supporters and all that. He lets you know what plans they've got for the future.'

Stephen Kingston, who edits a successful community magazine *The Salford Star*, was one of the principal fans of the club and a key media voice in the city. He was also one of the refuseniks. 'It was lot more than the badge and the change of colour,' said Kingston. 'I've stood on terraces and reported from there for seven years. I was just a normal fan with no special press privileges. We knew the Class of 92 were taking over. We had an exclusive on that. Then they called a fan meeting with maybe 35 fans, with Gary Neville. When he walked into the bar he had a power point presentation showing the new colours and crest. He just showed it and we were like: "What the fuck is that?!" There was no consultation or nothing. He gave his presentation, took about three of our question afterwards. One of the fans asked him if he was acting like the Glazer family, the owners of Manchester United, and he wouldn't answer it.

'It was presented as a fait accompli. Had they come to us or someone from the club had come to the hard-core fans – and believe me there wasn't that many of us! – and said: "We have people interested in investing, we can't take it any further, but these new investors want to change the colours and the crest. Do you agree or don't you?" Then we could have had a discussion. We could have said, "We don't like it but the club needs to move forward so we'll go along with it." Some people still might not have gone along with it. But had they asked us it might have been different.

'I don't wish them any harm. If they go up the leagues, I'll be really happy, because that's where they should be with a city of this size. I get what they're trying to do and I understand the club had to move forward. No-one wants to go to Yorkshire on a miserable Tuesday night to see the same grounds and same fans haranguing you for the next twenty years. We finished 11th or 12th every season. But it was the way it was done. I've spoken to some fans who still go and they say it's not the same. Not all of them, by any stretch, but some say that.'

Perhaps the biggest change with the club, though, was its success on the pitch. 'I remember going down to Moor Lane with 20 people and you'd get beat 5 or 6 nil,' says Terry. 'There was one season when we were in the North-West Counties, we went 21 games without getting a win. 21 games! Sometimes people who've come with an away team will have a drink in Manchester and then they'll get a taxi and ask to go to Salford's ground. And they'll go to where Salford rugby team used to play at the Willows on Weaste Lane. The taxis took them there. They've got out and gone: "No, this is a rugby ground." And that's a Salford taxi firm from Lower Broughton. They didn't even know where we were. But they do now.'

***

Gary:

One of the big reasons for coming into Salford City was the fact that there weren't many fans, so almost every fan was going to be a new fan. This was a club that had 80 fans and we knew that we'd have to look after those 80 fans. Those original 80 fans are our honorary members. I think there were 40 original season ticket holders and I think we've frozen season ticket prices for them until 2019, whatever level we're playing at.

We met them and I'd say we lost about ten fans when we announced our plans. Along with losing Phil Power and our mistakes in recruiting players, that would be a major regret and it wasn't easy to take. You might say it's only 10 fans but that's over 10 per cent of our crowd. They put it down to the colour change. It wasn't actually, I don't think, all down to that. To them, it was *their* club. They didn't want the razzamatazz, as they saw it. They thought we were going to come in and get rid of all the original committee. They thought we were going to wipe the club out. We'd take them out of Salford, we'd take them off Moor Lane. And then there was the colour change.

If there had been a long history of one colour we wouldn't have changed it. If there had been a stable colour for 50 years we would have probably gone with it, but there wasn't. Dave Russell will tell you that they played in claret and blue one season because the sponsors found a cheap set of kits. When we came over we just felt there's nothing about tangerine that represents Salford. There's no tangerine in the crest, there's no tangerine in the city's history. And, to be honest with you, we didn't like the colour. Salford, as we'd seen it, was always red. We'd always seen Salford as being red. Obviously we have the United connection, but it was as much about it having such a strong tradition in the workers' movements and the Labour Party. We knew we'd get some criticism for it, and a few of the fans, to be fair, used that as a sort of tool to rebel against us.

We knew full well that we had to go and explain the vision of the club to the fans. I went on my own. It was a bit hostile. There were three or four people who rebelled. I know some of them might say we should have discussed it with them. But we did run the changes – the change of the badge and the colours – by the committee. The committee backed it. Or rather I should say, some of them didn't want it but they supported it. If the committee had said, we're going to leave if you change the colour to red, we would have definitely not have done it. Once you got to 14 people who are the heart of the club, though, you can't then go to another 40 for another consultation. We had the support we needed.

There are still some old fans with their tangerine flags that go there on match days, and a couple of them are probably our biggest fans, but they also now wear the red shirts. I've had old fans come up to me and say that it's been the best two years of their life. They've had their best moments. There will still be that small group that probably won't come. Or even ones that are there that are tinged with sadness slightly. Their club's now going into a different level. It may be going away from non-league. There are some people who just love non-league and, to be honest with you, I'm actually with them. I'm already dealing with agents for players wanting five per cent commission. I've got some agent who is telling me he wants £600 a week and five per cent of his clients wage for the next two years. He wants sell-on clauses and all that. I'm thinking, 'Give me a break, mate, will you? We've got all that to come in a few years.'

***

Phil:

When we first bought Salford, my dad was totally against it because he'd been involved with Bury in League Two and his worry was the financial side. He has seen how clubs at this level can eat through your money. And his first question was: 'How are you going to fund this? It sucks all the money out of you. I'd prefer you to give the money to your kids.'

But when he saw what we were doing he went to every single game. He had great experience in football clubs, because he has worked for Burnley and Bury. And my mum's still working at Bury. So they know everything about that level, about how hard it is. I think my dad worried because he knew it's not money-making. Every time we'd buy a player, he'd say: 'How much did you pay? What contract did you give him? How are you going to fund that?' And then in the first year, when the FA Cup came around, that wasn't our goal. We wanted to concentrate on the league. But my dad would say, 'FA Cup: it's £100,000 to be on the BBC.' So he knew.

He has that business head on. He really offered great advice because he'd seen everything. He'd seen a club go bankrupt, he'd seen a club come back from the dead, he'd built a stadium at Bury. He's got a stand named after him there. He had raised the money, he had done everything really in a football club, so he passed on that experience.

My dad would take Gary and me to United. My first game was the day Bryan Robson signed on the pitch in October 1981. It was record transfer, £1.5million, and I remember he was wearing that brown suit. It's funny what you remember. We got to Old Trafford about three hours before kick-off and I remember walking out into the K Stand thinking, 'Wow, it's so big.' It was massive. It was honestly that moment in your life when you felt something change.

In the game, I just remember Mike Duxbury running down the wing and my dad telling me, 'He's tracking back here, he's overlapping there.' Mike Duxbury ended up teaching my son at school, so I was able to say to him: 'You were my favourite player. My first memory of Manchester United was of you.'

I remember my first ever game was for the team my dad ran, Ice Juniors Under 10s. It was absolutely pouring down and I think we were losing something like 12-0 at half-time. My dad was the manager, and we were getting beat that much and it was that cold and wet that he cancelled the game. So that was my first memory of playing – against a team that was about three years above us and were getting absolutely and totally hammered. I remember being so cold I couldn't move and at half-time my dad forfeited the game. So that was a brilliant start. I think I was seven, Gary was obviously two years older and we were playing in the same team, because I tended to play a couple of years above my age group until I was 12. I always played in the same team as Gary and, when I was 12, my dad put me back to my own age group. Looking back, it was brilliant because it toughened me up. When I went back down to my age group, everything seemed a little bit easier.

My dad would do that to us. He did it in cricket as well. We played for Greenmount Cricket Club in the Bolton League, which was a semi-professional level and where Test cricketers would often play in the summer. I was 14 years old and I was playing under-18s cricket. And then one day my dad says to me: 'Phil, get over to Farnworth, you're playing for the first team.' I hadn't even been selected for the second team. And they had Otis Gibson, the fast West Indian bowler as their club professional playing for them. He started bowling off about two paces because he felt sorry for me. Then about five, six overs later, when he wasn't getting me out and getting annoyed, he started bowling off his full length.

And then he bounced me. What did I do? I ducked! I was always taught to duck from a bouncer. But I wasn't like a duck out of water. At six or seven years old, my older cousin, who was a professional cricketer in the leagues, would be playing in the back yard with me and bowling bouncers with a hard, cork ball. And that was with no pads or helmet. Honestly it was the best upbringing you could ever have. Playing cricket, being bounced at 14 years old by Otis Gibson away at Farnworth, and having to fend for yourself. It's the equivalent to sending your son out into the forest!

Without the cricket I would not have made it as a footballer. I was learning discipline, mental toughness and honesty from international cricketers. They taught us the meaning of professionalism, training and toughness. Gary opened the batting. We had Mark Taylor, the Australian cricket captain, staying at our house. We had Matthew Hayden opening the batting when I was 12, Gary was 13. I mean you're talking world-class cricketers. Before they make it big they come over to the Lancashire leagues. Shane Warne's played at Lancashire. The top ones have all played there. Franklyn Stephenson played for the West Indies and had the best slow ball in history. He taught my brother how to bowl a slower ball. People might say, 'Oh, what's that got to do with football?' But he was teaching the art of practice.

We'd go to United and then when my dad joined Bury to work for them, we used to go up to Bury. My dad obviously was allowed to go in the directors' box but they weren't allowed to take kids in. We used to travel everywhere watching them, so we used to go and stand in the away end, me and my brother, with the travelling Bury fans.

My mum used to make the sandwiches and the buffets on match days, so we used to get down there early and have our lunch in the kitchen with mum and then go and watch Bury. That's what it's like now when you go to Salford. There's no bullshit. You just go to the game. Go to the game, have a pint, watch the match. You hear everything, every comment. The players are right there, on the pitch. There's an honesty about them. And you go home and it's the same feeling.

When we bought Salford, it was like a role reversal. My dad had taken me to games. And now I was taking him to games, to my club. There's a picture of us at Brighouse Town. It was freezing, snowing. And there was my son, Harvey, me, Scholesy, Gary and Nicky, and my dad was at the back. We've all got our hoods up and we're freezing. But it's a great photo. When I was young my dad used to take his dad. It had come full circle. Your dad takes your son and all of a sudden your son then starts looking after your dad. I'd say: 'Come to Salford today.' And every week he used to come down, park his car, and he used to pay to come in every week. He used to tell us that we had to pay to go in. Pay to go in. It's £7. So we still pay to go in now.

There are different types of people within a football club. There are those that give and there are those that work for you to take and he was very clever because he'd seen it all at

Bury over the last 20 years: those that were only in it for the short run, for their own gain, and those that were in it for the club. 'Stick with them,' he'd say. 'They're on the journey with you.' He was very sceptical at times because he'd seen a lot of people being made redundant or being burnt or taking advantage, and ripping people off. With our youthful exuberance, he was the one behind us with a bit of nouse. He'd say: 'Calm down. Just be careful about that. You're bringing that player in there. That will mean another player will want more money and then it'll cost you even more.' He was very clever that way because he'd seen it all.

My son still talks about the journey he had with Gary and my dad, because my dad picked Harvey up and they got lost. We would get lost going to every ground. They're all down little lanes. They're never on the side of a motorway. So my son will say, 'Do you remember when Granddad got lost going to Brighouse? Or do you remember that game when a director from the other club come out and started jumping on your dad's bonnet and your dad told him to eff off?' Stories like that. It doesn't happen in league football, but it happened to us.

Taking my son to Salford, it's like when my dad used to bring me here. All week you look forward to it. You wake up on the Saturday. 'Ah, we're going to Old Trafford today.' It's how it should be. There's a purity about it. A real genuine purity. The game at Prescot Cables, when we scored in the last minute. I'd left, we're going down the road and we hear cheering and my dad sprints back into the ground to see who's scored.

I left Wembley when United were getting beat by Oldham 1-0 in the 1994 FA Cup semi-final. I was so pissed off. There was a minute to go and my dad, my brother and me all leave. And then all of a sudden Mark Hughes scores, Nicky Butt chips in over him, we hear the roar and we sprint back into the stadium. And it's no different at Prescot. It feels no different. You leave the stadium dejected and then you hear a shout and your world changes.

24 MARCH 2015

PRESCOT CABLES 0, SALFORD CITY 1

It's a cold, spring night on the edge of Liverpool at a football ground bordering Huyton, where Steven Gerrard grew up. Paul Scholes is in unfamiliar territory among the plethora of Scouse accents. There was a time when Merseyside was only visited for hostilities, but it's not like that tonight. A row of terraced houses borders one side of the Prescot Cables ground and at the far end stands a man with a bugle, who bursts noisily into tune whenever Prescot win a corner or free-kick in a promising area. He stands alone amid the crowd of 187. Apparently, the neighbours have complained.

At half-time volunteers, club secretaries and officials gather inside the clubhouse, which is bedecked with team photos and pennants of visiting teams, and Scholes appears to be in his element. The spread of food is impressive. Quiche, cakes, sandwiches and sausage rolls are eagerly consumed along with cups of tea. Scholes sits in one corner while Phil Neville is across the table with his father, Neville Neville. Roy Keane once complained about the creeping culture of executive boxes of Old Trafford, saying the people there were more interested in their prawn sandwiches than supporting the team. There are no prawn sandwiches at Prescot Cables.

Phil Neville informs Scholes that they will be pairing up with One Direction at a forthcoming pro-am golf day, so Scholes might need to employ a stylist to keep up appearances. Scholes pulls a face and the group all laugh. 'Good food that,' says Scholes as they file out for the second half.

It is March 2015. The last month of the season is looming and automatic promotion, which requires the club to finish top of the division, looks uncertain. It feels as though a draw tonight will be terminal for those hopes. And Prescot Cables, one of the weaker sides in the Evo-Stik League First Division North, will not buckle.

'You never win away in mid-week,' explains Phil Neville. It's obvious when you think about it: the away team has to rush to wherever they're playing straight from work; they won't have eaten properly; after negotiating the M62, their mind isn't focused on the match in the same way it is at the weekend. That, and the fact that captain Chris Lynch normally has to come off on 70 minutes to work his night shift at the gas bottle factory.

Tonight ought to be different. Even though he can't be at the match, Gary Neville has taken charge and arranged for the players to meet at 5pm for a proper pre-match meal at the owner's hotel. And while some of the celery sticks and vegetarian offerings might have been eschewed, pasta is consumed. It ought to have stood the team in good stead. At least they've eaten properly, rather than grabbing a pasty from the petrol station en route to the game.

But Prescot Cables are seemingly unimpressed by this nutritional innovation. Fans, directors and locals have been as accommodating as can be for Scholes and Phil Neville. But the team clearly aren't about to roll over for this celebrity-funded football team, complete with their own TV crew shooting a documentary.

The temperatures dip below freezing as the night wears on, and Salford are no nearer getting the win they need despite having the better of the second half. 'This is going to ruin my week,' mutters Phil Neville.

Ninety minutes approach and Phil Neville and his father make their excuses and say their goodbyes. It's not so much that they need to beat the traffic; it's the fact that not being there for the final whistle somehow deadens the pain of a bad result. Scholes, though, is reluctant to leave. He makes as if to follow Neville but lingers at the corner of the pitch, just by the turnstiles, unable to turn his eyes off the game and unwilling to bring himself to give up on a lost cause.

Salford are attacking the far end of the ground and the view is obscured. There are 90 seconds remaining when the ball breaks for substitute Gareth Seddon, who has not been a first-team pick because of his decision to take a mid-season modelling job abroad which ruled him out of a number of games. Seddon is around ten yards out with only the goalkeeper to beat. Even from Scholes's long-distance position near the turnstiles, the ripple of net is visible as the ball beats the goalkeeper and Seddon turns away to celebrate.

Scholes, too, punches the air, his face beaming as it once would have done when he scored a last-minute goal for United. He turns to a friend, embraces him, but within seconds is composed again, yet beaming now. Phil Neville is on the phone, bemoaning the fact that he missed it. A physical change has come over Scholes; the worry lines have eased and his whole body has relaxed. 'We had to win tonight,' he says. The tension of watching this must compare to playing for Manchester United during a title run-in. 'It's the same,' he replies nonplussed, before reconsidering. 'Tonight's been worse.'

***

The first season of ownership of Salford City had not quite run as scripted. The Class of 92 had big ideas. Stability and loyalty would feature. Maintaining faith in your manager would be high on the agenda. Nurturing a core of players was a priority. 'At the start of the season we had a perfect vision that we'll have the manager now for the next 20 years and we'll have a set of young players and they'll see us all the way to the Football League,' said Phil Neville. Yet after four months they sacked the incumbent manager, Phil Power. Within a year the playing staff had been almost completely changed.

Gareth Seddon, Danny Webber and captain Chris Lynch were the only players who started the 2014–15 season and finished the 2015–16 season. Seddon was something of a star signing and had been approached by Gary Neville personally to ensure he came. Even though he was stepping down three divisions from the National League to play for them, he was initially excited about the challenge. Yet even with his levels of natural enthusiasm, he was soon finding it difficult.

'I don't want to sound bad here, but there was a non-league mentality when I joined in 2014–15,' says Seddon. 'I've worked under managers who can be absolutely relentless, whether it was in training or a game. We once went away to a game at another club and we got a last-minute draw. And we were 10 points clear in the league – top of the league – and we had the music on at the back of the bus. And we were laughing when the manager came back and he actually whizzed the stereo out of the roof window and onto the motorway, because he didn't accept that a draw was good enough. And it was big stereo. It might be a few hundred quid.

'I love that intensity because that's how I train and play anyway, but I've had that all my career with different managers, so for me to drop down to a league where players might have been out on a Friday night was hard. And no matter if you've won, drawn, lost, you were in the bar having a beer. People were drinking on the bus. It didn't seem really to matter that much. I found it really difficult.

'I started to question why I dropped down and ask whether this was what I really what I wanted. I was playing and preparing myself like I was when I was professional, and you can see the other lads not doing that. And we were losing games and it was really frustrating for me. It was that transitional period and for them that's how they've always done it. They can probably go out and play better than me. I'm not saying it affected them, I'm just saying from a mental side it was difficult for me to accept that.'

Seddon says that in the first half of the 2014–15 season the dressing room remained relatively united, however, and that he didn't experience any animosity due to the fact he was a significant signing. 'There was no bitterness. I did have a lot of pressure. I had to get the goals. I had to play well every week, because otherwise straight away, you know, lads at this level go, "Friggin' hell! You know, he's on that kind of money and I'm getting this kind of money . . ." But I think because I did score the goals, no-one has a leg to stand on. I'm not that kind of person in the dressing room anyway. I'm mates with everyone. I used to organise nights out. They weren't thinking, "He's on all this money and he's a tool." We were all friends. I just think there wasn't guidance or enough structure to the club.

'People were turning up late. People would turn up without tracksuits. When things were said in the dressing room, people were talking over the manager. Just things that you would never ever do, or I'd never do. As soon as the manager speaks you shut up and don't say a word. Little things like that were creeping in.

'There was a point where people were talking over the manager and they were arguing, and Gary Neville looked towards me and I was thinking, "Oh, he's looking towards me to stand up and get a bit of calm." So I stood up and said, "Look, everybody, shut up. Listen to the manager, what he's got to say." But I think we needed a change. We were five points clear; then I think we'd dropped down to second or third place, so we were in a bit of a meltdown really.'

On the wave of optimism created by the takeover, the club were unbeaten until November and were top of the Evo-Stik Northern League First Division North. Salford City then lost three successive games in November. Automatic promotion was slipping away. The team steadied but successive defeats on the 28 December 2014 and New Year's Day 2015 saw the owners take the decision to let Power go.

***

Gary:

We were the last ones to say yes to it. I think the fans were calling for it on the message boards. The chairman along with the committee was recommending to us that we should change and we probably left it another month, six weeks. We were sort of holding on and hanging on in there. That was the honest truth. If you speak to Karen, I know she'll say the same.

We were hanging on in there, hoping that there would be some change in that time, giving Phil Power a chance, and gave him two or three new players that would alter it. But Phil Nevile and Scholesy went to watch two games at Harrogate and Droylsden and they said that we ought to change. I would never have done it on my own and, to be honest with you, I'd never have done it just off the chairman's recommendation; I would have always wanted a consensus. I was in Dubai on holiday but we organised a conference call with the entire committee and Phil, Scholesy, me and Karen, and I said, right, before we do this I want some sort of overall consensus and opinion from round the room.

I asked three questions about the situation and took feedback from everyone. And there wasn't one single person on that call that said that we should keep Phil Power. I didn't want the call to be protracted, so then at the end I said, 'I don't want anybody to answer unless they disagree, so if you agree that we should sack Phil I want silence from everybody. If you disagree strongly, please speak now. I will take silence to mean you agree with the decision. And everyone went quiet. At that point I felt: Okay, that gives me the comfort that everyone in the club is behind it.'

I was away, but I texted Phil Power two days after he was sacked and I said: 'Phil, I'd like to get together with you next Thursday. I'm back on the Wednesday. And just go through everything with you and just sit down with you and have a few hours with you.' He replied back to me saying, no problem. That's fine. I've kept the text to this day. Then two days later he told the story in the newspaper and he said, I was really surprised that Gary and Phil Neville haven't contacted me. He didn't say anything about the other three lads. Just said Gary and Phil Neville; I was the easy one to blame, I think. I probably am the most vocal at the club in terms of the one that's sort of dealing with the business side of things, and I was the one that had contacted him and I was the one that had asked for a meeting with him and I was the one that actually had arranged a meeting for the week after, on the Thursday.

He said that he was disappointed that he wasn't told personally by me. But I was away, and the fact is I would never sack a manager. It's the chairman's job to sack the manager at a football club, not the owner. But I would always try to speak to them and have a meeting, because it was important to me to go and sit down with him and have two or three hours and go through the process that we'd gone through and how we'd made the decision and how difficult it was.

It's the one big black mark in our tenure that we've had to sack a manager, although Phil did get 18 months in the job. He'd had the previous season. He had six or seven months of the next season. So it wasn't as if he was sacked after six months, which is what's been portrayed. It wasn't as if it was just a shoot-from-the-hip decision. We went through a very thorough process and actually delayed the decision for longer than we were advised recommended to by other people.

But I still see it as a black mark and I'd never say, 'Ah, but look, it's proved to be the right decision,' because actually who's to know what Phil might have gone on and done. But obviously that's history and now I'm very happy that we have Bernard and Jonno along. I'm very happy with what's been created in that dressing room. And we didn't actually appoint them either. It was Karen who made the decision. I went to meet with them, as did Scholesy and Phil, but we trusted Karen and the committee to make that decision and to get it right.

***

Karen Baird is happy to take most of the blame for Phil Power leaving. 'I was going to every game and it wasn't right,' said Baird. But Gary Neville was saying, "I'm on television every week saying don't sack managers, give them time. I can't be doing it." But I pushed it.' Power hadn't seen it coming and Salford were still second in the division at the time. 'It just came completely out of the blue. I've often seen Gary on TV or in the newspapers saying that managers should be given more time. So yes, it's definitely a bit hypocritical now, isn't it?'

Baird conducted the sacking alone, but that was deemed appropriate given that she was the person who had employed Power in the first place.

'It would always have been me who told him,' said Baird. 'I'm the chairman. That's my role, isn't it? To be fair, it was me who pushed for Phil to go. Gary was probably the least keen. Paul, Phil and Ryan supported the decision. But Gary was probably more on Phil's side than anyone.'

For Phil's replacement, Baird had been keeping her eye for some time on two young managerial tyros wreaking a degree of havoc in the small world of non-league football. Anthony Johnson and Bernard Morley had certainly upset establishments along the way while taking tiny Ramsbottom United through three successive promotions, so that they were now in the Evo-Stik Northern League Premier Division, one division above Salford. An on-pitch brawl followed one of the games at Darlington in the promotion play-offs the season before. Johnson was serving a ban at the time of the appointment for violent behaviour.

Johnson and Morley brought with them a raft of players from Ramsbottom: Scott Burton, Gaz Stopforth, Jordan Hulme, Steve Howson, Phil Dean and Dominic Smalley. That meant there was no space for many of their original team. A year later, only captain Chris Lynch, Danny Webber and Gareth Seddon had survived. Turnover of players was at an all-time high, and initially there was a distinct rift in the dressing room.

In fact when Danny Webber walked into the dressing room before Johnson and Morley's first game at Bamber Bridge, it was as though a Berlin Wall had been constructed across the middle, with the original Salford players on one side and the new players from Ramsbottom on the other. 'It was like East Coast versus West Coast,' said Webber. 'And I just thought, "No, we've got a game to play out here. I'm not prepared to come here and let this season fall to pieces." So I jumped in the middle of two of the Ramsbottom lads and said, "Move up, lads." We didn't have time to have a bedding-in period. We had to start winning games together and we couldn't have done it with two separate teams being on the pitch in the same shirt, with Rammy lads and Salford lads.'

With Johnson and Morley's unique combination of charisma and drive, Salford turned it around, and the match against Prescot was crucial. Thereafter they only lost once more, and won their last nine fixtures. On a Tuesday night, the team and committee gathered in a Salford curry house for a club night out, though everyone was following Darlington against Warrington on their phones. Their hopes of winning the Evo-Stik First Division North rested on a loss by Darlington. When Darlington failed to win, Salford were secure at the top of the table and promotion to the Evo Stik Northern League Premier Division was confirmed.

For the Class of 92 it had been a bruising if ultimately successful first year. If there had been a loss of innocence, there was at least a better understanding of an owner's lot.

'You can understand how, when your emotions are running high, owners can make bad emotional decisions like bringing players in on big money and putting yourself under financial pressure,' said Phil Neville. 'I can see how it runs away with you. We want this club to run itself, and at the moment it is. But when you lose a couple of games you think, "Oh, we need a new player. Let's just push the budget out a little bit and we'll make it back here." But you never make it back. It was a massive learning curve. The biggest lesson we learnt was to take a step out of it, the playing and coaching side. We have to let the managers manage and let the players play. At this level, they're the experts, not us.

***

Gary:

In the first six months we learnt that even a small level of day-to-day involvement in the club is nothing more than interference from owners. Even when you're trying to help. We never did anything without good intentions, whether it was Phil and Scholesy going down during training sessions or me ringing up Phil Power and speaking about players and who had played well. But whilst the intention was to help, even those conversations actually hindered. If you call up the manager to say 'well done', but don't call the next week, he's thinking, 'Where's my phone call?' And whilst

Phil and Scholesy going down to put some coaching on to inspire the lads is intended to help, it hinders the manager because it undermines him. I think the big mistakes were all in the first five months.

Also, we made mistakes in recruitment. We didn't have a system in place and even though we're now at the eighth tier of football at the start, that still costs you. We reacted to seeing a player on a Saturday or to what a midfielder's mate had told the manager. We signed a player once and I'd say, 'Who's seen him?' And you'd hear: 'Well, our old midfielder has told the manager that he was a good lad and he was a good player.' That's enough for him to get through the Salford door. It was word of mouth. We had 52 players on the books in the first year. Now you always have more players on the books in non-league football but that was just obscene.

Those were our biggest mistakes, and to a certain extent Phil Power paid the price for those mistakes because it ended up in what has been our biggest regret since taking over the club. Sacking a manager in the first two years was never the plan. I have to say that by not having a system in place on recruiting players and by us trying to help and actually hindering, you could argue that that mistake sort of mutated into something bigger. It put more pressure on.

At the start of the season when we bought the club, we invited 25 potential players we were going to sign to a restaurant; we met them and sold them the vision for the club. That's not how you recruit. It was almost like a bad version of *Pop Idol*. It's not the way you do things. It just felt a little bit like cramming animals into a truck and hoping four or five of them would be good.

Now we have three scouts. One of those is directly employed by us and even at our level that's important. The other two report to the managers. One of the manager's scouts watches the opposition; the other two watch players. It's a much more systematic and precise process. We don't always get our man but we know what we're going for. We know who he is. We know who he's played for. We know his injury record. I suppose that was the first big change in the structure we made.

Scholesy and I went to the game at Northwich Victoria once. We'd just signed a centre-half on loan for three months on a guaranteed £280 a week, which is a lot at that level. And I think we looked at each other after five minutes and said, 'What have we done?' Ten minutes later we were watching a Northwich Victoria player called Bohan Dixon. He was fantastic and we're thinking, 'Well, let's sign him.' You can see straight away how being an owner becomes like *Football Manager*.

Now our system is that the managers have their scouts and we have our own scout as a club. The managers' scouts recommend players, but our scout has to go and verify them and do reports on them. That's the way we run it. There's the odd time that you fall outside that system. But all I want is verification and validation; that our scout has seen the player the others want to sign. I think there's only once or twice since they came that we've signed players that have fallen outside of that system.

***

Paul:

Your career is enjoyable, of course it is. But the only real, real enjoyment is at the end of the season when you've won something. That is the only time. The rest of the time there is always a nervousness. 'Can we beat this team? Can we play well? Can I score a goal? Can we get to the end of the season winning something?' That's the only time as a footballer that you really, really have time to enjoy it: when you actually win something.

When you're playing, you're so engrossed in winning a game, thinking about the other players you're playing against, thinking about the fact that you don't want to let your team-mates down. It's just so much more relaxing being a fan.

You don't really get nervous, that feeling in the stomach. I suppose we had it a little bit for the Notts County game in the second half in those last 15 minutes, when you're trying to hang on. But it's not your reputation or your performance to be relied on. It's everybody else's, which takes a bit of the pressure off you. Winning the league last season was brilliant, but the biggest sign of the fans coming back was the FA

Cup game. Notts County is a big club, isn't it? And wherever I went at that time, people at school, parents in the yard, people in shops, they were always asking about Salford City.

When you've been playing for 20 years you lose that feeling of being a fan. It's a different type of passion when you're a player. Of course you want to win and you want to celebrate when you do well. But against Notts County, it reminded me of being nine years old and going to watch Oldham and then their FA Cup and League Cup runs in the 1990s. It felt like those days again.

When I was 16 Oldham reached the League Cup final. And although I'm not from there – I'm from Middleton, about 10 miles south of Oldham – my dad Stewart was an Oldham fan and used to take me. I was always a Manchester United fan but I suppose it was easier to get tickets at Oldham. And cheaper.

I remember when we beat West Ham 6-0 at home in the first leg of the semi-final. For some reason I then went to the away game in London. I don't know why. Oldham were 6-0 up! That said, we were getting beat 3-0 at half-time, so it weren't that pointless. It was a bit worrying at the time. I had a mate from school, Mike Halliwell, who was a big Oldham fan so we used to go together. We went down to Wembley on the train for the final and there were 30,000 Oldham fans. That's how many people live in Oldham, I think. Now they get a crowd of 3,000. But you had that sense of community watching them. You always knew somebody who knew somebody.

It's felt the same watching Salford. It takes us back to when we were kids, I suppose. I didn't play in the greatest of places when I was a boy; the changing rooms and pitches and stuff were pretty basic. But it was just the way Manchester lads were brought up, the way me, Nicky, Ryan and Gaz and Phil were all brought up playing, really.

It's been exciting watching Salford. Even this season it's been exciting in a slightly different way. We've known for a while that we're probably not going to win the league this year but there's still the play-offs. Last year we always had a chance. We were always in the hunt. This year has been a better standard, and we've still had a chance of going up. There's going to be seasons where we don't go up, obviously. We can't go up every year.

***

Eight months on from promotion, and Salford City have made an enormous leap into the mainstream of football. It's the FA Cup first round and their game against Notts County is live on BBC TV. The FA Cup actually starts in August for clubs even smaller than Salford with a preliminary round.

For Salford City what is known as the FA Cup first round qualifying was in September against Whitby Town. Including replays it has taken six games to get into the first round proper of the FA Cup, where you get to play against fully professional teams. Notts County are a big draw. Although they are in League Two, the lowest rank of professional football, they are still three levels above Salford City and are a club with a rich history, as the oldest football club in the world, having been formed in 1862 and having won the FA Cup in 1884.

Fifteen hundred tickets have been sold. Outside the ground people are clambering on boxes to peak their heads over the wall to get a view. Lowry should be here to capture the scene. Instead, smart phones will have to suffice. 'Can we have a selfie, Paul?' shouts one of the unpaying onlookers to Scholes as he meanders among the crowd. He obliges. Usually Scholes, Phil and Gary Neville, the most frequent attenders of games, prior to the Neville brothers' move to Valencia, will watch from the corner of the ground, where a lone white metal bar stands as an unnecessary crush barrier, and where on a normal match day they are left alone.

Tonight that would feel a bit exposed, a little public, so they watch from a grassy bank in the far corner of the ground, surrounded by friends and family, which is perfect, other than the fact you had to crane your neck past the obstruction of a small stand to see the goalmouth. They might be anonymous among the crowd, but a TV camera on the other side of the pitch is relentlessly trained on them to capture their reactions for the live television audience.

Nicky Butt is here with Gary Neville and Scholes. Phil Neville is following events on Twitter, holed up in the Valencia team hotel in La Coruña, on the coast of northern Spain, where his new team play tomorrow. Ryan Giggs is in The Lowry Hotel a couple of miles away. Manchester United play in the Premier

League tomorrow and his first obligation, as assistant manager, is to be with the United team. Still, there is some downtime and he has snuck away to the dining room, where there is a large television, to watch the tie. Wayne Rooney, Michael Carrick and Ashley Young, all England internationals, are with him. They are all aware of Giggs's involvement with the club. A little later Juan Mata, Ander Herrera and David de Gea, all Spanish internationals, drift in and start asking questions about the little-known team they are watching. 'Obviously the English lads knew anyway that the game was on,' said Giggs. 'But then slowly the foreign lads would come through and were asking, "What's this?" And a few of the lads would explain.' De Gea, Mata and Herrera settle down to watch. Salford have attracted an illustrious audience.

From the off, Salford are impressive. They are already going reasonably well in the league, in the promotion play-off positions, but the owners can't help being impressed by this display. On the back of two evenings training a week, they are matching a fully professional side for fitness. There is no sense of the team being over-awed. On the ball, as well, they are Notts County's equal. At the start of the second half, it gets even better. James Poole breaks down the right and crosses, and Webber is on hand to turn the ball in for 1-0. Moor Lane erupts. Scholes, Neville and Butt are bouncing around along with the fans. This was surely hoped for but not expected.

As the half progresses, the euphoria grows. Jordan Hulme hits the crossbar. All around, people are starting to believe that this could actually happen. Yet 67 minutes in, with Notts County barely having threatened, Steve Howson makes a calamitous mistake. Having been superb throughout, he now attempts a clearance which rebounds off a Notts County player close by. With goalkeeper Jay Lynch having come out to collect the ball, the rebound takes the ball past the keeper, falling nicely for the County player Adam Campbell to touch home into an open goal. He strikes the ball and is already turning to celebrate when Howson, sprinting, powering to the goal-line, lunges at it and somehow hooks it away before it can cross the line. Howson is redeemed, and six minutes later Richie Allen sets off on a darting run down the right, exchanges passes with Jordan Hulme and scores a superb second goal, sparking an outburst of leaping around and embraces among the owners. 'I've never seen Scholesy jump so high,' said Gary Neville.

And back at The Lowry Hotel, half the Manchester United team squad are also up out of their seats when Allen scores and are now roaring Salford home. Giggs is beaming with pleasure. 'I would love to have been down there when the cameras pointed to Scholesy and Butty jumping around in the crowd, I would have loved to be there, but I quite enjoyed watching it on the TV really.'

At the final whistle, a degree of mayhem ensues at Moor Lane. A pitch invasion is obligatory. Neville, Butt and Scholes join in, but in a somewhat more dignified manner, walking briskly across the pitch to get to the players. Inside the Portakabin, otherwise known as the home dressing room of Salford City FC, the scenes are predictable. 'Wem-ber-lee, Wem-ber-lee,' sing the players at raucous volume. No-one's going to Wembley; it's just what footballers do when they win a Cup tie.

Outside the dressing room Paul Scholes grins. It almost seems as if this might compare to those extraordinary nights of his Manchester United career, such as the 2007 Champions League win in Moscow, the very peak of achievement in the professional club game. 'It feels the same,' he insists. Then he qualifies his assessment. 'It's probably better than the Champions League. It's like when I watched Oldham in the FA Cup.'

Quickly, Scholes is swept up into the dressing room along with co-owner Gary Neville. Somewhere amid the rabble, the sound of Rick Astley's 'Never Gonna Give You Up' is being played. According to Anthony Johnson, Scholes was one of the worst offenders. 'I'm sure it were Rick Astley he was singing,' he said. 'I walked out when that went on.' In a corner, Notts County manager Ricardo Moniz is manfully attempting a dignified TV interview after the 2-0 defeat; amid the chaos County players stand isolated in the sea of celebration waiting for their coach to pick them up.

Reporters and TV crews are swarming around the goal-scorers, the managers and of course the owners. 'It's been the maddest 10 days ever, getting everything ready,' explains Karen Baird to a group of newspaper reporters. Gary Neville sympathises. 'Have you ever worked with me? I texted her at quarter past five this morning.'

'I think I'm the only one who replies to him at that time,' says Baird.

Eventually it will fall to Hartlepool, another professional team from League Two, to remove Salford from the FA Cup, though only after another televised TV tie at home in which they draw and take Hartlepool to a replay. Even then they will only lose in extra time and be applauded off by the Hartlepool fans. For now, though, interviews are drawing to a close and Neville is back in full control mode again. 'Get down the hotel,' Neville is busily ordering the players. The five former United players also own their own hotel opposite Old Trafford, Hotel Football. 'There's a free bar tonight,' explains Neville. 'We're taking the players out and they'll be in a right mess tomorrow. I hope they are anyway.'

He is reminded that they have a game on Tuesday against Trafford in the Integro Doodson League Cup. 'Don't worry about that,' said Neville breezily. The FA Cup can do that to even the most earnest owner.

***

Ryan:

The FA Cup run was brilliant for a number of reasons. First of all it's just a brilliant competition to be involved in. Secondly, it captures the imagination and that's why it's so special. It gives opportunities to the small clubs as well as the big clubs. It gave us the chance to play against Notts County and you don't get that opportunity in the league. And when you get closer to the real big guns, then you start dreaming. We came very close to getting to the big guns and playing Premier League teams. And financially it was great for us because the amount of money that you're able to make with the TV and the crowds really helps. And the exposure allows you to bring in more advertising.

At that time it felt like everyone was talking about Salford City. That's what it felt like to me. That's what people were talking to me about all the time. And not necessarily just football people. It just captured the imagination, which is what the FA Cup does. The momentum built and built and built, and it was just a brilliant experience for everyone involved in Salford. Not only for us, but for the players, the managers, the fans. We all got so excited. It was a brilliant experience to be involved in.

But after all the emotions and putting so much into the FA Cup, when it's over it's difficult to get that momentum back. It's difficult to go again. But you have to do it; you just have to. You have to work hard on the training ground and tell yourself, 'Right, the FA Cup's gone now. It's the league. What did we want to do at the start of the season? We wanted to be promoted. We have to put ourselves in that position where we'll get promoted.' You couldn't help but be affected by our experience in the FA Cup. But you see it in at any level of football, that a good cup run can hurt your league form. There's nothing you can do about it apart from work hard and try to produce results.

OCTOBER 2015

Gary Neville discovered he had been targeted for an occupation by the homeless on Twitter. A member of a campaigning community for homeless people tweeted him with the message: "We're in your building and we're not moving." A group of homeless men and women had taken over the old Manchester Stock Exchange which Giggs, Neville and Peter Lim were converting into a luxury hotel.

The project manager went down to determine the seriousness of the situation and called Neville so that Wesley Hall, a representative of the squatters, could speak to him on the phone. He informed Neville that they planned to stay for a few months and that they had targeted specific buildings in Manchester for occupation. Unbeknownst to Neville, the call was filmed and the footage of him trying to broker an agreement was later put on YouTube.

Neville's initial reaction, however, caught Hall off guard. He expressed concern that there would be no damage and impressed on the squatters that he needed access to the site over the next few months to survey it for its impending renovation. He also needed them out at the end of the winter in February as building work was due to begin.

Hall quickly agreed to those conditions. 'All the paperwork from your business I've shoved in a back room so that no-one can get to it,' said Hall. 'Every single day we're taking the bin bags out. There's a rota for food … there's not a chance in hell that I'd stop anyone from coming in this building. If you need to do test works, if you need to do anything, that's absolutely fine.'

Quickly it was agreed that they could stay until February. 'Thank you so much,' says Hall. 'Listen mate we'll be gone by January. I just want to keep these people out of the cold.'

***

Gary:

Helping that homeless community last winter wasn't something I set out to do. It just happened because of the occupation. So I can't claim to be particularly charitable or to be an expert on the issues. There are plenty of people who know a lot more and work tirelessly to help the homeless.

All I can say is that I wouldn't judge someone just because they're homeless or taking a drug or just because they've been to prison previously. Within a couple of days the community in that building had rosters of lists for cleaning. They had a pantry of all the food, it was immaculately lined up. They had security watch. They had curfews by a certain time. They set their own ground rules that they weren't allowed to drink or do drugs on site. And it was clear that there a real communal spirit among them.

I agreed with them that they would leave on a certain date and they did. I agreed it verbally and they did, they left, because ultimately I'd shown them some respect and they showed me some respect. And I suppose what touched me was that so many of the homeless people you see are young people. And I do believe that every young person deserves a chance in life.

Clearly some young people have a very difficult start in life and can end up homeless and that is an extreme situation. And my gut feeling was that I shouldn't turn my back. Because those are also young people with talents, abilities and maybe hidden skills and young people who need a foot on the ladder. But even in less-extreme situations, even among very privileged young people, such as some of the trainee footballers I come across, there is also the need for someone to believe in you. Every young person needs that. Our generation has to show belief in young people, whether they be homeless on the street, or trying to get to college or trying to become a professional footballer. Their situations may be very different but we still have a responsibility to encourage and nurture them. It's why we want to build an academy to run alongside Salford City.

It's easy to dismiss younger people, to claim that your generation worked harder, did more, had it tougher. But actually I never would have had the chance to have a football career if Eric Harrison, our youth team coach, hadn't believed in me. I was never anything like the best player. Obviously I must have had a basic level of ability but it was always marginal whether they would keep me on or not. And then Sir Alex Ferguson believed in me and gave me the opportunity to play in the first team. I'm not sure there are many managers today who would stick with a player like me. Obviously Ryan, Scholesy and David Beckham were extremely gifted and would probably have been given a chance anywhere in the world. I'm not sure I would.

Then, when I retired and I wanted to go into business in building Hotel Football, Peter Lim believed in our ideas when others dismissed them. So all along I've been grateful for the opportunities I've been given. That's why an essential part of Salford and the next phase is setting up an academy for young people to be given a chance. We want local people to play for the club. The model I ultimately believe is something close to what Manchester United achieved when we played for them, that the core of the team is from the local area or at least British. And then half of the team might be foreign, because every culture is improved by opening itself to outside influences. We all improved as players because of the example of Eric Cantona. The Premier League has improved because of foreign coaches and players. I would never want to pull up the drawbridge. That mentality is wrong.

Yet there is also a sense that in the dash for cheaper players and the overreliance on the transfer market, we have forgotten our own community and made life so much harder for young people to get a foothold. And that is also wrong. It's hard to grow your own. It takes years of emotional and financial investment. It's easier to sign a ready-made 26-year-old right back from France. Sometimes the economics will make a compelling argument for that short term expediency. But if you reduce everything to pure economics, ultimately you lose the heart of your community. So developing an academy, for young people to have opportunities at Salford City, is something we have committed to do and will now deliver on. In the next year or so we hope to have a structure in place, so that the core of our team is developed at the club. Even if they don't make it there, we hope we will instil values in them that will help them get on somewhere else. As well as footballers, we're looking at whether we can train up people in our media and marketing department, perhaps over time in other disciplines related to football. Maybe I'm so fixated on it because I am so aware of how lucky I was. But every generation has the responsibility to train up and build up the next generation. That's something we hope we can play a small part in doing at Salford.

***

They kill you kindly when they let you go at Manchester United. For Steve Howson, a central defender at Salford City, it came when he was 14 years old. And there were tears. His father knew first. United's academy coach, Paul McGuinness, had taken his dad aside before the crucial meeting. McGuinness didn't like children to be told in the formal surroundings of an office that they were no longer wanted. So Dad was told, so he could break the news at home.

'Obviously it was a bit of a shock to the system,' says Howson. 'You want to keep playing there because you've got your mates there after four years. And I got a bit upset, crying and stuff. You're not good enough in some respect. So you've got to accept that, but being told you're not good enough at that age, it is a bit of a kick to the teeth.'

Howson is six foot two, the archetypal strong, tough, aggressive non-league centre-half. It's hard to imagine tears, though off the pitch he is gentle, considerate and sensitive. He is teased by the rest of the squad because of the amount of time he takes talking to fans after games.

And he is forgiving. He signed for United at the age of 10, an extraordinary opportunity which should confer status among his peers. Yet at secondary school he was bullied because he was with United. 'We had quite a big school and I was moved from one half of the year to the other half so that I wasn't mixing in those circles. I think my confidence took a bit of a knock. To be fair, a couple of the lads who were verbally rude towards me, they're alright now. I see them in Ramsbottom. When I see them they'll be like: "Hi, you alright?" And they ask how Salford's going.'

Ironically, United let him go because he was too small, but he has fond memories of his time as part of that gilded elite and even of the manner they let him go. 'United said, "Come and have a chat." So my mum, my dad and me went in and Paul [McGuinness] was lovely actually because he had told my dad before what was going to happen. I just thought again it was going to be: "You're getting released, thanks very much, ta-ta." And so did my mum and dad. But he said, "Look, you've been great with us. You've been fantastic. You've been loyal. You've been here for four years. We're going to the Dallas Cup, first time this year, and we'd love you to come, to go with us as part of the squad before you go elsewhere." I didn't even have a passport. I don't think my mum and dad had a passport. So it was unbelievable. You're going to America with Man Utd. All expenses paid. We got boots, we got training kit, we got everything, and it were nice. It was a good touch really.'

***

Paul:

I was from Middleton, just outside Manchester, about five miles from Oldham, and I used to play for a couple of teams, Boundary Park and St Thomas More. My first memories of football are watching my dad, Stewart, play on Saturday afternoons in the Manchester leagues or Sunday mornings in a Sunday morning league. And being eight or nine years old and playing for my school team, St Mary's in Langley, Middleton. Mr Turner was the football teacher, I'll never forget him. He was an old man. I think he taught me English, or something. I enjoyed it.

We had one school team for years five and six, but I was playing in it when I was still in junior school, which was year four. So you're playing two years up at eight years old, playing under-11 football. I always remember that team. I think we won the cup every year. I never really played in a bad team, which probably helps. It wasn't because of me, though. The Boundary Park team was attached to Oldham Athletic and there were loads of lads there who were on Oldham's books, all lads that were capable of having a football career.

I don't think I was the best player. I never stood out really until I was about 15 or 16; I wasn't somebody special, like Ryan. He stood out massively with his pace and his skill. But I was never a tricky type of player, fast or strong. They're the ones that stand out when you're young. When I was around 14 there was a school cup final with my secondary school, Cardinal Langley, in Middleton. Brian Kidd and Archie Knox, Sir Alex Ferguson's assistant mangers, were there to present the cup. At that stage Manchester City were considered to be the best in the city for youth recruitment, but I think Kiddo changed all that.

I was already at the Oldham Athletic School of Excellence, but there weren't that many games in those days for Oldham or professional clubs. These days there's all these under-11, under-12 games for your professional club, but it was really just training and you played for other clubs, school and Sunday teams. And I didn't really like training. I think Kiddo and my English teacher, Mr Cott, said that United would like to see me. There was three or four of us invited in. You were a bit wary at first. I think my dad might have said you've got more chance of playing for Oldham than United. And you do think to yourself: 'Come on, be serious.' But really you were thinking: 'Jesus! I get to go and train for United. Who knows? One day, maybe?'

We had to go into Salford, to The Cliff training ground where United used to be based. I loved it. Every Thursday night we used to train in a big gym, which was freezing cold. Then I started to go two nights a week. Kiddo and Archie used to train us, and Archie was the assistant manager to Sir Alex. And Kiddo would be a few years later. Top people would come down, even to watch training. Sir Alex would be there often. You try your best anyway training for Manchester United but you give something extra when the first-team manager's coming, and sometimes you even had first-team players coming and training down with you. Players like Bryan Robson, the England captain, when he was coming back from injury, or players like Mark Robbins and Darren Ferguson, who were 18 or 19 and on the fringe of the first team.

Then we were all offered apprenticeships when we were 16. And that was when it became hard. You would be leaving home at half seven, getting back at five o'clock. It's like a normal job really, but the lucky thing was you were playing football at the end of it. I had to get three buses from Middleton to Salford and we'd have to be in at nine o'clock and we all had our jobs to do. I used to mop the floor of the hallway and clean the first-team bath. That was just what you had to do. It was all part of growing up, I suppose.

Once we'd done our duties, there was a bus to drive us to Littleton Road where we were training. But we trained next to the first team and all those players, like Bryan Robson, Steve Bruce. They knew who the youth team players were. We used to have all the first-team lads watching us on a Saturday morning. I think that's a big thing that's missing now from academies.

We were in a little building at The Cliff; it felt like there was just 50 players and three teams: reserve team, youth team, first team. And everyone knew each other. First-team lads would speak to you, they'd know you and they'd give you tips at Christmas. You're doing the jobs. You're cleaning up after them. You're cleaning their boots. And the ultimate aim is to get where they are. You want somebody cleaning your boots. You want somebody cleaning your dressing room. That's just the way it works.

Nicky played for Manchester Boys when I first played against him. They were a tough team. I say a tough team –

really what I mean is they were a bunch of nutcases, including Nicky. He was a tough lad. One of the hard lads. He'd tackle anybody, wouldn't he? A brilliant tackler, a brilliant player. They were streetwise; exactly what kids aren't these days at football clubs. They're mollycoddled, aren't they? They get driven to school and taken to games. But we were all streetwise because that's just what you had to be. You had to look after yourselves. Gary and Phil, obviously, were a little bit more reserved than Nicky, I suppose, but still, they were good players. I don't think I ever played against Ryan growing up through school or anything. I think Ryan from probably about the age of 11 was always playing up a couple of years because of his ability.

There were initiation ceremonies at youth team level. The older lads would try to get you in the washing machine. They would get a mop out and you would have to chat it up as though it were girl. It was all designed to embarrass you. I thought it was bullying. I never liked it. It was cringeworthy, really. I suppose every year every lad had to go through it. It's just part of it, but it wasn't a nice thing. I used to hide in the gym at dinnertime. It was probably around our age group that all that got stopped really. I think one of the lads complained. His mum rang up or something. I think from then on it just got stopped, which was good. People might see benefits, but I didn't.

I think there's a big problem with academies and kids' football. I watch academy football, under-18s football, and

175

it's boring, to be honest with you. It's unrealistic. They all want to try and play like Barcelona with neat little passes. These things go in fashions. The last couple of years all of a sudden they've got to be like Belgium because they produce a lot of players. Fifteen years ago it was France. I don't think there's enough mental toughness in young players. As a kid growing up when we did, you had to look after yourself. And if you couldn't look after yourself you were gone. You were finished. Our youth team coach Eric Harrison, he taught you to tackle and to look after yourself. Now it's not so much looking after yourself, it's the style of play that counts.

And the amount of people there are now looking after the academy players: masseurs, assistants, physios. What do you need as a footballer? You need a coach. You might need a physio if you're injured, or a doctor maybe. But all you need is one coach to handle your football team. Now it's two or three coaches, and a sports scientist comes out with you and warms you up.

***

Nicky:

We've spent an awful lot of time in England in the past 10 years trying to think hard about how we bring through young English footballers into the Premier League, and now, as Director of Academy at Manchester United, that is a huge part of my job. We have an impressive academy system and an awful lot of time and effort has gone into creating it. Boys come in to our training ground at Carrington at 12 years of age and they come in here five days a week.

But because they're deemed to be Manchester United professionals they come here every night. They don't play for the school teams; they give up playing for their Sunday teams; they don't play for their town any more, their county or Greater Manchester. They will give up any other sports that they were doing, like rugby or athletics. The thinking behind that was that when I came through the system and was doing all those things and sometimes playing five games a week for different teams we ended up playing too much football. Some youngsters burnt out. And it is true that perhaps you had less time to train specifically on technique in a non-pressurised situation. So there maybe was a need to redress the balance.

But Michael Owen made the point to me recently that he would never have been the finisher he was if he hadn't had 20 chances in a crap game, because then if you mis-hit one, it doesn't matter; or if you try a chip and it doesn't come off, it doesn't matter. You'll get five more within the next 10 minutes. You might win some games 13-0 and score seven and it might seem like a waste of time, but you're getting the ball all the time and you're trying out all sorts of different finishes. Then you go up to the next level and the next and you probably get one chance in a game and you feel that you really have to score, so you use the finish you rely on the most. But if that's all you do, then you become over-reliant on the one skill rather than trying out and developing others. And that was Michael's point: he never would have developed the range of finishing he had if he had played all the time at the elite academy level.

And playing all those games made you physically robust and mentally tough. You played a hell of a lot of football compared to now and you became a match-game player. Your football brain develops more if you're playing a lot of football games as opposed to just training. And also it gives you different learning experiences, because you were playing in a school team, where you're the best player by a million miles, so you would just dribble with the ball and take people on and shoot. Then you get your town team, where you're still probably the best player and you dribble with the ball and take some people on. And then you come into the Greater Manchester side and it's getting a bit harder so you become a team player. Then you've got North of England. Then you've England. Then you've got Man United. So different environments give you different learning and different ways to do it.

We bring these boys in at 12 years old and make sure they come in here every day at 5pm to train. They go to this nice school, they get picked up by the nice minibus and they get brought here and get put into that lovely facility and they're training the same way with the same boys every week. They don't have nearly as many outside influences in life really or any difficulties with the football because they're not playing different kinds of games.

We used to train at The Cliff training ground in Salford and we would have to make our own way there every day. I grew up in Gorton, near what is now Manchester City's ground. From there I would take three buses and spend an hour and a half travelling across town at the age of 13 to get to training. I'm not saying that's the way forward. Obviously times change, but I was a lot more streetwise.

I'd come in to United once or twice a week and then every other night I'd play at The Rec in Gorton, where they had some five-a-side pitches. And you would be playing with lads who were five, six years older than you and so you couldn't do what you wanted to do because you'd just get battered basically. But you learnt. You don't take him on because if you take him on, he'll just punch you. If you don't pass to him when he's in front of the goal, you won't play again; he'll kick you off the pitch, because he's cock of the pitch.

But these days you probably wouldn't trust children to cross the road so you accompany them most places. When I was eight, I was out until I had to be in. My mum made sure we had to be in at six o'clock for teatime. From when school finished, I'd be out for three hours and I'd cross the roads and I'd be going to the shop and I'd be going to the chip shop.

It's not that it was better in my day. Many things are better now. Life has changed and it's not going back to how it was. But we do have to get a better balance for our young people, to give them opportunities. Their lives are very different to how we were brought up, sometimes for very good reasons. Safety is paramount and they live in a much better environment. Somehow, though, we need to give them the opportunities to take reasonable risks on and off a football pitch.

Firstly we should let our trainees play in school football, because there's a lot of streetwise kids out there and they need to learn how to cope with characters like that. And you should let them play other sports, because if you're playing basketball, for instance, it's got to be good for your athletic ability, with the jumping, landing and the need for stability. That needs to be looked at because we're not helping our children at present. We've introduced more sports at the United academy. They do a lot of gymnastics. They do boxing exercises and swimming. And when they come to summer camps they can do more sport. We've got gym-based classwork that they do where they're basically rope-climbing and climbing trees and stuff that we used to do without supervision. That play develops important biomechanics. God knows how many trees I climbed before I was 12. My son has probably never climbed one. Never. Many schools aren't allowed footballs in the playground nowadays. We're not saying everything is wrong now and was right then. It isn't and it wasn't. It's more that society and culture is changing very quickly and we have to adapt to help young people have some of the opportunities that we had.

***

Those that were at Manchester City still remember the day that changed everything: 1 September 2008. Salford's striker James Poole was an 18-year-old getting ready for training at the Premier League club. He had just been awarded a professional contract at the club, the team he had supported as a boy, and life was replete with enormous opportunities. He wasn't yet on the verge of the first team but he had made the first important step. And that summer he had been part of a group that had won the prestigious FA Youth Cup, an indication that these young men ought to be among the best in the country. Daniel Sturridge, now with Liverpool and one of England's best strikers, played in his team.

'We had tellies in the changing rooms, and one day we're all getting ready and it pops up that City had signed Robinho for £32million from Real Madrid,' recalls Poole. It was a preposterous notion at the time. City were a running joke in English football, the perennial failures forever being beaten up by their big brother down the road. Though he would ultimately turn out to be an expensive failure, Robinho was one of the most feted players in the global game. City were more used to scouring less powerful leagues for bargains. Suddenly they were taking star players from the biggest club in the world.

Unheralded, Sheikh Mansour of Abu Dhabi had purchased the club and immediately signed Robinho as a statement of his intent. It would take some time for City to become the force they are today, but essentially the entire outlook of the club changed. Without warning, it had been transformed from a jobbing Premier League outfit into a global brand. More stellar names would follow Robinho. Argentine Carlos Tevez was signed audaciously from Manchester United in a deal that was reported to be worth £47million in total; Nigerian Emmanuel Adebayor was signed from Arsenal for £25million.

Robinho, Tevez and Adebayor were all strikers. Poole, 18, was also a striker. 'They'd signed all these players and as a City fan I was delighted, I was in dreamland really, but as a player I think we all realised from that summer things were not going to be as they'd been previously, which at times got really frustrating for a few of us.'

Under Welshman Mark Hughes, who was the manager at the start of 2008, Poole felt there might still be a chance of progressing to the first team. 'There was a lot of people there who wanted us to be involved with the first team, like the coach Glyn Hodges, who was under Mark Hughes and was really good for us, He'd had a football league career, and he was a really good coach, wouldn't let us slack off. He brought great intensity to our training.'

Yet Hughes wasn't cutting it for the new owners with their global ambitions. So, alongside the trophy players, came a trophy manager in Roberto Mancini, an Italian who had had great success winning three successive league titles at Internazionale in his home country.

'When Glynn and Mark Hughes left, it was a really bad time for the reserves,' says Poole. 'We almost felt that there was nobody looking after us. No-one was saying to us: "You're going to go on loan to a smaller club or whoever. Go for a month and play some games." I understood the situation. Why would a manager risk his job on playing a young lad, or take a real interest in the young lads, when the reality was he wasn't going to be there for a long enough time to get the rewards of playing and blooding these younger lads?'

The average tenure of a Premier League manager is just over two years. Mancini, who won the FA Cup, City's first major trophy for 41 years, and the Premier League, actually lasted three and a half seasons. 'We almost just became a training team, the young lads,' says Poole. 'Every couple of weeks we would play a game against another academy and you might do really well. But it didn't really matter if you scored or did well, you were back in the next day training.' Meanwhile, lads lower down the league were cutting their teeth playing competitive games in front of thousands of fans week after week, where points and the livelihoods of the staff were at stake. They may have been playing at an inferior level to an elite club like City, but they were at least playing proper football.

When Poole was told that his contract wouldn't be renewed at City at the age of 21 he had hardly any real-life competitive football on his CV to back up his considerable talents: some academy matches were behind closed doors, and there were reserve team fixtures, but they were artificial experiences compared with playing in the lower leagues where he would now have to attempt to make a career.

'Looking back, and obviously with hindsight, you really need to be in first-team football at 18, 19, and if you play that's a massive, massive thing, playing at that young age.' Poole did eventually achieve three years as a professional footballer at Hartlepool United in League One and Two, the lowest tiers of the professional game. 'There was a lad there, Jack Baldwin, who I was playing with who had been playing first-team football at 17. He played a year and a half solidly, maybe two years, done really well and then by the time he was 19 he had 70 or 80 first-team games under his belt. He went to Peterborough in a big deal. He did his knee, unfortunately, but he's back fit now, and he's very likely to get a move off the back of that and that all stemmed from the games he was getting at such a young age.

'You can't replicate playing in front of fans and playing regularly, even at this level at Salford. A lot of clubs are more interested in winning youth cups than winning the league. And in fact it doesn't actually mean anything. Those players need to be playing first-team football at any level. A lot of people would almost look down on Salford and think, "We don't want to send our players there, it's not the right environment," when in fact for a 17-year-old it's absolutely the perfect environment.

'You just wish there had been somebody there to almost get hold of you and mentor you really. I'm sure if you speak to all the lads around my age group that were in there at the same time they'd feel the same and it's not bitterness at all. I'm a massive City fan and I understood where the club was at that time, but it was a frustrating time and looking back I think there could have been a lot more done with us.'

After a spell at Bury and then at a higher level of non-league with Dover Athletic in the National League, one tier below the professional game, Poole decided to stop attempting to pursue the dream of full-time professional football. He is now studying for a business degree at The Open University. Brian Marwood, the current academy director at Manchester City and one of the most senior executive staff, invited him back for an internship last year. He impressed and now works in the scouting department, analysing matches from around the world to pick up players for City's sister teams, New York City, Yokohama F Marinos and Melbourne City. The academy has been transformed since his time; Poole's impression is that the academy works much better now to help young players then they could during the time when the club was in transition.

But he can't help having **regrets**. And he knows several talented teenage footballers still become caught in a vortex of comfortable contracts at big clubs where they end up not playing. 'We have access to the data which is all pointing to the fact that with players who make it to the Champions League and World Cup finals, the experience they had before their 18th birthday was massive, as was the amount of games they had played. If you're getting some sort of football at that period it's massive, whereas most of the lads in the academy are playing in front of 20 people.

'I think we just need to kick the kids out on loan moves and see whether they can handle it or not. Make life hard for them and make them really earn the right to either get in the manager's plans for the first team or to go and earn themselves a career in the game. Being at an academy like City and being sent out on loan to smaller clubs is probably the perfect way. I've played lower league football and non-league football for quite a few seasons and I've not lost that basic ability on the ball that I had when I was at City but what I've added to my game is that I know how to win. I know how to conduct myself in a team that's pushing for promotion, a team with big expectation on them. And non-league isn't the old school of boot it and people breaking your legs, like a lot of people think. You get some really good players at this level. It is aggressive, but you go and play in City's first team: that's aggressive. You go and play in the Premier League: that's aggressive. Go and kick the kids out for a month or so. Let them fend for themselves and they might come back to City and think it's actually not too bad here and I'm going to appreciate what I've got here and work hard.'

***

Gary:

When I think about English football, I think we need to take more care of the roots of our game and show a bit more pride in our culture and where we have come from. That shouldn't mean that we become insular and closed off from the rest of the world. Football is always evolving and you have to take on board different ideas and welcome the rest of the world. But we have completely lost confidence in our identity.

There are teams that I see now playing football in the continent which are more English than the English. I think Borussia Dortmund are a very good example of English football. I think Atletico Madrid are a very good example of English football. If we'd just stuck to being what we are, we would have teams in the Premier League emulating what Atletico Madrid do. In Spain, five out of my first six opponents played 4-4-2. And I'm not talking about a flexible variable of that formation with fancy little shapes. They defended in a rigid formation. Honestly, I couldn't believe it. Eibar, Getafe, Rayo Vallecano, Atletico Madrid, Athletic Bilbao and Real Madrid, they all played 4-4-2 against us. And that has always been the foundation of English football, or at least since 1966.

AC Milan took it up under Arrigo Sacchi and put some bells and whistles on it through the offside trap. I think that Atletico Madrid now are doing it probably pretty much as you would expect a fantastic English team to have done it. You look at the Liverpool team with a very tight four in midfield and the two up top with Peter Beardsley dropping off Ian Rush or Kenny Dalglish dropping off Rush or Keegan dropping off John Toshack. I didn't actually play a strict 4-4-2 at Valencia. In fact, if I were a coach, I wouldn't play a rigid system like that. I prefer a variation of that system, like 4-2-3-1. But those are our roots and it's important to recognise that.

I think at the moment we've become stuck wanting to overplay, growing a more technical level of player but losing our physicality. Fitness-wise, other teams have caught up in Europe. They're definitely as fit, if not fitter. And I think we're stuck a little bit.

The FA blueprint at present talks about dominating possession intelligently. And on one level I agree with that. The Manchester United team I played in did that. But we also counter-attacked. We also could fight. Borussia Dortmund can do that, like Atletico Madrid can. They're both good teams; they can both dominate you; or if they choose, they can counter attack. Leicester City have just won the Premier League with 43 per cent of possession.

We're just a little bit stuck at the moment, trying to absorb the best from abroad but forgetting what we're about. We see an amazing team, like Brazil in 1970 or Barcelona 2011, and then we think: 'Oh we have to be like them.' But imagine if you're sitting in a house at home and you've designed your house because you like these curtains, you like this carpet. But then you go over to somebody else's house and you think: 'Oh I need to change now because they've got that.' You would be forever redesigning your house. So you might re-evaluate as football is always evolving. But the idea of tearing up everything and starting again? Barcelona split the centre-backs and they go and put Gerard Piqué and Javier Mascherano and whoever it is on the six-yard box, and all of a sudden I'm watching someone like Crystal Palace do it. I'm thinking: 'What are you doing? What you doing?' I'm watching Martin Škrtel and Mamadou Sakho split at Liverpool and they're giving goals away because they're trying to copy Barcelona.

My experience of Spain between 1995–2003 was: 'Easy meat. Give us Spain. Soft, not very good technically, haven't got an identity.' All of a sudden, Barcelona create this wonderful team with this wonderful crop of young players and then Spain become the pinnacle of world football. And rightly so. It's incredible what they've done. Absolutely magnificent. But why would we in England look upon that and think: 'Right, we have to follow everything that Spain are doing? We now have to follow everything that France are doing. We now have to follow everything that Germany are doing.'

If we want to copy from abroad, why not Atletico Madrid? Or Borussia Dortmund under Jürgen Klopp or Bayern Munich under Jupp Heynckes? Is there a more achievable style for English football? Are we really going to play like Barcelona in this country? Barcelona have only ever achieved that level of play for this period in their history. Is that us? Do we believe English football is Barcelona? If we do then we need to transform everybody's thinking because it's not. It cannot be. For me English football is aggressive, it's going forward, it's positive, and it's pressing. You try to keep possession but if it's not on, you play it forwards. When I played for England it only happened in bursts in tournaments and when we beat Germany 5-1 in Munich. Possession with tempo, but not for the sake of it, possession with purpose. That, to me, is English football. And that is what I played in at Manchester United for 20 years.

And I do believe in English football and in English players. I see Jamie Vardy, Harry Kane, Dele Alli, Ross Barkley, I think they're the right type and that they will prove it internationally as well. Dele Alli made a tackle before his goal against France at Wembley in November 2015, when he smashed it in from 25 yards, that was the highlight of my four years with England. It gives me confidence that, a boy who had played at Milton Keynes just over a year before, who's been well coached by Mauricio Pochettino and given an opportunity, is now playing for England, smashing Morgan Schneiderlin to win the ball and then receiving it back and knocking it in the top corner at the age of 19. I wouldn't lose faith in this generation of players.

He's a little bit angry, Deli. He might punch a player off the ball. But that to me is partly what an English football player is, someone who has this in-built aggression, passion, fight — and a level of talent. Jack Wilshere has it. He has a level of ability but he's also a little narky, he's also got that fight. The English spirit and character is something of which to be proud and we should be promoting ourselves and we should be believing in our system and in our style of football because it will come back. It is coming back.

The same issues exist around the lack of English coaches. You could argue that there are no English coaches coming through any more. That's one end of the argument. The other is that we've completely lost faith in our own. The answer is probably somewhere in the middle. We have a globalised Premier League with a lot of foreign owners and foreign sporting directors, who don't believe in English football culture. They think we're behind the times. But why do we not concentrate on what our own strengths are, our own characteristics, our own style and coach our coaches to be that way? But there is a lack of belief in ourselves at the moment.

It is difficult to take control of our identity when there is so little English input at the top end of the Premier League. I suppose that brings it back to Salford City and the idea of setting up an academy. Here we have some control and we can influence what happens. We can grow something organically and hopefully have an influence that way through the grass roots. I would always want Salford to be a team that tries to pass and create but one which can adapt, which can fight its way out of a game when necessary and think its way through a problem when that's required. A team that can dominate you but which can counter attack quickly. A team with speed, energy, grit, aggression and organisation. I think that is English football. And I think some of the best teams in Europe play that way. The sad thing is, they're not even English.

***

Phil:

Scholesy and I are trying to devise a programme for an academy here for Salford players. We think we need a specialised programme of games, so they're playing at different levels and get to know different styles. If I was a manager of a Premier League under-21 side now, I would devise my own training programme. Obviously you would play in the Premier League under-21 league, which is for me pretty basic football, standard. Twice a month I'd play a team like Salford or Prescot Cables, away from home, Tuesday night. Play them against the full side, a men's team, so they're having to play against 30-year-olds. And I would go abroad and play teams there. I would also go to tournaments where you have to play maybe two games a day or five games in five days. Because once you've done that, you know you can do it and it toughens you up.

Clearly the facilities that our academies have over here now are fantastic. You don't want to lose that. But since I've been at Valencia, everyone keeps asking me: 'What is their secret for producing players? What have they got in Spain?' They just put two goals up and they play football. And if they do well, the coach gives them a cuddle. There's a purity to it and it's really nice. When the youth teams play a tournament, they go on a bus for seven hours, which is good as they're bonding as a team. They have to do their homework on the bus and do what we used to have to do. They're all lifting their bags into the hotels, there's three in a dorm. Good! At City or United they would certainly be flying or going by train for distances like that. And they would have a kit man to do the bags. In Valencia, they take their kit home and they have to wash it and bring it back for the next game.

So at academies now in England you're not allowed to do PE at your school. If you miss a training session, then you don't play at the weekend. My son Harvey was at the academy in Valencia and had to go back to England for a couple of days and he was panicking. He went to the coach and told him that he would be away on Tuesday, and he was worried, thinking therefore he wouldn't be able to play on Saturday. And the coach said, 'Why can't he play Saturday?' 'Because he missed Tuesday's session.' 'And?' says the coach. 'If he's there Thursday, he plays Saturday. In fact, he can miss Tuesday, Wednesday, Thursday and he'll still play Saturday.'

'Can he do PE at school?'

'Why can't he do PE at school? PE's good for him. It's basketball. That's good for his co-ordination.'

'They have 5-a-side competitions at school on a Wednesday. Can he play?'

'Yeah, it'll be good for him, that, 5-a-side competitions.'

'But then he trains that night as well?'

'Yeah. So what?'

I like that. We used to play two or three games in a weekend and not have a shower in between! I told my son that and he was bit shocked, I think by the not showering. In England they would all have a fitness programme but in spain it's 'yes, do your PE at school and play football with your friends.' It's a different culture because they're outside all year round but there's a purity about it.

I did some work at the academy in Valencia and I think it's as much about how you can help young people develop and mature as about the facilities you have and the technique you can teach them. We will do things that challenge them. For example, I will make the kids come and speak out at the front. You can take the most nervous kid and insist they make a speech. Sometimes I'll make them do it in English and then my son, who was at the academy in Valencia, will have to do it in Spanish. The quiet ones, the nervous ones will be: 'No, no, no.' But once they've done it, they'll sit back down and you can see them grow.

I hate being taken out of my comfort zone. But it's important.

In England I think we have lost something over the last twenty years. I would like to find a way of restricting foreign players in the Premier League. Or maybe it's better to say I would like to find a way to promote our own. Obviously I appreciate the enormous input foreign players have had to our game. And I've benefited from going abroad. So I don't want to be insular about it. But the way forward for football clubs now has got to be to produce their own players. We have the talent in this country. I'm convinced we've got the talent. I went to a tournament with a Valencia under-14 team and it wasn't even the same level as in England. The English teams were far better. Far better. So why in four years' time are the Spanish players so much better? I don't think they are intrinsically better. In four years' time, though, they will be getting better opportunities. The second team in Valencia plays in a league against men. And it means something. There's a crowd and it's three points and there's relegation and promotion. And the coach is under pressure to perform; the players are under pressure to deliver. In all levels there are league tables. It's a competition. They want to win. In England, we don't have a league table from the age of 12 to 16. It's nice. The result, does it matter? No. I just go out and perform. Yeah, performance is good but ultimately it's about winning. I think we need to help our own more. We could find a way to encourage home-grown players.

***

Gary Stopforth, Salford City's midfielder, who is something of a lynchpin in the team, knows that he bears some of the blame. He joined Blackburn Rovers as a 12-year-old – no easy decision to make when you are born and bred in Burnley and support that team. The two Lancashire football clubs have a fierce rivalry. 'I turn-coated,' said Stopforth.

But he realised Blackburn's academy was going places. Jack Walker, the local steel entrepreneur who had used his wealth to fund Blackburn Rovers' Premier League title in 1995, had invested massively in the dream of bringing young Lancashire lads through to play for the first team. Walker died in 2000, but his legacy was the academy training centre he built at the club, with facilities second to none. It was intended to be an investment in the youth of the area.

'The facilities at Blackburn were just next level, they were top class back then,' recalls Stopforth. 'The first team used to train down the bottom of the hill and the academy at the top, and they swapped the first team over with the academy, because it was better, which I don't think Jack Walker would have been too pleased about.'

On one level the opportunity was second to none. But Stopforth was released as a professional player at the age of 20. 'I probably went out too much on a weekend, whereas other people were staying in and going to the gym and things like that. I do all that now I'm 29, but it's well too late.

'I never went out before games, but after games I would. That's what every young lad does and, I suppose, maybe to make it properly you've got to sacrifice. You speak to Gary Neville and he made those sacrifices. But there was no-one in my family to say: "Right, this is what you've got to do." I could do my own thing. It was up to me. It's my mistake if I want to go out. I mean, I had some good nights and stuff like that, but it's a strange one.'

So he knows it wasn't all about the influx of foreign players to the Premier League at that time, even though he feels that played its part. 'You didn't really get a chance back then at Blackburn. I mean, why would they risk me when I think they were in a relegation battle and then, the second season, they were going for Europe? And why would you risk a young lad when you can just go and sign, I don't know, an experienced player for three or four million?'

At the time, in the position Stopforth played, Blackburn had Tugay, a Turkish international they had signed for £1.5million, who had played in the World Cup semi-final in 2002 and who ended up with 94 international caps for his country.

'They had Tugay, Robbie Savage, Steven Reid in my position,' says Stopforth. 'I mean they're all blokes, you know. When I was like 18 I weren't developed or anything like that. I didn't fill out or anything. Some people they fill out when they're like 16 and it gives them a massive advantage, but it didn't happen to me. But it's just the way it goes, I suppose.'

***

Gary:

When young players come into our academy, I want them to be stress-tested. I want them to be pushed as far as they can and feel uncomfortable. I want them to be tested in every single way because I know once they come through those tests as young players, then they'll be capable of understanding the requirements at a higher level. And that's what I believe an academy should be. It's a given that an academy should be about technical development. It's a given you have to practise your skills, your touch, your tactical understanding. To me, they're givens. But actually the other bits, the physical and mental robustness, is where I think we are sometimes failing young people.

I'm talking about actually pushing them mentally and physically beyond what you think you are capable of. Once you've stretched young people, to a point where they'd never believe they could go, football becomes easy. Please don't mistake this for me thinking, 'It's not like it was in my day.' I will never come out with those statements. It's more about what can we do today to help young people achieve their goals. We want to have an academy up and running in the next few years, and when young players come into that they will be tested mentally and physically. We might make you play three games in three days. Is it the right thing scientifically? No. Physically, it's probably not the right thing. But if you can play three games in three days you can play three games in seven. I keep being told in every meeting I go into at elite football, 'I'm not sure he can play three games in a week.' Well, I'm sorry, he can't play for England then in a tournament. He can't play for Manchester

United or Chelsea or Arsenal or Manchester City, because they're likely to be in the Champions League. You can't play for those clubs if that's your starting point. If we're building players that can't play three games a week, we're failing. When you're preparing someone from the age 16 to 18 you have got to make them physically robust enough to cope with what's going to come their way. Cristiano Ronaldo, Lionel Messi, Steven Gerrard, Ryan Giggs, Paul Scholes, Frank Lampard, Wayne Rooney, Andrés Iniesta, Xavi, Carles Puyol and Gerard Piqué can or could all play three games a week. So what's happened to them? It's not because of the skill that they can play three games a week. It's because of their robustness, their mental and physical robustness.

***

Nicky:

There's a danger of giving young people too much, too soon. If a young 18-year-old lad's on £2,000 a week, it's a hell of a lot of money; not compared to a first-team player, but it's a lot of money in the real world, even for a mature adult. They're probably living at home still, they drive a nice car and they have a bit of spending money in their pocket. And if we don't give him that contract, then Manchester City will snap him up.

The problem is that if I say to that young player, 'For your development, you would be better off playing at Bury for £250 a week,' they're not going to do it. But ultimately playing every week is going to get you to where you want to be more than sitting on the bench at an academy and not playing and not developing. There's a lot of rules with the Premier League, the FA, UEFA and all the governing bodies to protect young players. But in my opinion there needs to be some sort of agreement where if a young lad is not playing a certain amount of games, then his contract's cancelled. It's not right that young men are sat on their backside at 18, 19 or 20 years of age.

It's different if you're 35, when you've had your career and you're just looking for a payday. But at 17, 18, 19 or 20 years of age, if you're collecting money each week and you're not playing at least 50 per cent of the games, your contract should be cancelled and you should be moving on elsewhere. That's my belief. Even the games we do play in the Premier League's under-21 league, we're questioning now how good it actually is and what young players are getting out of it. There will be some games that are unbelievably good. Liverpool at Anfield is a game you want to play in. There's usually about 5,000 fans there. There's passion there on match day. You want to win. They want to beat us. We want to beat them. There's competitiveness. There's one or two injured first-team players coming back. So that's a great game. But then the flipside is playing a team like Blackburn on the training pitch because the ground's not available. So we'll be playing on the training pitch on a Tuesday afternoon at one o'clock and there's no crowd and the wind's blowing the ball 200 yards down the field. You have to go to fetch the balls back and you're thinking, 'This is just not developing footballers.'

If you were playing at Bury in front of a crowd, that's immense responsibility at 19 years old. There's something on it. People's jobs are on the line and the fans are passionate about it and you get relegated or promotion; it's a million times better than what we have in the reserves at the minute. When we played it was like what it should be: proper games. Reserve games were always at a stadium, so always at Old Trafford or away from home at places like Anfield or St James's Park. Derby's Baseball Ground comes to mind; that was always a good game. It was never like a training game. And there was no age restriction, so you would have an experienced professional like Gary Walsh, who was in goal for us, or top players like Brian McClair and Mike Phelan, who were playing quite a bit, because they couldn't get in the first team or they were coming back from injury. Bryan Robson, who was England captain, played quite a few games for us as well, so you're thinking, 'Wow, this is really playing with proper men, proper professionals here.' And if you messed about once you'd know about it. You would be getting a bollocking off Bryan Robson and then we'd be getting spoken to by the coach Jim Ryan. Two minutes later the door would get kicked down and Sir Alex would walk in and really give you a roasting. So even though it was a reserve game you had the first-team manager there giving you a bollocking all the time and you would have the senior pros getting on top of you, so there was never anything easy about it. It was a hard learning school, but it was the environment that I believe you should be brought up in. It wasn't just a reserve game on a training pitch. It was proper.

The Premier League environment isn't necessarily a healthy one for raising young players. Because of the kind of people who own the clubs, if a manager isn't successful within 18 months, or sometimes less, then the manager's usually sacked and a new manager comes in. And he's not going to worry about these young players any more. He will go and buy ready-made players. If it weren't for someone with the mentality of Sir Alex Ferguson letting us make mistakes, giving us our chance, there is no chance we would have all made it.

For any youngster coming in, there is an element of luck as to how far you go in the game, because you prepare yourself from the age of seven to play, first for the youth team and then the next step the Under 21s or the reserves, and then, you hope, the first team. But ultimately you have to have somebody who will put their faith in you; someone who'll give you a chance. And that manager has to have foresight, be willing to plan for the future. And there's not many people that'll do that nowadays. There is no way that myself, Phil, Gary, Ryan, Paul and David Beckham would have all have come through at the same time; no chance that all six of us would have got through the system were it not for Sir Alex. Maybe Ryan would have, whatever, because he was exceptional. Paul maybe; but maybe not. He had exceptional skill but he was so small; he was a late developer. He might not have had the time at another club.

Sir Alex knew all our names from the age of 12. He knew us really well from the age of 14. To be fair, he was extraordinary and had this amazing memory about everyone's names. But he also knew us personally and our parents, which schools we went to, who was our schoolteacher. And he was willing to take a chance on us. We were also lucky because at that time there was a rule that you could only play four foreign players in the Champions League; and foreign in football rules also meant Scottish, Welsh and Northern Irish. So very often we would get the opportunity to play in huge fixtures because we were the best English players available and would be playing alongside Peter Schmeichel, Roy Keane, Mark Hughes and Bryan Robson.

Then, when we went to The Cliff training ground every day from the age of 16, we would eat in the same canteen as our heroes and the manager. There would only be a few yards from our changing room to the first-team changing room. You would be friends with some first-team players and end up being comfortable around them. So when you were called upon to train with them you were un-phased because you knew these people. They were still your heroes, still your superstars, still international players, but you knew them because you'd see them every day. Now there's not many trainees who would know our first teamers and be comfortable around them. You have to have a bit of confidence to go on a pitch and play with those players and not worry about not passing to him when he's asking for it or vice versa. And yes, I think it's similar in any walk of life, isn't it? If you're familiar with people you're more comfortable and you can get on with your job better.

Louis van Gaal showed when he was at United that he was willing to trust young players. Maurico Pochettino is the same at Tottenham. I think he knows that he's got young players that have got no fear and a manager like Pochetinno thinks: 'Why go and buy a 33-year-old player who has been there, seen it and done it and got millions in the bank? Is he really going to run through brick walls for you?' There's some great, more experienced players who still will, but most times the answer to that is no.

There has been some criticism of United's academy recently. People see the facilities that City have, and there's no getting away from the fact that it's phenomenal. Their trainees attend a private school and are bussed in to train at a ground with facilities that are better than most Premier League players will experience. But is it right that they get that much at that young age? They obviously think that it's right, and who am I to sit here and say it's wrong? But we feel that we're on the right track. We have a brilliant environment here. Certain things we can improve and we're working on that. But when it comes to producing players we're better than anybody else in the whole of the country. We always have been and we always will be.

When you look at clubs like Barcelona and Ajax, with great academies that bring players through, we have always been like that. And we believe that's the way forward now. We're proud of what we have here. We don't get everything right but we tend to get it right 90 per cent of the time. We're not where we want to be, because we've got massive aspirations for the academy. But it's moving in the right direction, and even though we're not where we want to be, we're still producing players. I know that City and other clubs have got all this investment and they're still not giving young lads a chance. So I sit in front of parents and look them in the eye and say to them, 'We'll get your son to a level where he can go and make a living if he does it the right way. And the ultimate goal is to get them a living at Man-United. If he does all the right things and he gets to the level he needs to be, there's a pathway there for him to go and play with the first team.' And they can see players like Marcus Rashford getting that chance. And parents know that I'm not lying, because whoever's in charge, whether it's Sir Alex Ferguson or Louis Van Gaal, or whoever it may be, they've got a remit from the board that they must blood young players. It's part of our club history and tradition that they will do that.

3 FEB 2016

COPA DEL REY
SEMI-FINAL, FIRST LEG:
BARCELONA 7, VALENCIA 0

Gary Neville walks into the press conference at the Camp Nou stadium. He has been Valencia's manager for just three months. His business partner Peter Lim, the 50 per cent stakeholder in Salford, persuaded him to take the role in December. He was reluctant initially, partly because of Salford and his business interests. But it seemed too big an opportunity to turn down.

He arrived in early December and initially all seemed well; they were knocked out of the Champions League in his first game but they drew twice in the league and were progressing in the Copa del Rey, the Spanish equivalent of the FA Cup. Even after a short Christmas break, they drew at home to Real Madrid. But good form in the Copa del Rey and the Europa League, the competition which accepts the best of the Champions League losers, could not placate a restless fan base. They had yet to win a single game in the league. Neville was parodied as 'the intern' in local papers for his lack of experience and close ties to the owner.

The Cups looked to be the only way to redeem the season, but Valencia had been handed the toughest semi-final possible in the Copa del Rey, against Barcelona, who at the time were playing by far the best football in Europe. A tight result here at the Nou Camp might just give them a chance back at their own ground, La Mestalla, in the second leg. But it hasn't worked out that way. Luis Suarez scored for Barcelona after seven minutes and added a second after 12. Lionel Messi scored after 29 minutes and Valencia had a player sent off just before half-time.

Messi ended up scoring a hat-trick and Suarez four in a 7-0 win.

After the match, the manager will always conduct a press conference. Neville now has to meet an already sceptical Valencia press pack. He walks into the small theatre-like press conference room at Barcelona and he spots some friendly faces, amongst them Jamie Carragher, his one-time adversary at Liverpool but a colleague on Monday Night Football with Sky Sports. He catches their eye, gives a wry smile and settles down. Carragher, who is here coincidentally on a visit, has just messaged him to tell him he's 'the new Pepe Mel'. Mel, a Spaniard, was West Brom manager for a few months in 2014, never coming to terms with the English football before being sacked.

Neville looks smart and in control, dressed in black pullover, white shirt and with no outward sign of anxiety. The whole process will be complicated by the simultaneous translation, necessitating an earpiece for Neville as the questions begin in Spanish. He fixes his inquisitors with a stare, making a point of ensuring he can make eye contact with them, as he listens to a translation of their questions.

The first comes from a newspaper reporter from *Periódico Levante*. It will set the tone. 'The other day after the defeat against Sporting, you said that you would sleep fine that night. I would like to ask you if you will be able to sleep okay tonight and if you believe that your position at Valencia CF is still sustainable? If not, do you feel that the Valencia job is too big for you?'

Neville doesn't flinch but fiddles with his earpiece to hear the translation clearly. 'To clear one thing up, when I said I would sleep well the other day, it is an English expression, meaning the team performance was better; not that I was actually sleeping any better. No, I won't sleep well; for your information, I didn't like what I saw. The Valencia fans didn't deserve that tonight and we have to recover incredibly quickly.'

The next question comes. 'Good evening Mr Neville, Hector Esteban from *Las Provincias* newspaper. The adjective I'm going to use, and this is out of respect, is that Valencia hasn't had such a ridiculous performance since Karlsruhe years ago. We lacked initiative; it was all chaos; Barcelona could have scored 12 goals. Do you think you're capable of saving the season from relegation?'

Neville deals with it in similar fashion before the expected question comes. 'Nadia Tronchoni from *El Pais*. Have you thought or are you going to think about your resignation?'

'No.'

A full 12 seconds of silence passes, a lifetime in these circumstances. Everyone is waiting for Neville to fill the silence, to elaborate. He declines. Eventually someone unable to cope with the awkwardness asks a question about tactics, but the more robust of the Valencian press aren't going to be satisfied with that.

In Spain radio reporters dominate football discussion and tend to be extrovert characters who broadcast live as they ask questions of their subjects. The next question comes from a reporter with one of the most powerful radio stations in Spain.

'Hi, good evening. Carlos Martínez, from Cadena Ser. You said that you had not thought about resigning, but after tonight's humiliation, I'm going to repeat the question that was asked the other day which you thought was ridiculous. Would it now seem understandable to you if you were to be dismissed from the post of manager of Valencia, given what we've witnessed this evening?'

Neville continues to stare at his inquisitor. 'Next question, please.'

That won't suffice.

'Mister, over here. I'm sorry but I have to really ask the same question as my colleague. The mildest descriptions being used right now by the Valencia supporters are humiliation and total disgrace. They are ashamed of their team tonight and you are the manager. The question is a reasonable one and it's one that we are asking because we are obliged to do so. You say that you do not intend to resign, but would you understand if they were to sack you because, since you came here, the team have not improved, in fact they are actually playing a whole lot worse than when you arrived at Valencia. So I'm asking the question with the greatest possible respect, but it is what the Valencia fans are thinking right now, who you said the other day had not asked you to leave.'

'Next question please. I've answered that question.'

***

Gary:

I remember going to the press conference and there must have been 200 journalists in there. I was walking in thinking, 'This is probably going to be the most difficult press conference you're ever going to have to face in your life.' And I didn't feel that bad. I suppose since the age of 24, 25, I've always been very good at being able to put things into perspective, and that was something I had to do at Valencia. I always remember because there was a young woman that had asked almost the first question and said, 'Are you going to resign?' I said, 'No.' It was a one-word answer.

And then I got asked it another four times. Some of the journalists were getting frustrated that I wasn't flapping. I wasn't getting angry. I wasn't giving them what they wanted but I was being very honest and just saying, 'No, I'm not going to resign. I'm going to keep working.' That was it. From my point of view resigning was never going happen. Sacking? Yes, of course you can be sacked. I knew that when I went out there. Valencia have had 27 managers in 23 years. And Claudio Ranieri, Hector Cuper and Rafa Benitez account for seven of those years between 1997 and 2004. So take those years out and it's 24 managers in 16 years.

The Barcelona game was ridiculous. We were 3-0 down after 29 minutes and then had a player sent off just before half-time. I always remember Phil saying, 'You'd better get out there on the touchline and be with them.' I remember standing out there for about half an hour watching it. We'd already made our changes and gone to 4-4-1, so there wasn't a lot more I could do in terms of formations. There was nothing more to do than watch and hope really. I was right on the edge of the pitch, seeing Neymar, Lionel Messi and Luis Suarez as close up as I've ever seen them before. And I was thinking, 'I don't think I'll see anything like this ever again on a football pitch. I've not seen it before and I don't think I'll see it again.' Three players that were absolutely toying with good, professional players; absolutely taking the piss; so good, so quick, so skilful, so intelligent, so brutal. I had watched them before in the Champions League but this was graphic. This was almost like watching a surgeon cutting open the skin of the body and seeing inside. It was so close up. It was just so graphic and brutal to watch. Part of you is thinking, 'Well, admire it, because I'll never see it again. I don't think I'll ever see a front three like that again, so close up, so devastating.

I'm sure every manager and coach will have been there, when you're sat there where you're thinking, 'Okay, what can I do to change it?' But the changes were made, the system was set, it was as rigid as I could get it. Maybe we could have gone 4-3-2. Maybe. But we were just waiting for the end of the game. I'm sure every coach has that moment. It's probably the only game out there that I felt like that. After half-time, we had exhausted every tactical change we could make and literally it was just a case of hope. I hoped that Suarez, Neymar and Messi and the coach, Luis Enrique, would sort of say, 'Right, we've got a league game at the weekend, we can sort of step off it a little bit.' And that he'd make two or three subs. But he never did. He decided it was a good moment just to rub it in. Well, fair enough. That's fine. But they were unplayable with 11 men. And with 10 men at 4-0 down? We were lucky to get away with seven, to be honest with you.

The Valencia media travel on the plane with the team, so that guy asking the questions was getting on the plane with me half an hour later. I'd always shake their hands when I saw them on the plane. Ultimately they have the right to ask that question. I've never been one to say, 'Oh, the press are terrible!' I've always sat there and analysed: is that question justified? I always think when managers snap at the press or the reporters, they've lost the battle. I always think to myself, 'If you were in the media, is it a question that you would have to ask?' And sometimes it's the way a question is asked. And if I was in the mood I'd say, I think that that question was out of order and answer another question. But I genuinely never came out of the press conferences, intense as they were, thinking, 'They're trying to stitch me up here.' They were only asking questions that, to be honest with you, the fans were asking.

***

Phil:

You knew straightaway when we kicked off. You could tell by the body language of the players. And you know what? You can't do anything about it. Sometimes you just have to take it. And it was one of those nights where you've got to stand there and take it. Firstly, Barcelona were unbelievable and they could do that to any team, I don't care what you say. And I really mean any team. And you knew when the first or second goal went in that this could be six or seven, because you could tell your team had lost belief. They knew. I knew. Everyone in the stadium knew what was happening. It's no different for the manager stood on the touchline.

I think you learn more about yourself in those kinds of moments. You learn how to lose. There's a certain way of losing. And a dignity you need to show in defeat. And looking at the other bench, how they acted against a team that was 7-0 down. And you learn about your players. And then you just forget about it. It happens. Don't beat yourself up about it because they'll do something else soon. We've all had them drubbings. I got beat 6-0 as a player by Arsenal first day in the season with David Moyes. It happens. If you don't see it as a learning experience to get better then you might as well not take part in it, because you could sulk and mope and be bitter and twisted, that's not going to get you anywhere.

***

The team arrived in the small hours of the morning at Valencia airport. However, the idea of slinking back into the city anonymously was not really feasible. Hundreds of fans had gathered at the airport gates to register their disgust, so when Phil drives Gary out in a black 4x4 at 3am, they are met by a jeering, angry crowd. 'Gary, vete ya!' they chant. It means 'Gary, go now!' As the chant grows in volume, one fan shouts, 'Wait a minute! Does anyone know this in English?' No-one does.

Valencia would announce that Gary Neville had been sacked on 30 March after a run of five defeats in six games. He had spent just four months at the club. Phil would stay on as a coach. The decision would ultimately be made by Lim, the club owner and the man who hired him.

***

215

Gary:

It's not unusual for the fans to turn up at the airport and at the ground if there's been a bad result, and that night was as bad as it gets. So we knew they were going to be waiting when we got there. Which was interesting to note. You could argue it wasn't pleasant, but at the time I said, 'These people are unbelievably passionate, they're crazy, and imagine what a force they would be if you're winning.' I kept thinking that at the time, because there was no point in me feeling down about anything.

Mauricio Pochettino said to me, 'Gary, you took the toughest job in football.' I knew that full well, even though I know the owners and we have a very good relationship with each other – while we are also very honest with each other. If there is a problem we have to speak to each other and they have to treat me like any other manager. People think I got the job because of the owners, but I also got sacked by those owners. They weren't afraid to make a decision.

In the cups I think we won seven out of 11 games, but in the league we were suffering and that was where the pressure was coming. The cups were a release. But from the moment I arrived to the moment that I left, I never had one free week where we didn't have a game, apart from the Christmas break, which is a compulsory rest for everybody. From January, we had 23 games in 78 days. I felt like we were on a roundabout and just couldn't get off and couldn't recover the players mentally and physically. We couldn't get any work in them. There was never a point where I could give them two days off – even one day off was a struggle. I think we probably only had four or five days off in a period of about three or four months.

The toughest part was not being able to coach the team at all. Literally, we were selecting a team, recovering, selecting a team, recovering. Ultimately it was a situation that I knew I had to deal with. I knew when I went over there what I was getting myself into, but if I could change one thing really it would be the programme – it was just so intense.

And when you can't coach tactically, you're relying on your communication skills. And of course, I didn't have that. There were some team talks that were maybe 10 minutes long. And by the time they had been translated they were 20 minutes long. And by the end even I was bored of hearing myself translated. With England I would love doing the post-match debrief or the pre-match team talk on the opposition. But at Valencia, because of the translation, I couldn't do it.

I knew communication and language was going to be a problem. I've been on courses with the League Managers' Association where I have discussed how futile it can be to go abroad without the language. And the reality of it is, the mistakes were all mine. I don't look at the players, I don't look at the club, I don't look at the fans, I don't look at the media: the mistakes were mine.

But do I feel that period reflects on me as a coach? No. Do I feel as though it reflects on me as a person? No. Do I believe that actually it was a failure? I don't even look at it like that. It was an experience from which I have learnt so much. I wish I could have stayed for longer because I didn't feel my education was complete. I wanted to learn the language properly, I wanted to immerse myself deeper into the culture of football. Even in four months I learnt so much from the Spanish way of doing things and I would like to have learnt more.

The first day I was there, we were out on the training pitch, and in England the goalkeepers always come out first and start warming up and training on their own. They'll be diving around, doing ball work with their hands. So the first day we get out there and I said to Phil, 'Where are the keepers?' And he says, 'Oh, here they don't do it like that. The keepers come out and train with the rest of the players.' And I said, 'Well, I'm not happy. Get them out early.' But all through my time they would come out with the rest of the players and train with them. So they would join in the rondos, the passing exercise at the beginning of training, with the rest of the team. And when we played mini games, they would play as a sweeper at the back. Well, after a few weeks it was really bugging me and I called in the goalkeeping coach, José Manuel Ochoterena. And I said, 'José. Why don't you get them out working before the rest of the team?' And he explained, 'We can do all the work with the hands at the end of training. They're tired then and that's more like a match. And during a match they only touch the ball with their hands 15 times maybe. With their feet, they might have to touch the ball 30 or 40 times. It's more important that when they're fresh at the beginning of training they're working with their feet.' Of course. It's obvious. But I've never seen an English team do that, not even one coached by a foreigner.

I always remember we beat Rapid Vienna 6-0 one night in the Europa League and United lost to the Danish side, Midtjylland. Someone rang me to say that people were saying I should take over from Louis van Gaal. Seven weeks later I was sacked. That's the perspective that I put on it. My record was 10 wins, 11 defeats and 7 draws. If it had read 15 wins, 6 defeats and 7 draws people would say I'd done a good job. And I know how close we were to that. Ultimately every manager might have a similar story. But I'd put myself in a very difficult situation, with lots of handicaps, and we were close to getting it right. So I can always put things in perspective.

When it was actually announced that I was leaving and that I'd been sacked, I'd already moved on because I knew seven days before. I remember coming back to Manchester a week later and people had those little puppy dog eyes as if to say, 'Are you alright, Gary?' I remember saying to one or two of the people, 'Get on with your job! Everything's fine.' People were coming up to me saying, 'Oh, you'll recover, you'll bounce back.' And I was thinking, 'I've already recovered and I don't feel like I need to bounce back.' Genuinely that's how I felt. I can very quickly compartmentalise things, put things into a box.

***

Phil:

The only reason we bought Salford City is because we can actually have control and we can develop a football club the way we think it should be done. That's why we went down the football pyramid, because we can actually do what we want to do there. In football, unless you're an owner, you're in the hands of other people. Somebody could wake up and sack you. You could be working for a football club, they bring a new manager in, he doesn't like you and you could be sacked. You could have a bad bunch of players, get injuries: sacked. Your life is in the hands of other people. It's not a nice feeling, and sometimes I wake up and think, 'Is it actually worth it? I mean really worth it?' At Valencia I was the first in, last to leave, but I didn't get to do anything once Gary had gone.

Gary got sacked, and being sacked hurts you and it knocks you and you doubt yourself. And then you look at all these other managers – they've all been sacked. Claudio Ranieri, José Mourinho, Jupp Heynckes, Ronald

Koeman. They've all suffered. They've all got through it. When I left United, after David Moyes was sacked, for like a month I was thinking, 'If we had got a result there' or 'We should have done this.' But then you think, 'Bloody hell, just move on, get another job, and move on.' You have to protect yourself. The first sacking is the worst, but it's the best thing that could happen because actually you realise that everyone else gets sacked. You go into a job and you know full well at the end of it you're going to get sacked, so you can't doubt yourself and you stick to what you know.

Despite all that, I will do it. I will be a manager one day. I know I'm lucky to be in a position where I can choose, but I will do it and put myself in that uncomfortable position. That's why Gary probably had to do the Valencia job even though probably everything in the world was telling him not to. He's done it. He got the sack but actually it wasn't a disaster. It was actually a brilliant learning curve. And people were saying, 'Oh, he won't be able to go back on TV now.' Well, Graeme Souness has been sacked. Glenn Hoddle's been sacked. Great players, good managers and excellent TV pundits. They've all been sacked. Gary's always mapped his life out. 'When I finish football, I'm going to do this.' This was like uncharted territory. It wasn't in the plan.

***

Gary:

If you'd said to me would I have gone into coaching and full-time management before Valencia I would have said it would have to be a unique offer. And I think it was a unique offer that forced me to go. It was four months that made me even more knowledgeable. But it also reinforced thoughts that I had about English football, about where English football's at, and where I'm at in terms of my development. I think I can bring those learning experiences back to Salford. We have to have our own identity at Salford and we have to believe in it. I look at Salford and I think: passion, care, character, spirit, personality. These are the qualities we should be building on. And whilst we should always be open to outside influences, we should know what we stand for and build around that.

I want those words to run through the club because I think those qualities – character, personality, care and passion – define people. If you have players and young people who have that within them, you can achieve so much. People say to me: 'You should be a football coach.' But though I am sure I will do that, I do ultimately want to achieve more. Because as a football coach I can go and win five matches, I can go and win 10. I can get called an idiot, I can get called great. But by running an academy at Salford and owning a business we can affect much more. We can try to impact the most people we possibly can. Not just 20 rich football players.

In my time at Valencia we used to do a passing drill at the start of training. They call it the rondo over there. At Manchester United we called it boxes. Two players in the middle and seven around the edge. The seven around the edge have to keep the ball away from the two in the middle, using just one touch. We did it every day at Manchester United for 25 years.

In Spain, when a player hits a really slow, steady, safe side-foot pass, the Brazilians, the Spanish and the Argentinians will laugh and go, '*Pase Inglés*'. English pass. We're a joke to them. I was in meetings with agents over in Spain, and if they wanted some money for a player they would say, 'Ah, sell to the English.' When they talk about coaching, they won't even put an English coach up. They just laugh at us. They think what is happening here is funny and a chance to make money.

We've sold our identity. All the benefits of the Premier League, all the amazing things that have happened with the influx of great players, great coaches, the new stadia: it's come at a cost. There is a cost to the fan.

At Salford we're not looking to fight the establishment. We're not looking to be outlaws, but if no-one stands up to some of the things that are wrong in English football, how is it ever going to change? If we just sit there and say, 'Yeah, that's the way it is,' then we're stuck with the status quo. There's one small example at Salford, but you could find a hundred examples of this kind of thinking in English football.

We've frozen ticket prices at Salford and we've said that at the moment we're not lifting them at all. It's still £7 and £1 for a junior. We don't believe in lifting our ticket prices. We want it to be affordable. I believe football should be affordable for people to come and watch. There'll come a time where we'll have to lift our ticket prices, but I hate the idea of charging £75 for a ticket. I hate it.

We had a big important game, a play-off game against Ashton United. So we wrote to the Evo-Stik League just to check, as we have to, that we would stick with our usual ticket prices: £7 standard, concessions £2, under-16s £1. The reply we got back was that we would have to charge £8 and £4 for under-16s with no further concessions. Because the gate money is split with the opponents and because it wasn't a usual home game, ultimately the Evo-Stik league had jurisdiction.

But as a club we emailed back to say we wouldn't be increasing our ticket prices for the play-offs, as we deliberately kept our prices low this season to attract more fans, which has worked.

At that stage we were told it was an Evo-Stik League decision and we had to comply. So I got involved. I contacted the league and asked them to reconsider. We even agreed to increase the percentages that Ashton and the Evo-Stik league get to ensure they didn't lose out. But, still, the answer came back: No.

How can that be right? We made a commitment to our fans that we would always keep our pricing low but the authorities are telling us to charge more. On the night we charged £8 as instructed so Ashton got their full amount. And from our own money, we gave £1 back to everyone. So when you came through the turnstile, you received a voucher for £1 back. And went over to a table to collect your £1.

The reason we keep going down to Salford is not just because we own the club. We actually like it. It's real. There are kids playing behind the goals. There are people walking round with a pint in their hand. It's cheaper than going to watch League Two football. Once you start getting up to £10 and £12, which some clubs are doing, you're into £50 for a family day out. How can we justify charging people that with the facilities that we have? I just find the whole thing bizarre.

We were looking to play a part in the league. We didn't want Ashton to lose out so we agreed we would subsidise their extra pound or whatever it might be. But if you think about a family bringing three kids to the game tomorrow night, they're actually taking an extra £10 off them. They've doubled the price. I think £10 is a lot to a family who come and watch us all season when they're normally paying a pound. They've also told us our season ticket holders can't come in for free. Our season ticket holders that have watched us all season and now have to pay, which just seems crazy. Why don't they make easier for the fan? I don't get it.

There'll be people listening to this saying, 'Gary you work on Sky; Gary you work at the FA; you benefit.' Yeah, I do, but it doesn't mean to say that I have to abide by everything that happens. It doesn't mean to say I have to like it. What do you want me to do? Just not work in football ever again? We're trying at some point to make a stand about things that actually we believe are important. And we believe it's important to support your team and that grounds are fully accessible to all people, which they're not any more, because we benefited from that as kids. We turned up and paid at the turnstile and queued to watch United and other clubs. From our point of view, that's something that was a big part of our childhood. Kids now have to order tickets in a ballot two months in advance. It's mad!

I'm sure people will look at Salford and say that we've got a very big budget relative to the league and we have. But we're spending the extra money on players and we're keeping the prices low. So the fans are getting a better quality of player for the same price and I think we've got to try to keep it as affordable as possible. Of course we'll have to put our prices up at some point, but when you've got fan groups marching on 10 Downing Street, when you've got the Premier League capping away tickets at £30, yet for our FA Cup games against Hartlepool and against Notts County, the FA forced us to put our price up to £10. Why? What's £3 going to do to them? It's probably £900 extra.

Clubs need to make money, they need to be sustainable. I understand that. But let's take Aston Villa as an example. Their ground now has a capacity of 42,000. The Holte End holds 13,000. Why can't half of that be made available for local people paying between £10 and £15 a ticket? Because football was a working man's game, a working-class game, and was located at the heart of the community. People still use those phrases, but the reality is that it's no longer true. But actually there still could be a quarter of the ground or a stand in the ground that could remain the heart of the community.

Let's say the rest of the ground is £50, £60, but that stand is £10, £15 a ticket just for people that live within a certain distance. And the same goes for the Kop at Liverpool, the Stretford End at United and the Clock End at Arsenal. I believe football needs to do that. The Premier League has capped away ticket prices at £30. It now needs to go that step further. It needs to stay true to its local roots and its community. It should be globalised. We should accept fans from all over the world, and corporate boxes and executive price tickets will always be part of the model now. However, there should still be that thing that we look after our own. This is our club and it's born out of our streets, whether that's Manchester, Liverpool or London. That may be an old-fashioned principle but that's what I believe.

13 FEB 2016

· ·

As winter crept into spring, Salford struggled. Gary Neville was now in Valencia, where Phil was already working as an assistant coach. In theory, it should have made no difference to the day-to-day running of Salford. By February though it was clear that something wasn't right in the dressing room.

Perhaps the euphoria of the FA Cup run had worn off; maybe opponents were taking them more seriously; or the club was missing the unique brand of Neville enthusiasm. Whatever the reason, the team was falling away. A home defeat by Stourbridge was followed by a narrow away loss to leaders Blyth Spartans. The Blyth defeat was perhaps understandable. The opponents were a good side in fine form and Salford played well. But then there was a disappointing home draw against Frickley Athletic. February starts with a 4-0 home win against bottom club Ramsbottom which seems to be have broken the poor run of form. That hope, however, proves to be an illusion.

The nadir comes at home to Darlington, when Salford are 3-1 up with 20 minutes to play. They lose 4-3. At training on the Tuesday, Johnson and Morley make the team run and run. It was a punishment for the laxity of the Saturday before. Several players are unhappy and Danny Webber, the club's most experienced player, a man who has had a long professional career in the Premier League and the Championship, picked up on the growing discontent. Before training that night we all received a message saying not to bring our football boots, he said, 'We knew then we'd be doing only running that night.' I had probably eight text messages saying, "Webs, you've got to have a word. Why are we doing that?" I looked at the dressing room and I thought, "The lads are going here. They're on their way out mentally and we've got a big thing to achieve. We've got a league to try to win and I'm watching people disengage. They're there in body but they're not there in mind, and the more they feel like they're being punished, the less they're going to give back."'

Webber spoke to Morley. Morley took the message back to Johnson. Johnson wasn't happy. Webber, though, was relaxed about his role. 'I'm not scared of any situation. I don't need to be. You're speaking to people and if people take it the wrong way, that's their choice. All I did on the day was put across the lads' point of view and I just voiced that to the managers. I just said to Bernard, "I'm 100 per cent in and I don't want this season to fizzle out, so you need to know how the lads feel, because this is how it is. And I didn't let him know who it was or who'd spoken to me – it was all in confidence. But I just said, "You need to know that, because if you lose the dressing room, you've lost everything, so I'm giving you the information. What you do with that information now is totally down to you."

'I'm not the sort of character or the sort of person who would go in moaning every day. I don't say a word. When the managers came in last year they expected me – and they've said this to me – to have a bit of an ego and be a bit big-time. They came in and gave us a level of work, running and hard graft, which they didn't think that the likes of me and Gareth Seddon would put up with. And as hard as it was, it wasn't harder than anything I've ever done before. I didn't enjoy it, but I showed them: "That's not how you're going get me out of here. There's no amount of hard work you're going to put in front of me that I'm going to buckle under. My body would have to physically stop. I may not do the time you want me to do it in, but there's no amount of work you're going to put in front of me that's going to break me." And that was how they sorted the wheat from the chaff very quickly. The people they brought in were prepared to do the work because they knew what they did at Ramsbottom. There was a select few of us, a handful of us who were like: "Okay, throw what you want at us. We're here because we want to win and we want to be here." That was another thing that unified everybody at the time. Like I say, Jonno may have been unhappy with what I said. It was Bernard I spoke to, and if you actually sat and spoke with Bernard, he would know that I did it not for my gain.'

'We still ran the next time we trained but we had a big talk at the end of it. I'm not going to be everyone's cup of tea. You can't be liked by everybody. But you need the masses pulling in the right direction. And once you see the masses are starting to fall off and not buy into what's going on...It's my last year of my career. I'm not here to waste my time. I'm not here to waste the last six months. I may as well have not been involved if people are not going to be on board with what we're doing. So I thought that something had to be said, and if that meant I sacrificed myself, and Jonno and Bernard isolated me, I would have just held my hands up and said, "You know what, I tried my best, thank you very much," shook hands and walked away. But it was taken in the right spirit, it showed that I cared and it also showed the lads that I would back them and I would go in and speak on their behalf if the need arose.

'The managers are younger than me, but I'll say this for them: from the very first day they came in they've shown me a level of respect, so it's not a case of I'm the manager and you must obey. They've also shown me a level of respect as a person and said: "Look, we can't tell you how to play football. You, by far, know how to play football better than we do. Basically, all we ask is that you put the work in." And I'm alright with that. I've always been okay with that. They'll be pretty straight with *their* opinion and if you are a player and you understand the dynamics of the dressing room, their opinion is actually the only thing that matters because if you don't go along with it you don't play. If you don't agree with it, it doesn't really matter because there's not much you can do about it. At this level, you can be gone in a heartbeat. Most of the lads who aren't contracted can be gone tomorrow, so it is very much a like it or lump it.'

Some home truths may have been aired, but if anything the performance on the pitch gets worse. At Ilkeston the next weekend, in a game they would be expected to win easily, the team lose 2-1.

***

Danny Webber found out Sheffield United had let him go when his friends saw it on *Sky Sports News*.

It had been a tricky season. Sheffield United were a prominent Championship club in 2008–09, and they had reached the final of the play-offs, a chance to be promoted to the Premier League. They were on the verge of the elite, and Webber had been led to believe there would be a new contract for him in the summer. But the warning signs were beginning to flash. In the play-off final, at Wembley, a game worth around £80million to the winner, he wasn't in the team or even on the bench. Then Sheffield United lost, 1-0 to Burnley.

'You come to realise that you're dispensable in football, and I think the moment I realised it was when I was at Sheffield United in my fourth season, my final year. I was told I was going to get a new deal. Okay, happy days. But I'm thinking, well, what does that look like, how long's it for? I'm not stupid enough, if I don't see the paper and the pen, to think it's done. The closer you get to having no contract the more insecure you start to feel. This is where I say you become aware that you're more of a commodity than anything. I could tell by people's behaviour towards me. You can just tell that people don't fancy you at that moment in time for whatever reason and it can knock you as a person.

'We left Wembley after the play-off final and I drove back to Manchester, booked myself a flight the next morning to LA. When I landed in LA, I didn't have any missed calls or anything like that but somebody texted to say, "Gutted to see you leave." I was getting a lot of messages like that, so I googled Sky Sports. And it's up there: "Danny Webber, Ugo Ehiogu have been released by Sheffield United." And I thought, "Oh, that's a great way to end the four years, you know."'

All professional footballers know it deep down, but few express it publicly because to do so would be deemed ungrateful, and thus even more out of touch with reality than they are already perceived to be. Working in a profession which many young men idolise, earning money few can dream of, is meant to soften the edges. But ultimately, a player is a human asset listed on a balance sheet.

'I'd say probably in my mid-twenties the shine was taken off football as a game,' says Webber. 'And you can probably tell in my performances to a certain extent. You grow up and it's the dream and people tell you it's the dream, and you go out onto the field and you're living your dream; and then you realise that with everything that's such a big business, there's so much politics involved, and you become a pawn in the whole game. So that side of things I came to terms with very young, where some people like to believe that dream even into their thirties, and people daren't look at the fact that you are a commodity. You are a commodity, and when it's time to dispose of you, you're disposable.

'You realise that when you're not playing in the team and you think, "I'm doing everything I've been told to do as a young boy." You sacrifice your lifestyle, you're going to bed early, you're eating right, you're giving 110 per cent in training every day. And then you notice that somebody who gives 50 per cent, who has come into the club through a different route, gets treated differently. Some managers would pick you and they'd tell you one thing to your face in their office and then make the decisions opposite from what they just said to you in the room. And you're meant to sit there and just accept it. You wouldn't accept it from the man in the street. But you're almost told: "We're paying you, so put up with it and shut up."

'And some of the love goes, it does. It's not the love of the game, because I'd still go and kick around in the street and love the actual game. Once you've crossed the white line or you're kicking around with your mates in the park or whatever it is, that is the game to me. But once the shine gets taken away from that sometimes it's a little bit: "Oh, right, this is really what I'm involved in." Some people don't care and just get on with it. Other people become aware of it and I'm very aware of that kind of thing. That might have been to my detriment, but I'm very aware of how people acted towards me. I'm competitive, I'm driven, I'm all those things, but I'm not one for treating people badly and that goes down to my upbringing. Obviously you're never going to please everybody, but certain people don't care. They don't care as long as *they* get ahead.'

Webber is quiet and unassuming off the pitch. In the dressing room, though, he is a forceful, authoritative presence. There he can exert an influence with just a look here or a word there. If you wanted to improve the image of professional footballers with the more sceptical section of the general public, Webber would be your ambassador. Calm, sensitive, intelligent, engaging and a good father.

Yet even with brains, it's easy to get sucked in. Young men acquire unimaginable piles of money to spend. 'I don't think if you'd met me on a one-to-one it would be the case that I had an ego, but if you saw me from afar I would have appeared to have the trappings, if you get what I mean.'

By the trappings he means the five cars, including a Range Rover, BMW M6 Convertible and a Mercedes C-Class. And then there was the clothes. 'It was beyond ridiculous the amount of clothes I had. And trainers. I would say into the hundreds of pairs of trainers.'

And then the football comes to an end and the big money steps. For Webber that was 2012. He was scrabbling around trying to get Championship contracts – still good money – and had played for Leeds, probably the biggest club outside the Premier League, and was waiting to hear whether he would get another year when he injured his knee on the last day of the season.

When that happens you don't need to ask what comes next. You know you're expendable. You just get your bags and leave. Webber had an operation on the knee in the summer and instead of starting the new season, he embarked on a new phase of life.

'I quickly realised how fickle the industry actually is, because my phone stopped ringing. All of a sudden I was without a club and I had an injury, so my days consisted of getting up and going to the gym and trying to do rehab with a physio. But the physio would be with me for an hour and then I'd have to do it all myself.

'Being a professional footballer disables you. Unless you're aware of it, it disables you from being a capable 35-year-old man in the world. It's all well and good when you've got a level of money that can take care of everything. So when you're playing it's: "Can you help me a buy a house?" "Of course I will, but here's the fee." "I'm not bothered about the fee, just sell me the house." I need a car. Here's a fee. That's fine, just take it out my bank. You know, it's very easy when you have that level of money. But then all of a sudden you may have that level of money when you finish and you may have looked after it very well, but it doesn't account for the person who can't make dinner for themselves or the person who's got a lot of time to fill.

'You're used to a routine. You get up and you train. Suddenly you get up in the morning and there's no routine, there's nobody demanding you are somewhere. It can be a lonely place. I see a lot of people who seem to sit in their house with the realisation that you're not actually that valuable to everybody in the world any more. It's a big deal and a big ego slap for a lot of people. The bigger people's egos are, the harder it hits. There's no amount of money that accounts for your mental health. I've seen more and more people struggling with the transition.

'So I thought, what can I do within football? Media maybe. Coaching. So I applied to do my coaching badges. Obviously media, but you're one of so many people that want to do it, so you need to go away and learn. I wasn't like Scholesy who would go straight on to BT. I had to go away and learn the craft. I thought: "Okay, that's what I'll do." I accepted a lot of free work with local radio, with Sky Sports Radio, with different newspapers, shadowing people, just watching to learn how it works from that side of the game. People think they know, but you don't until you're actually stood in it.

'And I started trying to trade commodities. I was just basically putting a deal together between two people. It was things like sugar, oil transactions and so on. Also I know a lot a people within football and I had three, four, five different agents coming and saying would I come and work for them? At the time it was almost like: "Be a football agent? Are you crazy?" Because I knew the players' perception of agents and I just thought, "I don't need to tarnish my reputation or be involved or be branded like that." So that year sort of went by and it was actually a year of earning no money from football for the first time since the age of 16. I thought, okay, that's what it feels like to not earn any money from football.

'And I just had to cut my cloth accordingly. Drop any form of ego that I had. And it was very good for me, probably one of the best things that could have happened, in a way, when I look back. What am I doing with all these things? I looked at the amount of clothes I had. I just started to strip everything back in my own mind and go back to what I was when I was 16 years old but with all the knowledge and education that I'd learnt. I stripped my life back.'

The cars went, the clothes downsized to a more manageable level. Life came back down to earth. There was an offer the following season from a League Two club, Accrington. He met good people there, but overall didn't enjoy the experience. So professional football was pretty much over for him by the summer of 2014.

Webber would have a last throw at League One club Walsall. He did all the pre-season training, got himself fit and played in the pre-season friendlies. All was going well. But he was a striker and he wasn't scoring. Dean Smith, the manager at the time, told him, 'I need to be able to justify this to my board. I need a striker but I can't really say I need a striker that's not scored a goal since he's been in the building.'

Webber didn't mind that. It was straight talking to his face and a justifiable decision: not the norm in football. So he threw himself into media work. BBC Manchester asked him to work with commentator Bill Rice at a low-level game. Salford City had just been taken over. They were playing a friendly against their owners, the Class of 92, at Salford's rugby league stadium, which holds 12,000. Because of the celebrity involvement, a large crowd was expected, meriting local radio coverage.

Webber went and worked the game. It was quite an event; unexpectedly the stadium sold out. There was traffic chaos on the motorways, people abandoning cars to make kick-off. More importantly, the Class of 92 were struggling on the pitch against their employees. The years had rolled by – only Giggs was still playing professionally – and they needed reinforcements. 'At half-time I came down for a cup of tea,' Webber recalls. 'The dressing room door opened and it was Gary, Giggsy, Scholesy, Butty and they said: "What you doing?" I told them and they basically said, "Forget the radio! Come and play the second half!" So, off the back of that, at the end of the game Gary and Scholesy said, "What you doing next year?" Carlisle wanted to sign me at the time but I thought, "I don't want to be in Carlisle, if I'm honest." So I said to Gary, "Alright, let me think about it."'

At 6am the next morning Webber was awoken by the familiar ping of a text message arriving on his phone. It was Gary Neville. 'Come on, Danny, you going to do it? Do you want to do it?'

'I texted back, "At least give me till I've had my breakfast! I'll give you a shout." I spoke to him later on in the day and he said, "Look, if you don't like it, you can go. But we'd love to have you and I think you'd help us massively. Come down to training. If you don't like it then you don't need to come back. So I came down and then, you know what, it was the first time for ages I was with a group of lads where I enjoyed the atmosphere. I enjoyed it: egoless people who wanted to just have a graft and work together. For me it was like stepping back 15 years to a group of lads who weren't bothered about money, cars, anything like that. It was just, let's play football, lads. I thought, "This is great!"'

***

There are few more beautiful places to take a Sunday morning stroll than the Andalucian city of Granada, with the thirteenth-century Alhambra, built by the Moors, dominating the skyline. The sun is relentless, but in February the winter chill provides a pleasant counterpoint.

Gary Neville was enjoying one of the short good periods in his management job at Valencia. The team had finally won a game in La Liga at the tenth attempt under Neville, beating Espanyol. They had then won 6-0 at Rapid Vienna in the Europa League. It seemed a corner was being turned.

Neville was making his way for a mid-morning coffee to collect his thoughts before the game that evening when a text came from Karen Baird. 'I'm not sure we'll have managers next week,' it read. Neville called immediately. After Salford's loss to Ilkeston, Johnson and Morley wanted to quit. It seemed they had had enough. They felt the team wasn't delivering for them so it would be more honourable to go.

***

Gary:

It's probably one of only two conversations that I had with Karen whilst I was in Spain, because obviously I was just completely immersed in the Valencia job. Apparently after the Ilkeston game they'd said to Karen: 'That's us done.' She thought there were rumblings around senior players. I said, 'Look, Karen, the idea of them walking out is just absurd. It's ludicrous. We won't accept their resignations. Tell them to calm down. They're going to have bad moments.' I suppose having had three promotions in four years upto 2015 and then the FA Cup run, they've not experienced a poor season. I had taken over at Valencia on 9 December and I didn't win a league game until 25 February! We were winning in the cup and we had drawn at home to Real Madrid but still... My feeling was 'This isn't a bad moment, trust me! Losing a couple of games and losing against Ilkeston away isn't a bad moment. They need to calm down.'

They had signed Josh Hine, a centre-forward, in January. And I was talking from afar and had absolutely no detail; I'd not spoken to any of the players. But I was just looking at the circumstances that could have arisen and caused some offence or conflict in the dressing room. And I was thinking, 'Hang on a minute, we've got four good centre-forwards and they've signed a fifth.' I said, 'Ask them to think about how James Poole, Gareth Seddon or Danny Webber, who are the three most experienced players in the team, and Jordan Hulme who's done really well for us, how they might take that.' All of a sudden, you four are sat there thinking, 'Hang on a minute, they're signing another centre-forward, they mustn't fancy us.' They might have been thinking or saying, 'The writing's on the wall for me. I'm going to be leaving. I'm not going be here. I'm not going to play any more.' And once you've got two or three saying that in the dressing room, if that's what was happening, you've then probably got a situation where it spreads to six or seven because negativity just spreads. I said to Karen, 'Tell them to deal with that situation. Tell them to hit it head on. Speak to the lads who they think might be the cause of the problem. And start to think on what have *they* done to create it rather than thinking it's others, and look at it in the round.' Karen then had a further conversation with them that night, I think, and calmed them down.

***

Not many players are spared the wrath of Johnson and Morley if they make a mistake. But sometimes it seems centre-half Steve Howson gets more than his fair share. Bizarrely, Howson, Johnson and Morley have all known each other since they were 16; they were all at Bury FC together as teenagers. Howson appears to be the player they trust the most. Yet he is often picked on.

'If you sat there with Steve Howson after he made a mistake and put your arm round his shoulder and said, "Never mind", he'd do it again second half,' says Johnson. 'And then, if you did it again, he'd do it again the same game. If you fuck him, he won't make that mistake for quite a while. But because he's a semi-pro player he *will* make that mistake again and then you fuck him again and then he won't do it again. So every three or four weeks you need to do that to him. Jordan Hulme's the exact same type of player. Gary Stopforth's another one, whereas you've got other lads I can't have a conversation with because they're not as strong.'

Howson, Stopforth and Hulme all came with the managers from Ramsbottom. They are all used to their ways by now. They seem to like it. 'They create a siege mentality: us against them,' says Stopforth. 'They portray themselves as the thugs of the league. Everyone's against them, but they'll stick up for you on the pitch and you can feel it. Say someone puts a tackle in on you, they're ready. They're ready to jump on. It makes you want to play for them and want to run through a brick wall or play 60-odd games like I played this season for them. And I think it goes a long way, that. I mean, they've had to maybe adapt a little bit to certain players that they've never had before, a bit like Danny Webber and people like that, but I think slowly but surely they've got exactly the same thing with them.'

Stopforth doesn't mind the dressing-room confrontations. 'It's just football. You kind of know it's coming. I suppose the sting gets taken out of it sometimes. I say to them, even sometimes when we win a game, to have a go at us, because sometimes you rest on your laurels, don't you? I think Alex Ferguson did it once at Aberdeen. They won a cup final and he went mental afterwards. But he's right. Because another day you get beat. I usually ring Jonno on a Monday and we have a little chat about football because we do have the same views really.'

Howson views it similarly. 'They seem to get the best out of me by bollocking me. He's gone over the top a few times but on a Sunday morning after the game he'll ring up, we'll have a chat about things and he'll apologise or I'll apologise and play on the Tuesday, you know, back to normal. It's fine.'

Howson's fiancée Vicky Thompson sighs. 'Jonno usually does ring him first thing on a Sunday morning and wakes us all up.'

Howson grins. 'About half seven on a Sunday morning.'

Vicky mimics the conversation. 'They'll be like: "What do you think you did wrong? What did you do there?"' She is rolling her eyes, but it's clear she knows and appreciates how important this is to him. And she understands football. Her father works for Manchester City and she has a season ticket at Salford. Admittedly Howson bought it for her, but she enjoys going.

'At times he has gone over the top, to be fair,' says Howson. 'I've been upset a few times when I've been blamed potentially for something that might not have been my fault, but they're entitled to do that. It's their job. And, in fact, if they get the best out of me that way then fair play to them.'

Vicky interjects. 'He does get upset. He just goes quiet when he gets home. He's not *usually* that bad. I've seen him bad maybe once or twice when he were going through that little bad period in football where they weren't really winning anything and I think you'd got a bit of a bollocking, hadn't you? He came back and he was actually upset that night. I didn't really know what to do. I remember picking him up in the car and he literally came straight out and just said, "I've had a right bollocking." Then he kind of went from there, but they're the main two times, but other than that he's not usually that bad. Because like I said, Jonno usually does ring him first thing on a Sunday morning and wakes us all up.'

Howson concurs. 'I probably get it more than anyone else, but I am a football geek and this is why I probably take it on board maybe more than others, because I love football too much, in a way, really. Because I watch it, I listen to it. All day, every day. And I'd love to work in football in some respect. So I want to learn. And if they're telling me something and I'm not doing it right, then if I take it in I should be learning, if it take it in and act on it.

'Against Workington at home, they were soft goals and we should have dealt with them. And I just thought, "Ah shit, I'm going to get pinned up against the wall or something here." Because I'm one of the senior figures really in that line-up. I like to act on it. I like trying to prove them wrong. But there have been occasions where maybe Jonno had just gone on at me a few games and it has got me down a bit. The playing's great but sometimes, when you get the shit you think, "Ah, fucking hell. I'm going to get bollocked again here for some reason." Some of the lads turn round to me and say, "How the fuck can you take all that?" Experienced lads have said that to me. I was like: "Dunno, I'm just used to it."

'Once or twice I think I've said something back and I've learnt not to because I ain't going to win. They're in control. And I wouldn't try and undermine them in a situation like that really. There's been a lot of phone calls on Sunday mornings, Mondays, Tuesdays, whenever, Wednesdays after games, and we'll sort it out if there's been a problem. He's great like that and Bernard's great like that. So I'm happy. A couple of times I've told him he's being unfair and he'll listen to you then. It's just man on man, isn't it? And they're big enough to hold their hands up at times.

'They're driven and they're honest lads. I think people buy into honesty sometimes, because you get managers who are bullshitters and they'll bullshit you. I've played for a couple of them and they tell you what you want to hear and sometimes they're sucking up to you. It's like: "Why?" Just be honest with me. These two are full-on and a lot of the characters are like that in that changing room, so I think, yeah, people buy into what they're about. Their honesty – and they're just one of the lads. You see them on the coach trips and they're in the back with the kids, they're having a few beers, they're playing cards with the lads. Yeah, and lads who come into the club I think possibly haven't seen that kind of managing, and I think that's why people enjoy it.'

Gareth Seddon, the team's star player in 2014–15 but injured and dropped for much of 2015–16, is also surprisingly supportive, though with some reservations. 'I think if you spoke to the managers they'll admit that they've let the standards slip. They've lost a bit of their fear factor in the dressing room. That's just because of the lads they are. They're funny. So everybody sees the funny side to them and you automatically lose the fear factor. Every now and again they snap and you think, "Oh God, there it is." But I think they lost a little bit of that and it was only towards the end they brought it back again and it showed in results.

'At one stage in the season we went 17, 18 games away and were never beat, setting a record, and then we lost away and then the managers were like: "Oh well, you know, there's the record. It was going to happen some time." I feel the lads accepted losing, and then the next game we lost again and it was that acceptance of losing that drifted into the dressing room and that should never happen. You shouldn't accept losing a five-a-side game in training in my opinion. And it was just that that crept back in and it's hard to get that winning mentality back. And I think that's why they brought in a couple of new players. They then started talking about going on another run, setting it right, and they set little plans for the next few games.

'And before that they were really emotional. So we'd win and we were the best thing ever. We'd lose and we were the crappest players ever. When you're a manager you're a bit like a parent talking to your child, and if you bark at your kids all the time they just switch off. They don't learn. And I think they were probably reacting emotionally, bollocking us. You can only have so many and then you switch off and you don't listen.

'I think they have evolved, analysed the game and said, "Right, we didn't play well" or "We had seven or eight good chances which we should have scored. We were the better team but we've lost or we've drawn." And they analysed it and put it into how to improve the team, and I think players respond a little bit more to that, like children do. My dad never shouted at me but if he said, "I'm really disappointed, son, in what you've done," it was like: "Oh my God, I'm sorry!" It affects you more. And it's the same with football players. They say, "Gaz, you didn't hold the ball up today. You couldn't let the midfield join in. That's one of the reasons why we had to play long and we lost the game." And you think, "Oh yeah, yeah." So the next game you take it in. Instead of going, "You was effing crap today, Gaz." When they say that you think, "Well, yeah, but why was I?"

'I think they have become better as managers and realised that we needed to have a set plan. Footballers are thick. Or rather they need to just follow a plan. You're performing on the pitch and the only thing you want to concentrate on is your performance. You don't want to be thinking, "What foot does that right-back play off? Does he cut inside?" A little information like that is alright, but players just want to have one thing in mind when they go on the pitch, no other worries. That's why if they have troubles off the pitch, footballers just crumble on the pitch because they're not relaxed. I think once Jonno and Bernard simplified it for us and said, "Right, this is our plan for the month: we've got these six games coming up..." and it improved.'

Danny Webber concurs: 'It's a bit more tranquil. There's not so much panic and we have a way of doing what we do. We've just gone back to how we were pre-FA Cup and in the FA Cup run. Everyone's digging in for each other. Everybody's grafting and you don't win anything if you don't do that. They're also learning on the job. Everybody's learning on the job. And they're very aware of where we are. We play for Salford. They're managers of Salford. If results go on long like this then you're out of a job. That's the nature of football nowadays. You become very aware of what you're in. We had quite a few conversations. I did openly say to them, "Look, I'm not going anywhere. I'm here. I'm all in. We've got this amount of games to put it back together and fingers crossed we can do that in the next five games. End in a good way." We played 60-odd games in a season – you don't want to walk away with nothing to show for it.'

PART 3

PART 3

Phil:

We've made great strides in this country with all the facilities and the sports science, even the analysis side of the game. But do we now focus too much on it? Do we give the analytical side, do we give the sports science side, too much power and too much of a say? Where actually the most important thing is what happens on the grass. And that's probably where I would say probably we've gone too far in terms of the little things. Maybe we call it the marginal gains. It's part of it, but the players in Spain are probably equally as professional, go in the gym when they need to, stretch the same. But they don't have an obsession with it. There's no fancy drawings on the screen. There's no massive meetings that go on for an hour. It's just five minutes here, 20 minutes there. You do all your work on the grass.

Marginal gains is perhaps one per cent or even half a percent of your performance. That's what a marginal gain is. I think in England we've come to rely too heavily on those things and expect for it to account for 30 to 40 per cent of performance. Whereas in Spain they would focus on coaching better. We're hiding behind the sports science, the fitness, the analytical side, when really we should be focused more on developing technique and coaching styles and improving players.

I wouldn't say the coaching ability is better over there. What I would say is that because they spend more time focusing on the football side of it, their attention to detail in terms of the sessions they put on is far greater. There's more thought to what they're doing, both tactically and technically. There's more meat on the bone. So their marginal gains would be around the body shape of a player, your shoulder position, the place you connect with the ball on your foot. That, to me, is coaching.

We can all put on a possession training session. We can all set out a 40 foot by 40 foot square, but it's actually what you do within the 40 by 40 square that's more important than the actual cones that you put out.

I think what I've learnt is that the detail in possession probably needs to be greater. So, if your possession session is not working, why is it not working? Is it a tactical thing? Is it a technical thing? Because, if you're playing in a 40 by 40 square and you're not using the full area, why are you not using the full area? Go in there, coach it. Why are the players not getting any fluidity? Is it their body shape's not right when they receive in the box? That is detail. Not just: 'Oh, that's crap. Come on, run more, work harder.' I would not probably have looked into as much detail previously as I would now. That's what has changed in my coaching.

And that's not being down on English football. There's many reasons why their training is like that. The climate helps. You can spend more time on the field, which is a massive thing. You can stop the session and stand around for a few minutes explaining your technique. You can take your time. The actual pace of the football is slower. In England, everything is done fast.

***

Gary:

I remember going to watch Aston Villa at the start of the 2015–16 season and they had signed five players from France for £38 million. It was their first game at home against Manchester United and we're watching them and I couldn't work it out. I was thinking, 'Am I being harsh because they've not settled in and need a bit of time? Or are they just not very good?' But I thought, 'What a risk. All those players from the French league.' The French league isn't as competitive as our league. It's not a measure of our league. I'm not saying you can't get a player from there – N'Golo Kante and Riyad Mahrez were both from there and among the players of the season in 2015–16. But to think you can go there and just get a raft of players at cheaper fees, cheaper wages and expect that it will work out?

Has Scotland not got any football players any more? Has Northern Ireland and Republic of Ireland not got any football players any more? These were hotbeds of the English league. Have Belfast, Glasgow, Manchester, Newcastle and Birmingham not got footballers? I've not fallen out of love with football but I've become more jaded, worried about what I'm seeing. I want clubs to bring kids through.

The 2015–16 season in the Premier League was a special season in that it gave you the impression that a side outside the elite can succeed. Leicester are not a small club, but you would never have thought a team from the Midlands – Birmingham City, Leicester, West Brom, Nottingham Forest, Derby – would ever win the league again. Maybe Aston Villa if they had investment. But without what we'd call huge investment, the idea that Leicester would win the league seemed ridiculous. And maybe it's showing two fingers to some of the things that *are* going wrong at the moment with excess recruitment, overpricing fans and driving passion out of the game.

When you see the most passionate, spirited team in the league with one of the best atmospheres winning the league, you think maybe people will realise actually it's not all about the most expensive player. Football is about spirit, passion, character, care for your club, working hard, having people in your team who are representative of the fans. When you look at Jamie Vardy, for all his faults, for all his strengths, he absolutely represents lots of people in England. I always remember when Rickie Lambert scored against Scotland in 2014; I've not heard Wembley roar as much for anyone. The reason was that he'd worked his way up from Macclesfield, Stockport County, Rochdale and Bristol Rovers and people felt that he represented them. There was a feeling that Ricky Lambert was one of them. There's the same feeling that

Vardy is one of them; and it's the same with Harry Kane and Tottenham fans.

Steve Bull had that for England, as did Stuart Pearce; a sense that 'the boy done good'. And I'm not someone who's nostalgic and forever saying, 'It was so much better then.' I always believe in today. I always believe in the player of today. But I think if you asked every coach, they would want the physique and athletic capability and technical ability of a player in 2016 combined with the mentality and toughness of a player from 20 years ago. And I'm sure in the 1990s, when I was breaking through, people probably thought I wasn't up to it mentally in the same way that Norman Hunter was; or that David Beckham wasn't like Johnny Giles; that Nicky Butt wasn't as tough as Nobby Stiles. You always want that player who's moved with the times from a technical and physical capability point of view but who has got the mentality of someone from 20 years ago. And that's what the likes of Vardy do; they take you back. Wayne Rooney has an element of that in him, the streetfighter football player who can connect with the person from 20 years ago, and he's a throwback. That to me is what Salford is. Salford is a group of players who have got the physical toughness of players from 20 years ago – not necessarily the technical ability of the top player, but it's almost like going 20 years back.

The time I spent in Spain made me more knowledgeable but it also reinforced thoughts that I had about English football, about where English football's at. And that's why

Salford is important to all of us. We have to have our own identity at Salford and we've got to believe in it. Whatever that is. So I look at Salford and I think: passion, care, character, spirit, personality.

And when I see Salford play in front of 500 people, I do see a connection between the team, the committee and the fans. I want that to stay. If that goes we've lost the soul of the club. That's why those 14 on the committee, they are the club. Because those 14 people have another 200 people that they know in the ground. I've seen owners come into clubs and they've taken away the soul of it. We don't want to do that. We have to change some things. We've got to make the facilities better. We've got to improve the team budget. We've got to set up an academy. We have to help commercialise the club and make it sustainable. But the operation of the club is the people. My mum's worked at Bury for 25 years and my dad did so before, and my mum has a friend, Jo, who has worked there for 50 years. And I can go in today and she's still got the 1960s calculator, which is the old till-style one where you press the buttons, and it makes me giggle and smile but in a nice way, in a respectful way. She's still working there after 50 years. I go to Manchester United's training ground at Carrington and I see Kath at reception, who's been working there for 50, 60 years, and it makes me think, that's what a football club is. And we can't afford to lose that at Salford.

15 MARCH 2016

HALESOWEN 0, SALFORD 1

'Money talks,' croons coach driver Ian Corrie. 'But it don't sing and it don't walk.'

Corrie has got hold of the microphone on the team bus and Neil Diamond songs are being enthusiastically covered.

'And as long as I can have you here with me...I'd much rather be...'

'Shut the fuck up!' comes a voice from the back.

The club committee, all over the age of 50 and sat at the front of the coach, mutter about an unappreciative younger generation. Ian laughs.

Salford's team bus is stuck in traffic, having come off the M6 on the way to Halesowen, on the outskirts of Birmingham. The coach pulls off at a Shell garage to allow some players to eat before the match. Coca-cola, Luzocade, crisps and pasties are all consumed.

Danny Webber isn't impressed. He has his own pre-match food prepared, a mix of protein and pasta designed to get him through 90 minutes of football. It is evident who was a full-time professional. The players eating this service station food of minimal nutritional value will struggle in the last 20 minutes of the game tonight.

Steve Howson is nursing a minor injury above his eye. He works in an adhesives polymer factory that makes liquid glue, hauling huge packets of powder into big vats. His shift started at 5.30am this morning. Most of the players will work an early shift on a match day.

It's been a two-hour journey, starting from Salford City's ground with pick-up points at the TGI Fridays in Prestwich and the Holiday Inn off Junction 15 in Stoke. The 3-1 defeat by Skelmersdale on Saturday is weighing heavily. Everyone knows it has been a poor performance, and the play-off position suddenly seems uncertain.

Cards are played, spirits seem superficially high, but there is an underlying anxiety. The end of the season is approaching. Bernard Morley says all the other clubs will be looking out for Salford tonight, expecting them to lose and to spiral out of the play-off places. When you're running out of games, the stakes grow ever higher.

The Halesowen ground is an old-fashioned stadium on the edge of town, with terracing on three sides and a small dressing room tucked under one of the terraces behind the goal. As Salford disembark from the coach and walk to the dressing room, the stereo is turned up to full volume. They are marking their territory. 'They've got a bigger speaker than us,' says one

Halesowen player. 'They've more fucking money than us,' retorts a Halesowen official.

Inside the dressing room physio Val McCarthy is about to get to work massaging Webber. McCarthy eyes the treatment table. It is broken. It stands up, but one of the supporting rods underneath has snapped off from the beam which connects the table legs. And the rod which is meant to support the stabilising beams and which runs horizontally the length of the table has also fallen away and is no more.

McCarthy winces, but Webber jumps up on the table anyway. It rocks one way, then the other under his weight. McCarthy seems to be considering whether it is worth the risk of continuing the massage and having to tell the managers that their star striker is out for the rest of the season because a massage table has collapsed. But he goes ahead, and Webber relaxes on the rickety old table as McCarthy massages. Meanwhile, Gary Stopforth giggles as he unties Webber's shoelaces, the striker oblivious as he lies on his front with his muscles being prodded and probed.

The warm-up is completed outside, but prior to the announcement of the team, Gareth Seddon is taken to one side. He won't be on the team tonight. Johnson and Morley wouldn't normally single out a player to let him know he has been dropped. No-one knows until they announce the team in the dressing room half an hour before kick-off. But Seddon, 35, is a senior player and Morley and Johnson want to deliver a key message. They feel he let them down two weeks ago when he came on for the last 20 minutes against Darlington.

In retrospect, it seems clear to them, he wasn't fit. They feel he should have been more frank about his injuries and that his lack of contribution was one of the reasons why they lost the game in the final minutes. Seddon is told all this before Johnson goes into the dressing room to announce the team.

Morley takes care of the pre-match team talk. 'We need to go back to basics and start enjoying our football,' he says. 'Getting the best out of individuals.' Morley and Johnson are worried that their players are worried; that the players have stopped playing as they can; that possibly the managers' approach is inhibiting them. They're trying to strike a new tone tonight.

'I'm not making excuses,' continues Morley. 'I rung Scott. And I told him, "Stop putting them fucking messages on that group because I'm sick of it." The team have a social media app where they can see each other's messages. The idea is that it builds team spirit, that they can cajole each other after a defeat or congratulate each other after a win. But Morley feels that Scott Burton's messages to the group have been counterproductive of late: making excuses after the poor run, telling the team that they're still great, even when they have played badly.

'And look, I understand it,' continues Morley to Burton. 'You've got a big heart. But, boys, we're men. We're fucking men. Every single one of us. We haven't got anyone any more that you have to put an arm round and say, "Unlucky". We've gone past that stage of being unlucky.

'It's not unlucky. It's four good games, two bad. As individuals, two good games, one bad. Let's go back to basics and enjoy ourselves. I don't know if any of you have heard Gary Neville's interview? Did anyone read it? Or is interested in it? Because we are.'

Morley will amplify this point later but for now he moves on. 'First and foremost, all we want to see is 11 players work hard. Yeah. Blow up and you can put your hand up if it's half-time and say, "I'm fucked." We'll take you off. But work fucking hard. And be organised. And, listen, the rest of it comes with it, because when Scott Burton sees Tunji Moses or Gary Stopforth going into a tackle, he then mentally thinks, "I'm going to go and do the same thing."

'If Chris Lynch puts the ball into the stand, you then think, "Yeah, I'm going to do that." And we start to do the right things. We go back to basics and we'll start winning games again and start going unbeaten, six or seven, instead of winning two, drawing one and losing one. Jonno says it every week, about that siege mentality, boys. Go back to basics. Work hard and enjoy it. If we lose, we lose. But let's not have excuses for why we lose. If we come back into the changing room and say, "Listen, boys, you've run through a brick wall for us today" and you can't pick fault in anyone's performance, then we've got beat by the best side. But we haven't been able to do that for the last four months of this season.

'We haven't been able to say we got beat off Darlington twice because they're a better side, because they wasn't. We're still defending you and we'll continue to do that until the end of the season. Hand on my heart. Because I still believe that on our day, when we're fully fit, we've got the best side in the league. But tables don't lie. And we're not the best. We're fucking lying third. We can drop to sixth. They're facts, and we have to put it right and we only do that by eliminating all these stupid excuses about new players coming in, about our training methods, about telling me and Jonno you're one hundred per cent fit when you're not, Pooley, which you have done. Everything.'

He is looking at James Poole now. 'We pulled you last Saturday and I said, "Are you right?" And you say, "Yeah, great, gaffer." But you wasn't. But you want to play football. I've just had the same chat with Seds. We understand you want to play football for this club but you let me and Jonno down by conning us. Do you understand that? It's not just you – you're looking at me…' Poole is looking directly at Morley quizzically, but not quite hard enough to be a direct challenge. 'Tunji's done it; he got told. Seds has just been told. You have to be honest with us, boys. One hundred per cent fit means, "Yeah, I'm one hundred per cent." If Gaz says, "I've got a bit of a dead leg but I can get through this game," I believe you could. But muscle strains? Boys, you can't. You can't do it. Val will tell you.' He gestures to physio Val McCarthy. 'That man has had more shit off me and Jonno this season than it's worth the job to him. Val, am I right?'

McCarthy nods. 'And he must be banging his head against the wall because we'll put someone on and he'll say, "I told you he weren't fit." So from now on, nine games to go, we do things right. No excuses. Enjoy it, right. Like I say, it's going to be a fucking scrap. That's what it's going to be. Whoever wants it most tonight will win the game. Yeah? Come on!'

He's done. It's 30 minutes before kick-off. 'Fucking love that,' says Anthony Johnson of his co-manager's speech. 'Jay in goal; right-back Lynchey, left-back Hally; Daws, Howson the two centre-halves; Gaz and Scott starting in the middle; JJ to the right, Richie to the left; Pooley and Webs start up top. Yeah? Come on boys!'

There has been a change in tone. Morley seems to have softened. Maybe the intensity has been too much for some of the players. He believes they have assembled the best team in the division and he is convinced if they simply start playing as they can, a run of victories will follow. 'I just want them to relax,' he says out of the players' earshot. 'Take the pressure off. Eliminate excuses.'

Excuses such as the players' complaints about training. After the 4-3 home defeat against Darlington, the infamous game in which they were 3-1 up after an hour, and which started this inconsistent run, there had been hard running on the Tuesday night.

'We're old school, me and Jonno,' says Morley. 'If you're a naughty boy, you get slapped. They did do a lot of running after the Darlington defeat and I got a call from Webs saying some of the boys weren't happy. They'd got sore backs and they felt they were being punished for the defeat. Jonno heard about it and wasn't happy. Running isn't nice, is it? But the fittest team normally wins.'

Morley watches carefully what Gary Neville has been saying in his role as Valencia manager. Neville's side lost to Levante on Sunday. It was a terrible defeat to local rivals and a dismal performance, and Neville admitted that the defeat was his responsibility. 'We were interested in what he said,' says Morley. 'He takes responsibility. And you have to. But ultimately the players have to perform as well.'

The players run out of a narrow, fenced-in gap between the small terraced stands behind the goal which makes up the players' tunnel. For this game 746 fans have turned out on a cold, spring night, including a smattering from Salford. It's enough to make an atmosphere. 'You can stick your documentary up your arse,' sing the Halesowen fans, followed by 'You're just a shit Man United.' But this is gentle, nothing like some of the hostility from a section of fans at Darlington. Everyone is pleasant here; even at pitch-side, a few yards from the fans, there is no vitriol.

As the match starts, substitute Jordan Hulme notices that there are some water bottles stacked in a crate behind Johnson. They are so close that the manager is in danger of tripping up over them. He dutifully gets off the bench and moves them to a safer position. 'If that was me, you wouldn't have moved them,' observes Craig Dootson, the goalkeeping coach. 'I would have put something else there to trip you up, you dick,' responds Hulme. Everyone is laughing.

The first half is tight, no quarter given by either side. Halesowen hit the underside of the bar, but Salford create some good chances. Full-back Steve O'Halloran, a former professional in the Premier League with Aston Villa who won two international caps for the Republic of Ireland, brings the ball down with a delightful piece of skill, beats a man and heads off on a run down the left. Johnson is delighted. 'He could play for Ireland, him,' he says enthusiastically. O'Halloran's next touch is to mis-control the ball and send it squirming out of play. Johnson turns and pulls a face to the bench.

John Johnston gets involved in an argument with a Halesowen player, who has fouled him. He squares up, swearing. It seems out of character. Johnston is physically smaller than most on the pitch; the tricky, skilful, quick player as opposed to the muscle. Gary Stopforth is impressed. 'JJ. Keep pretending to be hard. I love it,' he says at half-time. Johnston looks at him, unsure of his sincerity. 'I'm not taking the piss!' insists Stopforth. 'You're playing better for it.'

And the dressing room at half-time is a much calmer place to be than it has been of late. 'Really pleasing, that,' says Morley. 'There's an identity to what we're trying to do. I can't nit-pick it too much because I can actually see what we're trying to do. We've not won the battle; but we're competing. And we've not lost it. But we've looked good there.'

Johnson is similar, commending Webber, Pooley and Richie Allen's work down the left side of the game. 'Fucking brilliant, that. That is how we'll cut them open. Short, quick, incisive football, into feet. Not lumps up there. Keeping fucking feeding the ball into here, into feet, into Webs, into Pooley.

'They've got the best first touch in the league, Richie,' he says, turning to Allen, the winger. 'That is when you come alive. Bang! It looks good. We look like a good fucking side. It will come. These lot will tire.

'Hally,' he says, looking at O'Halloran. 'That's fucking great that, that is. As good as you've been for a long time. And I'll finish with exact same thing we said at the beginning. It's not about shape; it's not about being tacticians. It's about outworking these now. Not chasing the win, but wanting to win each personal battle. Wanting to win it more than them. Doing the right things for another 45 minutes. We're not going to finish with the same eleven, so for the next 15, 20 minutes, blow yourselves. Put everything in to it. If it's 0-0 at that point, they'll be fucked. It's good stuff. Start right and go at them.'

The second half progresses well. Salford continue to create chances. Poole has one, with just the goalkeeper to beat. He attempts a chip, but scoops the ball harmlessly up in the air and over. 'What the fuck was that?' asks Johnson, more to himself than anyone else.

A turning point is coming, though. On 53 minutes Richie Allen receives the ball on the right-hand side. Allen attacks, cutting inside the penalty area. Everyone expects a cross, as the angle is so tight it precludes shooting. But Allen does shoot, a low, hard strike which shocks everyone and ends up in the roof of the net. From the Salford bench, substitutes, kit men, coaches and managers leap to their feet in celebration. Allen has continued his run and is now grabbed by his team-mates congratulating him. Webber gets to him first. 'World-class cross, that!' he says incredulously. Allen looks hurt. Webber is laughing. 'There's no way he meant it,' he'll tell his team-mates later.

It gets better for Salford. Captain Chris Lynch is advancing when a Halesowen player dives in with his foot raised. Lynch is on the floor injured and Salford players surround the referee. Morley is demanding that the Halesowen player is sent off. At the same time he turns to the bench. 'He's a drama queen, Lynchey.'

The red card is shown and the Halesowen player trudges off. Johnson and Morley are as relaxed as they have been for some time. Morley is pointing to captain Lynch, still hobbling a bit from the challenge. 'He's a drama queen,' he repeats, smiling.

That said, it is still only 1-0, even if now against ten men. JJ, John Johnston, who has had a fine game, attempts a delicate if perhaps self-indulgent skill to cut back on his man rather than get down the wing to cross. He loses the ball and Halesowen launch a counter-attack. 'Put balls in the fucking box, JJ,' yells Jonno from the sidelines. 'That's twice I've told you!'

Johnson had made a conscious decision tonight to calm down; not to give too many instructions to the players on the pitch. He wants them to play with less pressure. However, JJ's step-over skill has tested the limit of his self-control.

'He's thinking: "I'm doing alright so I can start doing stuff now. I can do a step-over,"' says Johnson. 'No you can't! Do your step-over in the opposition's box, you do what you want in there. But not on the halfway line or when you make a yard you don't need to do a step-over. Deliver the ball into the box.

Them players have made a run for you, you've checked back then lost the ball, they've made that run, they can't get back into shape.' JJ is substituted.

The game is drawing to a close. Stopforth, who has been ill for three days before the game and barely eaten, comes to the bench to ask physio McCarthy for some energy tablets. 'Fuck off,' orders Johnson. 'It's all in your head.' Stopforth plays on without his tablets.

The clock stands on 86 minutes and with four minutes to play the linesman on the side closest to Morley and Johnson flags for a Halesowen offside. But he quickly changes his mind and puts his flag down again. In the confusion, Halesowen continue to attack. Before they can finish, Johnson is marching down the touchline towards the linesman.

'Keep your fucking flag up!' he is yelling. He stops, pauses, and eyes the assistant ref, who is around 30 yards away. 'What the fuck is going on? You just flagged offside!'

'Shut the fuck up,' shouts a Halesowen fan.

Johnson spins round. 'You shut up,' he says, eyeing the fan. He stalks back to the bench, angrily.

'Fuck off!' shout the fans.

'Oh that's lovely language that, with ladies and kids here,' replies Johnson, gesturing to the fans close by. 'Sorry about that,' he adds, to the fans. Standing close to the pitch is a middle-aged woman with glasses, a pink coat and a fluffy bobble hat; next to her is an 11-year-old boy. The woman is giggling uncontrollably at it all. The controversy turns out to be unimportant. The final whistle blows and Salford have ended their poor run with a 1-0 win.

The dressing room is a haven of contentment. Morley takes control. 'Listen, boys. I know we've had six or seven-goal thrillers, boys, but you need to understand how satisfying that is for me and him: a one-nil win away from home.

'It was comfortable, but listen: they were dangerous at times, weren't they? But the red card came down to basics. Pooley, you did your job, into Danny Webber. Two touch out to your skipper and he rode the tackle and it's straight red. Basics. That's all it is. We do the right things in the right areas and they're down to 10 men, which I'm not saying wins us the game because we was always in control. But it's just about doing the right things, boys, and that's what we've done tonight, haven't we? If we're honest, everyone's done their job.'

He turns to goal-scorer Richie Allen. 'Richie. Listen, you took a lot of criticism for your attitude and what not. That's a fucking brilliant performance, mate. From the first minute to the last, you grafted. That's what's expected of you. There's no denying the ability, mate.

'We changed the side tonight and one or two will be disappointed, but the spirit in the changing room before the game and now, listen: there's been a bit of a difference, hasn't there? Everyone stick to what we've got to do, yeah. Eight to go. Yeah? Well done, boys!'

'Let's have a look at these results now,' shouts a voice as they check up on the scores of their play-off rivals.

Everyone is happy. The stereo goes on. Will Sparks's 'Ah Yeah' is playing, a simple house music track which builds to an intense crescendo, allowing everyone to shout out the two-word chorus. Jordan Hulme strips down to his underpants and is gyrating, thrusting his groin in various directions and leading the merriment. Gaz Stopforth joins in the dancing and eventually Steve Howson, who is completely naked, does too. But Hulme is centre stage throughout.

In the Halesowen bar, Morley and Johnson are beaming. 'One-nillers away from home,' says Morley. 'I love them. They're better than a 5-0 win.' Chairman Karen Baird has given them money to buy drinks for the team. Morley appreciates the simplicity of her style. 'Karen always hands us cash for drinks if we win. I like that. If I'm good, tickle my belly. If I'm naughty, put me in the corner.'

***

Phil:

As the season progressed, I started preparing myself for disappointment. We had started well, had the FA Cup run, but January, February and March were really difficult. I worried we might even fall out of the play-off places. So I started telling myself: 'Well it can't always be plain sailing. We only ever planned for a promotion every couple of years, so we're still on course.' But inside I was feeling a bit empty, to be honest.

And I felt the distance, being in Valencia. Like with all owners, if we're not fully there and on the ground, then I don't think it's fully successful. That's what I felt in Valencia. 'We're not there. We're not helping. We're not there for the managers when they need us.'

Halesowen felt like a good solid 1-0 away win. Perhaps it was changing. But there was still a 0-0 draw at home to Whitby Town after that which didn't sound too good. I think the turning point came that week at the end of March though, just before Easter, when we signed Billy Priestley, the centre-half from Bradford Park Avenue.

We have our scouting set-up and Billy's signing fell outside of that. We probably hadn't done as much due diligence as we should have done. We hadn't got our usual three reports. I was worried about it. I had a big thing about it upsetting the togetherness of the dressing room. He was coming from a National League North side, which meant relatively big money. And the fact that it was outside our normal process made me more nervous.

But the managers wanted him and we had to back them at that stage. It was our way of saying to them, 'You've done really well, you've earned the right to ask for this.' They had literally earned it, in that they had taken us to the second round of the FA Cup, which meant the money was there. It wasn't like we were borrowing money.

I think it was a big thing for the managers when we backed them to sign Billy. They had just lost twice to Darlington in quick succession, and I think they feel those defeats more than any other. They've always used Darlington as a benchmark by which to judge themselves. They have been our closest rivals for two years in the league, and even when they were at Ramsbottom they were rivals. I think those two defeats knocked them a little bit. They're street fighters and they don't want to be wounded.

And, regardless of how successful the club was, there was always the impression that they were thinking, 'I wonder if these lot like us?' I think that was a vote of confidence which helped them get their mind back on track.

Billy came in and played against Ramsbottom on Easter Monday and scored the opening goal in a 4-0 win. Then we beat Grantham 5-0, and went to Ashton and won 3-0. We kicked on with Billy. It wasn't just that it helped us defensively but other players started lifting their game. It's as though it lifted the whole mood. Danny Webber, Jordan Hulme and James Poole were scoring goals. It felt like we had momentum.

Before the Ramsbottom game I had been texting the managers, and in their replies I could tell they still weren't happy. But around that time I started texting them, 'Well done.' And the reply was, 'We can smell it now!' I've played in championship winning teams and you can smell momentum changing. And then, once Gary came back in April, I felt more secure. We were winning games again, scoring goals and Gary was back on the ground. We were on a charge coming into the play-offs.

26 APRIL 2016

EVO-STIK PREMIER LEAGUE, PROMOTION PLAY-OFF SEMI-FINAL: SALFORD CITY 1, ASHTON UNITED 1 (AFTER 90 MINUTES)

This hasn't gone to plan. Salford City have gone into the game in a confident mood. They have finished third in the league overall, which means they will not be promoted automatically. Instead the teams from second to fifth play off in a mini cup competition to see who will be awarded the second promotion spot. Because they finished above Ashton, who were fourth, they have the home advantage in the one-off game, which is effectively a semi-final. They have already beaten them twice in the league this year, 3-1 at home and 3-0 away, so it would be something of a calamity to fail now.

Yet there is something unnerving about the day. It's late April and the match starts in the clear light of a spring evening. Yet it might as well be January. It's been snowing during the day, the pitch is freezing up and the temperatures are dropping below zero. And though they start well enough, with a headed goal on 25 minutes from Jordan Hulme, they fade, looking sluggish and nervous, and are unable to impose their authority on the game. An Ashton equaliser comes on 69 minutes. It's well deserved. Johnson and Morley start conferring on the touchline. On the bench in the corner, smothered in as many coats and blankets as space allows, sits Gareth Seddon. Outwardly, he has been joking, cajoling, encouraging. He struggles to hide the hurt, however. His face contorts with repressed disappointment.

Still, a substitution is coming. There are 12 minutes to play and a goal is needed. Seddon is the obvious choice. John Johnston, the winger, is coming off. The managers turn round and call out to Richie Allen, who is recovering from injury. Allen is a winger, quick and, as the game at Halesowen showed, capable of the kind of individual creativity that could win a game. Allen is being summoned to come on. Seddon doesn't react other than slumping lower into his seat. The fate of a substitute is to suffer a thousand public indignities and never be allowed to show it.

Full-time comes and the game is still 1-1. Thirty minutes extra will be played to decide the tie and then, if necessary, penalties. There is no time to return to the dressing room. The players gather around Johnson and Morley close to the bench for their team talk. A drum beats incessantly as a group of fans chant: 'We're the Salford boys…making all the noise.'

'Heads up,' says Johnson as Morley calls the players to gather round. 'Good reaction when they scored. Because I'll tell you what, they're fucking fired up here. But it's the same thing we tell you week in, week out. Set pieces and the ball in behind – that's all they've got.' He catches the eye of Steve Howson, captain because of Chris Lynch's injury. 'Howson – fucking outstanding.' He turns to Luke Clark, the midfielder who came on late as a substitute. 'Clarky, you've come on for your 40 and so far you've not given it to us. Now's your time for half an hour. Get on the ball. Listen, listen in here. We've been here and played extra time before. We've been there and done it. We've been there and we've won games and we've matched sides in League Two. Now what we're asking you to do is to go against a side that you've been better than for 90 minutes. Work your socks off for each other. We'll get chances here.'

There is one substitution left for the managers to make, but still no Seddon. He goes through the ritual of encouraging players for the last 30 minutes. He does everything right. He even puts his heart into it. But, to those that know, it is obvious what he is hiding.

***

Ryan:

Gareth Seddon is a character and that's what I like about him. He's loud and he can rub some people up the wrong way, but he actually produces for the club when it matters. Some players are quiet and produce. But he's the same on and off the pitch. He's larger than life. He likes to have a laugh. He likes to have a joke. He's got those model looks, but actually when it comes down to getting on the pitch he produces. He's been enormously important for the club in the last couple of years, especially in that first season when he scored the goals which took us up.

But in 2015–16 it was hard for him. He was injured for much of the season and those are the worst moments of your career because you're not able to do what you want to do. You're simply not able to do it. It doesn't happen in any other jobs really, where you're not actually able to do your job and then you have to watch others doing it. It's frustrating. It's not that it affects your ego, but obviously you want to be out there playing. You want to be out there doing what you do. You want to influence the game. You want to help the lads. You want to help the club win games. You can't do that when you're injured. You have to deal with it. You have to get on with it. It's particularly frustrating when the team lose and you can't influence it. When they're winning it's not so bad. I could imagine that it's been a tough season for Gareth.

***

It's not just the cash; it's the little moments that make it all worthwhile for a professional footballer. Gareth Seddon has had a few, but one sticks out. It was at Bury, shortly after he had been signed from Everton at the age of 21: a goal at Blackpool on a

Saturday afternoon in late January 2002. He was just settling in at Bury in his first season as a professional, but he was already popular with the fans. A couple of hundred Bury supporters had travelled across to Bloomfield Road in Blackpool for the game, and this goal against Lancashire rivals seemed to consummate the fan-player relationship. In the immediate aftermath of the goal, a song starts up from the Bury fans. Sung to the tune of Dean Martin's 'That's Amore', it goes: 'When the ball hits the back of the net/It's not Shearer nor Cole/That's Seddoni!'

'I'd never heard them sing it before,' remembers Seddon. 'And then they started to sing that and my mum was in the crowd and she was like, "Ahh". When Seddon, who is originally from Padiham, had signed for Bury from Everton, the local newspaper had misprinted his name, adding an 'i' to Seddon. 'For some reason they put Seddoni, so I was always known as Seddoni. And when I signed, people have told me that they were googling maps of Italy to see where Padiham was.' It's a couple of miles north-west of Burnley.

Seddon has had a good football career but more bad luck than most. A rare debilitating illness forced him to quit professional football at the age of 25. When he eventually recovered his strength, he forged a semi-professional career. He couldn't afford to go back to the full professional game as it would have compromised his insurance pay-out. All of which might leave many people with a heavy burden of regret.

'People say, "You've been unlucky in your career, you could have gone on to this, you could have gone on to that,"' says Seddon.

'But I've had the best footballing career ever. Obviously I've never played in the Premier League, but I don't know if I'd have enjoyed it as much if I did, because you're more in the spotlight, you're not close to the fans. Some of the best moments that I've had in football have been with Hyde, Kettering, in the FA Cup, big giant-killing wins. And you can't get that if you're a Premier League club.'

Corporal Seddon's RAF commission was bought out by Everton. It's unusual for a serving member of the armed forces to be given a break in the Premier League, but Seddon had previously been with Blackburn Rovers as a youth player and was released when he broke his sternum. 'One of my friends had joined the RAF and said, "Look, Gaz, if you're good at football just join up, you'll travel the world." So I joined the RAF as a PTI, which is a Physical Training Instructor. Did all my basic training and passed out as a Corporal. I was playing in the Southern Conference at the time for I can't even remember who – it might have been Nuneaton or something like that. I can't remember. Because I was so fit as well I scored something like 20 in 12 games.'

He knew as soon as he arrived at Everton that it was a step too far. 'It was brilliant. But I knew when I was there I wasn't good enough. I could just tell. You just knew, physically as well. I was six foot one but I was very slight, and these guys were six foot two and 13 or 14 stone, and quicker than me. Kevin Campbell was there, and Paul Gascoigne. I'd been in the RAF. These guys had been in full-time training for the last 10, 15 years. When I was 25, I was ten times better than I was when I was at Everton. I think if I'd gone from school and been with them I might have progressed.

But I was there for six months playing quite a few reserve games. I played quite well. We played Man. United reserves at Bury's ground, Gigg Lane. Bury's manager Andy Priest was watching. He enquired about me and I just signed for Bury.'

Just before he signed for Bury he contracted a tropical disease on a holiday in Thailand. It didn't seem too dramatic at the time; merely unpleasant. He recovered well enough. However, this particular strand of the disease lingered in his body, subsiding but then mutating into something worse. In his second season at Bury he was out for 11 months with a bad back. Eventually, though, physiotherapy appeared to have sorted the problem and he was back playing so well that at the end of his third season he was top scorer at the club and earned a move to Rushden & Diamonds, a team which was funded by the Doc Martens boot business and which was a level up from Bury, in Division Two or what is now known as League One.

Seddon was one of the big-money signings designed to take Rushden & Diamonds to the next level. As such he was something of a local hero, with lots of fuss surrounding him in pre-season. Yet he never even played for the club. 'I never trained, never ran. I was just really ill from when I got there,' he recalls. 'I couldn't keep any food down. Every single joint in my body would swell up.'

As August drifted into September and on into the autumn and winter, Seddon could sense the club's sympathy wearing thin. It was understandable. He was Rushden's major signing on decent money. Even though the club was well funded, he was taking up a chunk of the budget that could be used elsewhere. 'I was having loads of blood tests. The club knew I was ill but they just couldn't work out what it was. I said to them, "Look, I don't care about my football, I just need you to help me find out what it is before you release me." So we spent about 11 months going for blood tests, CT scans, tests for bone cancer, leukaemia, HIV, anything you can think of. Having the tests and then the waiting to find out was just horrible. Horrible. I lost so much weight. It was the worst time of my life. It might have been life-threatening, but it came to a point where I wished something was wrong with me just so I could find out and I could get my head round it and handle it. It was the uncertainty. Then they came back and said, "No, it's not leukaemia, we need to look at HIV." It was just horrible. I was very low. I was living on my own down in Northampton. I didn't tell my family. I told them that I had a damaged cartilage, because I didn't want them to fret and worry. I didn't know what was wrong, and my mum's a panicker anyway.

'I suppose I handled it by just going out every weekend. I didn't get into alcoholism or gambling or anything like that. I just handled it as a lad would. I just tried to smile it away. I'd go to watch the game on a Saturday and then we'd all go out together, and I just tried to keep involved in that way, but I was really ill. There were some times where I couldn't even move off the settee. My hands would swell up and I couldn't eat my tea. Just weird things like that.'

When the diagnosis came, the best that could be said was that it wasn't life-threatening. He had spondyloarthrosis, a disease of the joints, which had lingered in his blood since the tropicol disease and attacks the spinal cord. Suddenly at least some of the mysteries became clearer. The sciatica at Bury in his second year was down to the disease. That was the first major attack. It then subsided and came back at Rushden. 'You get two or three major attacks in your life, so it kind of attacks you and then it dies down, stays dormant, then it attacks you again. So I'd had two major attacks and obviously, touch wood, it's gone from my system now, I'll never get it again but it does affect your immune system. I've always got a cold because it's just really weak.'

However, there is no place in professional football for a man carrying a disease which affects his joints. He received an insurance payout from the Professional Footballers' Association and returned home to Padiham to live with his mum. He worked in a boiler factory. 'My dad used to work in a factory, so he said that he would get me a job, as I needed to earn some money. It was on the production line at Potterton Myson. I had a belt on with a drill in it, and I had 47 seconds to put the gas valves into each boiler before the next one came down. It was the worst job ever, but it was money and I was living with my mum, Julie, and I had to pay for my board. So I'd gone from being a professional footballer to making boilers and being back home in Burnley. And there was a lot of bitterness from people as well in my area. They were pleased to see me back. I think there had probably been a bit of jealousy.

'It was a hard, really difficult period. But I just kept seeing the doctors all the time and I kept having blood tests and they'd say, "It's still in your body." I'd go for a run and I'd get about seven minutes in and then my knees would start to hurt, my elbows, every joint and they'd just blow up and I'd have really bad, burning-like arthritic pain. Then, because it was in my blood, it used to affect my eating. So then I wouldn't be able to do anything for a week. I'd let it die down. Then I'd try another run and it'd get to seven minutes and it'd happen again. They told me it could last anything from six months to six years but it will eventually go. It got to about two years, and on my run I would get to eight minutes, nine minutes and then 10 minutes.

'I was on auto-immune deficiency tablets to build my strength up, and anti-inflammatories, really strong ones. I had injections into my sacroiliac joints, because everything runs through your spine. I had fluid drawn. I went for injections every six weeks. Eventually it just started to go and I could do more and more training. I went back into the boxing gym, got myself super-fit. I contacted the manager at Padiham, a local team, and said, "Look, I haven't played for 18 months. Can I just see how my body is? Let me play in the last few games of the season." I think I went in January or February.'

Padiham were playing in the North West Counties league, two divisions below where Salford City played the 2015–16 season and seven levels below where he was at Rushden & Diamonds. 'It was brilliant,' says Seddon. 'My first goal for Padiham was brilliant. I never thought I'd get back playing football any more and I was just glad that I could run again.' It was almost as though he had rediscovered his identity. He was a footballer again. Not a professional, admittedly, but a footballer, nonetheless.

In 2006, Seddon signed for Hyde United, who played in the National League North, which is two levels below the fully professional game. He scored 67 goals in 82 games and met one of his closest friends, Steve Pickford. 'It was one of the best times of my life,' he recalls. Seddon represented the England semi-professional side made up of non-league players and was sold to Kettering for £50,000. Kettering play in the National League, one level closer to the professional game, the Football League. But many of the teams, including Kettering, are actually full-time professionals. The terms of Seddon's insurance pay-out meant that he could accept a contact in the National League but he could not go up into the Football League. Kettering, coincidentally, is around nine miles away from Rushden & Diamonds, where he had experienced his lowest point.

'It was weird because I lived two streets away from the home I had when I was at Rushden & Diamonds. I never thought I'd see this place again and now I've just been sold for £50,000 and gone into the Conference with Kettering. I was back full-time with Kettering, and within that four years I'd come full circle and after all the horrible bad times I'd had at Rushden, I was two streets away, and having one of the best times in my life.'

In 2008–09, Kettering Town were the FA Cup story of the season when, as a non-league club, they made the FA Cup fourth round. Seddon scored the winner against Notts County live on ITV in the second round and scored again in the third against Eastwood Town. Kettering finally went out to Premier League Fulham in the fourth round, but Seddon earned a move to Fleetwood Town. He was gaining a reputation as one of the best strikers in non-league football, the man you signed to score the goals to win promotion. That was the premise on which Fleetwood Town, in the National League North, bought him. He was dropping down a division but on more money, as Fleetwood had big ambitions. Indeed, with Seddon's goals, they went up to the National League and reached the play-off semi-finals for promotion to the Football League, losing to Wimbledon. The club then decided they needed something more to make that final push into the Football League, a strike partner to Seddon. So they signed a raw 21-year-old who had failed at Sheffield Wednesday and had a conviction for assault: Jamie Vardy.

'I'd never heard of him. He signed from Halifax, who were a league below us. They were in the Conference North and we were in the Conference. We played 40-odd games together. And, yeah, we won the league that season. We won the league with a record amount of points. We played like a three up front, so I was central and we had Andy Mangan (who went on to play professionally with Shrewsbury Town and Tranmere) on one side and Jamie Vardy on the other. We had a brilliant side. I'd say we were probably the best non-league side ever.

Seddon wasn't immediately impressed, however. 'He probably still had too much of a lad's mindset and didn't realise how good he could be. He just wanted to play and have fun with his mates and have no stress. But I think once he'd come to Fleetwood and was full-time, he then realised how good he was. We were playing against sides like Luton and Wrexham and we were battering teams and he was the outstanding player. By the end of the season we were like: "This lad's phenomenal."'

Vardy set a record for a non-league player when Leicester City, then in the Championship, signed him for £1million. 'I didn't think he'd have moved into the Championship. I thought he'd get a good League One deal and do really well. I thought, "He's going to struggle in the Championship." And I think he did struggle in his first season. But then he obviously stepped up again. I think people in football don't look past the decision they make about players as teenagers. If they're not in the net at 14, people think they're never going to make it. But I think a lot of it with Jamie was mental. Mentally he wasn't at the right place then.'

When Fleetwood were promoted to the Football League in 2012, Seddon had to leave, because of his insurance pay-out. Instead he played for Conference North side Halifax and then Chester in the National League. But at the end of the 2013–14 season with Chester, Seddon was with his fiancée Melissa on a Sunday afternoon when the Salford call came. 'It came up "No caller ID" and I was, like: "Hello?" And the caller says, "Oh, hiya, Gareth. It's Gary Neville here." "Yeah, okay, who is it?" And he says: "No, it's Gary." And as soon as he started to speak you then recognised the voice. And I'm thinking, "Oh my God, it's Gary Neville!" And he just told me what the Class of 92 had done, and about their ambition for the club, where they wanted to take it. They wanted to sign a striker who would get them the goals to win promotion, who had experience, who would nurture the young players coming through. He offered to put me through my 'A' licence for coaching and loads of things like that. But it wasn't about the money because I'd dropped my money because I was at

Chester, which meant playing in the Conference (one level below the professional game) where they trained full-time. But I was just kind sold on the journey and being involved with them guys.'

***

Gary:

It's a signing we supported as owners, but it was step further than we ever wanted to go. It was £400 a week on a two-year contract. Phil Power, the manager at the time, said that he felt he would get the goals which would take us up.

I said I wanted to hear from him that he was committed. He was in the National League with Chester, which was three tiers above where we were. It was a big step down. I wanted to know he was committed, and I think he wanted to know we were committed to him. So I made the call to him. It was just about sounding each other out and telling him how excited we were about the club, that we wanted to go up but that we need committed players.

There's always a danger with players dropping down a couple of levels. The perception is that it's always for money. And I think Gareth is coming to the end of his football career and starting to build the next stage of his life. So it wasn't just money; it was case of transforming his personal and professional life to make that transition to life after football.

The fact that Gareth is a happy-go-lucky character who likes attention is one of his strengths. I've played with many players who thrive on the attention, the thrill, the hero moments, the Hollywood moments. He wants to be the one up in lights. I believe you need all types of characters in a team, including someone like Gareth.

Our conversation on the phone was more about me getting comfortable with the idea and reporting back to the lads that we could take this leap of faith on a two-year contract. At the time it was reported that he was on £1,000 a week; he never was. But £400 a week was further than we wanted to go. I could never have believed we would have paid that and given someone a two-year contract within our first six months of taking over. We never could have believed that these were the sort of demands with which we would be met. Maybe we were victims of being famous owners and being the new moneybags of the league. But also we did want to attract talented players and generate some enthusiasm and excitement at the club. Most of all, we wanted players who had the quality and commitment to take us up.

* * *

When Seddon arrived at Salford he was, again, the big money, high-profile signing. And though the salary was £400 a week rather than £3,000 a week in League Two or £250,000 a week in the Premier League, everyone knows their place in a football dressing room, even if salaries are meant to be confidential. And in the 2014–15 season he was the absolute star of the show, scoring 28 goals as the team won the league and playing a key role in holding the dressing room together when the manager, Phil Power, was sacked.

He first met his new managers in compromising circumstances. Seddon was standing naked in the dressing room when Anthony Johnson burst in. The pair had just been involved in an altercation on the touchline. At the time Johnson was manager of Ramsbottom, who were playing Salford in the cup. 'There was a bit of a scrap at the side of the pitch and me and Jonno got sent off,' remembers Seddon. Johnson had punched Salford player Sam Madeley and was subsequently banned for five matches.

Seddon returned to the dressing room and was going to shower when suddenly Johnson came through the door. 'I'd heard of Bernard and Jonno but never met them before. But then I got sent off. I went into the dressing room, stripped off and was just about to get into the shower when the door burst open and it was Jonno. I thought, "Oh my God!" The last thing I wanted to do was to try and fight him naked, because he's a big lad.'

Seddon glared for a split second, feeling threatened. Johnson looked at him, strode over and said, 'Gareth, you didn't do anything wrong out there. It was out of order getting sent off. It was something and nothing.' And then he left. Seddon was pleasantly surprised. 'He shook my hand, walked out and I thought, "What a top guy." And then the week after that he was my manager.'

Seddon was initially pleased when Johnson and Morley took over from Power in January 2015. 'When they came in, we had a set way of playing. They had rules. Nobody dared turn up late or not put it in during training because they were on you. And I thought: "This is brilliant. This is exactly what we needed. Exactly what *I* needed." My game stepped up a hundred-fold. Everybody else's did. And we ended up winning the league and I'd put that down to those two. We would not have won the league if it weren't for them. They were brilliant.'

Yet in the 2015–16 season Seddon was no longer the star. He missed much of the first half of the season with a knee injury, including the FA Cup run. The dressing room was changing with the influx of Ramsbottom players. He was relegated to the fringe of the team. Everyone sensed his status had changed. He was almost 36 years old. His contract was up at the end of the season.

'I was injured for I'd say close to six months and even when I got back it didn't feel right. It's coming to maybe your last couple of seasons, you start missing games and you're out a long time…I really started to get a bit anxious – I started to panic. I don't want to sound depressive, but I was thinking, "Oh my God, everything that I've always known is coming to an end." And when you're injured you have more time to think about it. It really hit home that I was approaching 36, all my best years, basically, were behind me, and I just wanted to try and get on the pitch to prove that I still can offer something. In 2014–15 I scored 30-odd goals, I was the star player, it felt amazing because everything was going right and you believe in yourself. Then you get injured and as soon as things start going wrong you just lose your confidence and you stop believing. You start thinking, "God, am I past it?" Physically, my body hasn't changed. I'm probably fitter because I've been working really hard, but mentally you just lose that confidence, with the anxiety and all the stress.'

Seddon has planned well for retirement. He has properties, he models professionally, he's just opened a boutique cheese and coffee shop in Ramsbottom and he is developing a bespoke concierge business, providing the kind of service to the rich that a personal assistant would, only remotely by phone. 'I've opened up two new businesses, including this shop. I've shelled out a lot of money and then you start thinking, "Well where's that money going to be replaced from if football ends? My football money has been that norm every week, that regularity, since I left school, always on a contract no matter what, getting paid every single week whether you're injured, whether you're ill.'

At his worst he has felt as bad as he did during the worst days of his illness. 'I kind of closed up. I never told Melissa about how I was feeling. Never told my family and that anxiety, again, built up. It's really hard to explain but I kind of went back to that place when I knew I had to retire when I was getting ill. But I had an excuse then. I was ill then. Whereas this time I'd felt all the same feelings but it was because of my age and it was just coming to an end. You start thinking, "I'll never be on this money again. I'll never have this adulation again. What are people going to talk to me about?" Because everyone sees me and they're like: "I saw your goal at the weekend! Or, I've seen you on TV! How's Salford doing?" When I was at Chester and Bury that's what everybody knew me for.'

At Darlington away, the game the team lost 3-2 after being 2-1 up with seven minutes to play, it was Seddon who got the blame. He had come on with 23 minutes to play, failed to make an impact and the game was ultimately lost. 'I'd just come back from pulling my groin and the managers said to me at Darlington, "Are you fit enough to play?" And I said, "No, I'm not, but I'm fit enough to go on the bench if you need me." I came on at 1-1, we went 2-1 up. But then we ended up losing 3-2 in the last four minutes but I actually held the ball well when I came on. I didn't really influence it as much because I did set off and I felt my groin. I couldn't really make runs, but as a player you don't know that until you come on. You can come on 100 per cent fit and still pull your hammy. It's just one of those things. They said to me that I'd lied to them and told them I was fit when I wasn't, but in another breath they said they thought that I wasn't committed enough. They thought that I had other things going on off the pitch with my businesses and modelling.

'I said, "I don't really understand your argument. On the one hand you're saying I'm not committed enough, and then on the other you said I'm lying to get on the pitch because I'm too committed. They kind of looked at each other and I just think it was a bit of an excuse really. Managers can do this to shock you into thinking you've been left out the squad, and you need to improve, which at the time sometimes you don't realise, but when you take a step back you think maybe they just wanted a reaction from me, which as a manager I might do. But when it's being done to you, you don't realise it sometimes. I took it in my stride. I texted Jonno a couple of days later and I just said: "Look, I don't agree with the things that you've said but you're the manager. I take it on board. I just want you to believe in me that I will contribute to the season. And I'll win you the league."'

Johnson didn't reply.

'Bastard! It was like, I've just held an olive branch there for you and you didn't text me back. It killed me and I thought, "Shit, can I take this message back now? I want to delete it." And he never mentioned it.'

***

In the play-off semi-final at Ashton United it's just one minute into extra time and Allen comes to the touchline to talk with the managers. He had hoped he had recovered from his hamstring injury but he tells them it is constraining him; he can't sprint. Morley turns around. 'Seds,' he shouts. Before he can get the word out, Seddon has leapt from his spot, where he has been sinking deeper and deeper into his seat, and is springing up and down the touchline warming up. It's the last change for the managers. They need something now and they're trusting Seddon.

He sprints on to the pitch, but there is very little time to make an impact. He's struggling to get an early touch in the first minute he is on, but then Salford win a corner and James Poole lifts it in the direction of Steve Howson at the near post. Howson jumps to head the ball, surrounded by a clutch of Ashton players, but they all miss it and it bounces two, three times and falls to the edge of the box. Seddon shifts his body position a yard or two to meet the ball. Ashton have failed to mark him properly. He is around 16 yards out, just inside the area. As the ball bounces, he pulls back his leg to strike it. He connects cleanly and it gathers pace, accelerating towards goal. On the touch-line, Morley and Johnson strain their necks in anticipation, like meerkats. The ball's trajectory clears all players, and it heads onwards towards the very top corner. It doesn't appear to lose speed. It just continues, seemingly unstoppable.

Seddon is already turning away as it hits the net. His head is down and his body convulsed into the sprinting mode. Behind him slower players are reacting and attempting to catch up. There is no chance. When he reaches the touchline, Danny Webber has rushed from the bench and is there to greet him first. Webber knows something of the despair Seddon has felt this season. They embrace as Scott Burton jumps up and down like an excited child next to them. But quickly they will all disappear under a bundle of bodies: players, coaching staff, physiotherapists, substitutes. All of human life is in there. Seddon has been on the pitch for around 90 seconds.

'I nearly started crying,' says Seddon. 'It was relief, like the feeling of a whole season where I didn't feel I had contributed, going in one moment. Straight away people then were like: "Why haven't you been playing this season? You were brilliant!" instead of thinking, "He's been crap, him." I'd never wanted to dwindle away and keep playing, so people get to a point where they look at me playing and think, "He's crap, him, how's he ever made it as a footballer?" I always had it in my head that when I'd finish, I'd finish on a high, and not keep playing when I know I can't. That will stick with me for a while. It was brilliant. It was just a massive, massive relief that I've still kind of got it.'

The Saturday before the play-off semi-final, Morley and Johnson had rested key players for the final game of the season. Salford had already qualified for the play-offs and there was no point risking the likes of Poole and Webber up front, so Seddon finally had a start. 'I played really well and the manager said to me, "Gaz, you were a different class today. Well done. To come through what you've been through and do what you did today, your attitude's been brilliant."

'I have been professional all season. Obviously I've come home and moaned like mad to Melissa. But I'm 35 and I've been a professional footballer and I do try to carry myself like that. I want people to look up to me and I think if I start showing a bad attitude and moaning, that's only going to rub off onto other people. In the long run people are always going to look back and go, "What a dick he was. He wasn't in the team and he was being a baby." I never want people to think that of me. I held it together loads of times where I've been upset, and now because of what I did towards the end of the season people are going, "What an amazing attitude he had." I think Gary Neville saw that as well. He's commented to a couple of people that he was really impressed with the way that I handle myself, and I've come on and done alright because I could have quite easily blown up, which I wanted to loads of

Danny Webber opens the scoring against Notts County in the FA Cup first round in November 2015… (© Gareth Lyons)

… And Chris Lynch and James Poole help him celebrate (© Gareth Lyons)

Gary Neville congratulates Gary Stopforth as Salford beat League Two Notts County in the FA Cup. (© Ian Hodgson/Daily Mail/Solo Syndication)

Paul Scholes sings Rick Astley in the wake of the Notts County win. (© Getty)

Goalscorer Richie Allen with happy owners Gary Neville and Nicky Butt after the Notts County game. (© Getty)

The gaffers. Morley (left) and Johnson. Real men can kiss.

On the touchline at the Nou
Camp, Barcelona 7, Valencia 0.
'I remember Phil saying:
"You'd better get out there
on the touchline and be there
with them."' (© Getty)

Chris Lynch gets stuck in during the 2015-16 promotion run-in. (© Gareth Lyons)

Barbara Gaskill, or Babs: seller of the finest pie, mash, mushy peas and gravy north of Watford.

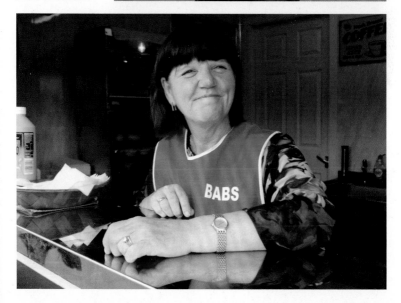

April 2016: Extra time looms in the Play-off semi final against Ashton United and Jonno asks for one, last effort from the team... (© Gareth Lyons)

... and Gareth Seddon sets off to celebrate after scoring the winning goal while Gary Stopforth dances a jig in the background. (© Gareth Lyons)

April 2016: Karen Baird (far left) celebrates as Jordan Hulme scores against Workington in the Play-Offs. (© Gareth Lyons)

Ah Yeah! Jordan Hulme performs the dance to the Will Sparks' track to the delight and bemusement of the Moor Lane crowd after the Play-off final. (© Gareth Lyons)

The Evo-Stik Premier League Play-off winners in 2015-16 celebrate with their trophy, a cut-glass vase. (© Gareth Lyons)

times but I think as you get older you get that experience and you think in the long run it's only going to look bad on me.

'So when it's 1-1 against Ashton in the semi-final, I'm thinking, "You should be looking at me first." You get to the 80th minute and I'm looking at him and thinking, "I've just played on the Saturday for you." But then he looks to Richie Allen, who's just come back from a hamstring and tells him to come on. That was a kick in the stomach and it really wound me up. I think that was my anger when I came on. And when that went in it was kind of like: "Fuck you! You should have brought me on. This is what I can do." And, yeah, it was a big relief.

After Seddon makes it 2-1 in the semi-final, another goal will come deep into extra time when Jordan Hulme beats the Ashton goalkeeper, who has come way too far off his line, and crosses for James Poole, who heads in at the far post. This time everyone comes to celebrate. There are eight minutes to play and everyone in the ground knows there is no way back for Ashton now. Poole's hamstring has tightened and he is lying on the ground. Physios Val McCarthy and Steve Phillips are ticked off by the referee for joining the throng on the far side of the pitch, but he might have picked on anyone – Morley, Johnson and Craig Dootson are all there. The job is halfway done.

Afterwards, the club bar is alive with people basking in the glory of the victory. Fans, directors, managers, players all mix here. Plenty have contributed to the win, Jordan Hulme and James Poole not least. Poole stands away in a corner chatting to his girlfriend, sisters and parents, quietly content. Seddon, by contrast, is surrounded by a throng. He wears a huge, permanent grin. Everywhere he goes, he is congratulated. He looks happy tonight, as though he has rediscovered who he is.

***

Ryan:

It was a difficult game against Ashton. It was only the second game that I'd been to and it was nervous times, obviously. One goal and your season's finished. And to be fair to Gaz, he produced at the right time. He's had a frustrating season. He hasn't played as many games as he did last year. But at the right time he came and produced a brilliant goal. That's what centre-forwards do. That's why people love him.

***

Phil:

Danny Webber and Gareth Seddon were our two big signings at the start. We paid them the most money. But they won us promotion last year, both of them. And in the play-off semi-final against Ashton, Seddon won us that game really. He came on and produced a moment of magic. They're game changers. They're game winners. It's what was missing. And you know, that's why we pay them the big money, because they score the goals at the right time in the big games. They produced the best moments.

***

Gary:

In that first year we committed to Jason Jarrett, Paul Linwood, and Gareth Seddon and they were the spine of that team. They all played a big part in taking us up, and Gareth's goals at the end of the first season were absolutely critical.

Last season was more frustrating for Gareth. But still he scored that second goal against Ashton in the semi-final. No word of a lie, Scholesy and I were stood there in our usual position at the semi-final and I genuinely thought we were going to lose that game. I thought it was running away from us until he came on. In the two years we have had our money's worth from Gareth and I think he's had his money's worth out of us and I think we've been true to each other.

The likes of Gareth and Danny Webber have set the tone for the club in the first two years. The players who have typified the club, who have been with us from the start, have been Gareth, Danny, Chris Lynch, our captain, and Jay Lynch in goal, who joined very early on in September 2014. With Chris, you always felt he would run through a brick wall for you from day one. Danny was an opportunistic signing after that friendly game with the Class of 92. I was nervous about him because I thought he would find it hard to motivate himself to get up on a Saturday and travel to Brighouse or Buxton. But he was a model pro for two years. I think Gareth found it difficult in his second season with injuries. And he had professional commitments outside the game, and he had to have that transition.

At every level in football, a player has to find something inside them which motivates them. It can be that you have it inbuilt in you, that you are a hard-working character, committed to the team, who will never drop below a certain standard. Other players will find outside motivations to get themselves to that level: it could be a new contract; it could be that they're building a better life for their family; it could be that they have to be the star or the hero and the new pin-up boy. There are many different ways of getting to the end result. And Gareth is one of those who is driven by the hero moment, being the star and walking off the pitch with the cameras on him.

I've never really minded how a player finds a way to motivate himself to get to that level, as long as he finds a way to get there and maintain his level and is valuable to the team. I don't elevate the lad who seems to be the dream professional and who wants to do it for the team, or the one who wants to do it for the new contract or to get the attention. As long as the performance is beneficial for the team and they find something to draw the best level of performance out of themselves, then it's never really concerned me how they get there. In a perfect world maybe it would all be inbuilt in your character. But in the real world, not everyone is like that.

30 APRIL 2016

EVO-STIK PREMIER DIVISION PROMOTION PLAY-OFF FINAL: SALFORD CITY 1, WORKINGTON 2 HALF-TIME

The dressing room is quiet. Everyone knows what is coming. 'You listening?' says Bernard Morley. He looks at Steve Howson and Billy Priestley. 'You two listening?'

They nod.

'This is going to be the last fucking bollocking I give you, because at the end of the game, it's irrelevant. It's irrelevant. The preparation, the information, the way we've done things, talked about how to beat a side and what not to do...you've just done the total fucking opposite.'

Morley is angrier than he's ever been. Usually it's Johnson who operates at this level of aggression. Morley looks at Howson, who is captain now that Chris Lynch is injured.

'You, Steven,' he starts and points the captain's armband he is wearing. 'You've been given that for a reason. And you might look at me again and go, "Oh, fucking hell." But both goals, you stand off the ginger kid and you think, "I don't want to get tight because he's going to turn me." Am I right or am I wrong?

'First goal, he drops in, he gets on the half-turn and it's "Fuck that, I'm not going with him." See Kyle May . . .' He is referring to Workington Town's centre-half, who plays in Howson's position and who scored the opening goal. 'What does he do to you when you drop in?' He is now talking to the Salford City strikers now, Webber and Poole. 'Danny. What does he do to you? He's fucking laughing.'

He turns to Howson again. 'You? You don't do that.' Morley turns to the subject of the ginger kid, Workington's Scott Allison. 'He will hurt you. He scored eight goals in his last four games. Listen to us? We do not do our homework for fuck all. Second goal, you let him get on the half-turn. He actually squares you up. You cannot let that happen. You cannot let it happen. Get your arm out and he won't go past you. You're too slow for him. Stand off him, he'll do what he did. You've got to think up here, boys. We've banged on about it all season. About concentration levels, that's all it is.'

Morley will now turn his attention to his forwards. 'Now from that, to what we we've got going forward. You're bang on. It's as bad as we've been. Everyone wants too many touches.'

302

Webber, the former Manchester United professional, is usually above direct criticism. 'Danny. I'm not sticking up for you because on two occasions you've had too many touches. See when that ball comes into his feet, he's had 10 touches. I'm not sticking up for you because 10 touches is too many. You have got to go: "Fuck off. Past him."'

He points at Poole. 'He did it one occasion. Go past him and then I can say, "Danny. Too many touches. Give the ball to JJ."

'You've got to want to win. You've got to repetition. And want to score. We're putting balls in the boxes and they're heading them. They're not bigger than us. They're not bigger. They want it more. And I'm stomping up and down on that side-line thinking: "Why in the final do we roll over? Why?" Go out with a fucking fight. And they've got nothing. Apart from one good ball in the box: goal. They switch off. Second goal, we show too much respect: goal. That's it.'

Now he turns to midfielder Gary Stopforth. 'I don't like doing this, but I tell you what, son, you are one person who is trying to impact the fucking game. Getting into areas, getting on the ball. And he should be the last person doing that. Wake up!'

The players are responding, A couple shout, "Come on, boys!" like it's the expected response.

Morley continues. 'I'm angry, because you've done the opposite of what I wanted you to do. What we wanted you to do. Jordan, you've done alright. That has got to be better. And I know it will be, because you're body language says you know it hurts. I can tell. You can tell in your own head. You don't need me to tell you. It's got to be better, boys. JJ. Come alive.'

Left-back Stephen O'Halloran is being patched up by physio Val McCarthy. He has a deep gash in the back of his head which has been bleeding. Billy Priestley has ice on his left eye, which is swelling and so bruised he looks like a punched-out boxer. The pair collided attempting to head out a long ball from Workington.

'Billy, Howson, O'Halloran. Communicate. You've come 20 yards, Billy, to head Hally in the back of the head. Fucking communication. We're looking at being two players down. Get it together. Yeah? Massive 45 minutes. Massive. The No. 10's dropping in. He's a very clever player. Scott. You've got to look after the No. 10, yeah. Gaz will do the other kid, is it the No. 6? He's not doing anything. What he's doing, he's getting on the end of our balls. It's that defensive they play like a 3-5-2. But he's winning the headers in their box.

'We've got to play at pace. The more touches and the more we slow the ball down, the more we let them get back in. And boys, listen to me. They'll run through brick walls and I know you will. But they're doing it. I don't know how long they can do it for. But they're doing it and it's a good half without them doing 'owt. We've got to wake up and play to our strengths. If it doesn't come off, it doesn't come off. Yeah? Don't let us come in here, going, "Fuck me, what if? What if?" That's not what we're about. We've come a long way. Don't throw it away to this.

304

Cheating twats. Diving for every yellow card, red card. That's what they're trying. That's what they've come to do. Box clever. Come on.' This outburst comes despite the fact that Workington don't appear to be any more prone to gamesmanship than any other team at this level.

Anthony Johnson steps forward. 'Listen, you've got 45 minutes of your season left. Maybe another half-hour on top. That is it. Some of you are just watching as if to say: "If we have a shit half, we'll put it right the next game." Forty-five minutes!'

Johnson turns to Stopforth and Jordan Hulme, who are sitting together. 'I'm glad you've pulled Gaz out there. And I'll single you out, Jordan. Because you're occupying players. You're going, "That's my fucking man, I'll deal with him." But the one thing he's just touched on: we've got to move the ball quicker. The defender is a carthorse. Very, very aggressive. Excellent in the air. But he can't turn. So if we're dragging players out and we know he's there, let's set the ball quicker. Because we drag them out of play.

'That can only happen if you go beyond the forwards. Because if you don't, and they have to go back in there, you have to beat two men. Yeah. People have got to occupy positions and areas on the pitch. We've got to be smarter, boys. Because you looked in that first half like: "We'll lift it when we fucking want to and need to." That's how it looked. "Oh, we'll up a gear again now." It's a final! They're not going to lie down for you, boys. They don't do that. Sides don't do that at this level of football. They get a third goal, it's goodnight sweetheart here. We're lucky we've come in 2-1 down and could put things right. But your energy, your work rate, your movement, isn't fucking acceptable. You look caught in the headlights, boys, some of you.

'I can't get my point over about how important this is, now, in the whole scheme of everything. That's not to put extra pressure. You've got that anyway. But if you're not going to perform in a final, boys, what's the point?'

'Come on, boys,' someone shouts.

Johnson: 'Up your fucking game, up your tempo, up your work rate. Work for your pals.'

Morley wants one last say. Johnson has referred to the unspoken fear, a potential third Workington goal. One more goal and an entire season would, realistically, begin to slip away. Another season's slog in the Evo-Stik Premier would beckon.

'Listen in, everybody,' says Morley. 'Listen. I mean it. If we go 3-1 down, we continue to play the right way. Because if we go 3-1 down, I still back us to get in the game. Don't go to pieces. The next goal's massive. They'll think they'll win it if they get the next goal. We continue to do the right things. Or at least try. Alright? Come on, boys!'

***

It had started so well. Coach driver Ian Corrie is on the microphone again, at the front of the coach. He is leading a chorus of 'Sweet Caroline'. Everyone joins in. Even less ebullient players such as James Poole are singing. It's 1pm, two hours before the play-off final starts. Salford City have hung in there all season and have this one, last chance to win promotion. Win, and all the fall-outs and disappointments will be irrelevant. Last year the club won the Evo-Stik First Division North. A second successive promotion would take them to the National League North, which is two levels below the fully professional League Two. They are on the cusp of becoming a fully professional club.

Lose, and it will feel like it's back to the beginning. It isn't, of course; they have one promotion in the bag from last season, and they reached the second round of the FA Cup this season, heights previously unheard of for Salford City. The season has been one of continued progress. But having come this far, having to do it all again, to again scramble to get out of this division, will feel awful. 'It's not the feeling of losing,' says Gary Neville. 'It's the feeling that I've got to go through it all again in the same league. Ever since the semi-final, I've been saying it's a huge few days for the club. It's the biggest few days in the club's history. Forget the FA Cup. Going up is everything to us. It's what we want. It's what we strived for.'

Coach driver Corrie is launching into another chorus of 'Sweet Caroline' when the music is suddenly turned off. He is left exposed, singing the chorus with gusto but without the back-up music. The players scream with derision and laughter. 'Fucking nob!' shouts someone. Everyone laughs. Corrie laughs.

Pre-match salmon, chicken and pasta have been consumed. The coach has been booked in to take the players the few miles from Hotel Football to Salford City's Moor Lane, where the final is taking place. Early that morning Johnson and Morley were driving over to the hotel when their car pulled up alongside a new Range Rover. Inside is Nicky Butt. They wave to get his attention. He waves back. He is used to fans doing this kind of thing. Suddenly he recognises his managers and winds down the window.

'Where are you going?'

'To the hotel,' says Johnson. 'Pre-match meal and coach.'

Butt makes a face. 'You're costing us a fortune!' he complains. He smiles and wishes them luck. He will be along later with Gary Neville and Paul Scholes. Phil Neville is in Valencia and Ryan Giggs has training with Manchester United.

When the team arrive at Moor Lane, the ground is already filling up, which is unusual. It's raining but everyone is happy: a wet pitch allows them to play the quicker football they like. And the pitch needs softening anyway. In the dressing room, Hulme is voguing. Diplo & Sleepy Tom's 'Be Right Here' is playing. Loudly. The bass is thumping. It's an up-tempo house music track. Format: B's 'Chunky' follows. More of the same. But then the music is switched off and the mood is quiet.

'There are some fucking nerves in here,' says Anthony Johnson, smiling. 'It fucking stinks of it!'

There is a smattering of laughs.

'Everyone's got fucking big skid marks in their undies!'

More laughs.

'Relax!' he screams. 'Chill the fuck out!'

Everyone laughs.

He turns to right-back Evan Gumbs, who hasn't said a word. 'Shut the fuck up! I can't a word in edgeways with you, fucking tennis ball head.'

Gumbs is giggling. The whole team is laughing.

'Come on, gaff,' Johnson says to Morley.

Morley takes over. 'Boys, go out and enjoy yourselves. I'm nervous, I'm not going to lie to you, but so I should be. It's what dreams are made of. We said it before on the way here. It's what we aim for all season. We've had our ups and down, we've had our fall-outs. I said it on Tuesday night, go out and enjoy yourselves. Don't go out there with the world on your shoulders thinking, "What if?" Go and do it. Don't leave anything here. Webs, Seddon, Tunji. It might be your last game. Who knows what they're going to do next year? Might retire. Who knows what he's going to do.

'Go out, boys, collectively – for this group let's go out with a fucking bang. All of us. And we'll say: do you know what? We got promoted with Danny Webber in our squad. Gaz Seddon. And Tunji Moses. And fucking Scott.

'Don't fuck it up. Don't leave anything in here. Listen, we don't know what's coming next season. You might move on, we might get rid of you. Shit happens, doesn't it? So today's a special day for us. With this squad. We've been through war, haven't we? We've been through the trenches together, boys, and we're here. All them doubters. People saying it won't work, joint managers. Everything. All comes collectively for today. Don't let yourselves down. Listen. We trust you. You know that. And we back you all the way. So it's about you boys today. We pick a side, boys, so it's down to you boys. Attitude, discipline, hard work. Desire. Determination. And we fucking win the game. Simple as that. Yeah. We go down 1-0 don't worry about it. How many times have we come back from 1-0 this season? Yeah? Come on. Enjoy it.'

Johnson takes the stage back. 'Listen, boys. On a personal level I'm proud of everybody and I'm glad everyone is here.' He begins addressing players who won't be in the team today. The captain, Chris Lynch, is injured; others just haven't made the team. 'Dom. Lynchey, you're part of today. Sam. You picked up an injury and went out on loan. Michael played your part last game of season. Keiran's been part of it. Ben, you've been in goal all the time with Jay. Every one of you, every one of you in the dressing room. Rushy. Make me proud.

'On a personal level, I'm a proud man today. No matter what happens – and I know what will happen – but no matter what happens, I'm a proud man. They'll be no coming in at the end of the game and dressing things down and analysing things, because that's it. It's done. So this is my point. Listen. Thanks for the best season I've ever had in football. Don't start crying now, because I know it's a fucking emotional speech and I'm on the way here. I'm serious. The best fucking year I ever had in football. And it's all down to you lot. You've all played a part. I want the same thing we've asked for every single game – effort. And you can control that, boys. You can control how much effort you put into it. Go out and enjoy yourself. Come on, boys!'

Morley takes over. 'Same starting eleven. Tunji will come onto the bench for Richie.'

The team has been announced. The warm-ups commence. The sun is out, the pitch drying too quickly. Morley is away from the players now, checking the grass. 'So many people have doubted us,' he says. 'That's what you remember. People doubt us as young managers. And there have been so many ups and downs with this team, this group of lads. We got to the second round of the cup. We've had a promotion.' He pauses. 'I don't even want to think what I would be without football. Outside of my family, it's everything. And this is an opportunity to go one better, to a better level. And every level I go to is for the betterment of my family.' Five years ago Morley was starting out in the North-West Counties league, which is just above Saturday afternoon parks football.

With 10 minutes to go, the managers deliver their final thoughts. 'Listen,' says Johnson. 'They're likely to play 4-4-2-ish. Two wide players. So they're playing into our hands with that formation, yeah? In the middle of the park, Scott, Gaz, we've got so much more energy than them it's not true, but it's important we win those second balls. Alright, Gaz?'

'Yeah!' shouts Stopforth. He needs to shout to be heard. He has left the team talk and is sat in the toilet.

'He's had six shits in the last hour by the way, because he's fucking shitting his pants,' says Johnson. 'We're on the front foot. Webs, Pooley, Jordan: shape. As soon as it breaks down, let's get our shape. Here's the most important thing for me. How fast we start. They've just travelled three hours and got here at two o'clock. We start fucking well and we put them on the back foot for 95 minutes. It's how we start. Pooley, Jordy, JJ, Webs. First 10, 15 minutes chase things down. Chase fucking lost causes. We play from there.'

Howson, today's captain, stands up, ready to leave. 'This is us, boys,' he says.

Now Webber, the senior pro. 'We don't come all this way and give it away now,' he says, looking round at each player. 'See it through.' It's a calm, assured voice.

On the stereo, Neil Diamond's 'Forever in Blue Jeans' plays. They're ready.

***

Five minutes into the game Workington have a corner. The ball sweeps across the face of Salford's goal. Howson comes to head it away but misses. The ball drops at the far post. Kyle May, the Workington defender, has pushed Billy Priestley out of the way and lost his marker. He simply sticks out his foot and directs it in. It's Salford 0, Workington 1.

There is, however, a swift reaction. On 14 minutes, Poole's corner is met by a fierce header from O'Halloran and it's 1-1. On the bench, players and coaching staff relax a little. It's been unusually quiet. The ribald chat and piss-taking has receded. The nervousness is almost palpable. Then a poor kick out by goalkeeper Jay Lynch allows Workington a throw-in. Scott Allison, the ginger kid, attacks Howson and slips past him. He rolls the ball across to the far post where Workington striker Gareth Arnison is free. He taps in for 2-1.

There isn't much of a response from Salford City. Priestley has a looping header that the Workington goalkeeper Alex Mitchell does well to save. Webber attempts a chip that is collected by Mitchell comfortably. Half-time comes, the team trudges off. Over the PA they're playing 'Forever in Blue Jeans'. But everyone knows what the half-time team talk will be like.

***

The second half is little better. There are chances. James Poole strikes one wide. Jordan Hulme has a header. Gareth Seddon comes on for Danny Webber on 65 minutes. The bench is even quieter now. Johnson and Morley are less vocal from the sidelines. The season is slipping away.

And yet, finally, on 77 minutes John Johnston lifts a cross to the far post where O'Halloran is unmarked, a few yards from goal. He has a clear header, with just the goalkeeper to beat. It is the outstanding chance for which they have been waiting, the equaliser. All of the bench are jumping up. Morley and Johnson have tensed up and are leaning forwards in anticipation.

O'Halloran heads it wide. He buries his head in his hands. Hulme looks across to the bench. Morley is squatting on the ground, head in hands. Hulme thinks, 'Shit. It's not our day.'

***

Jordan Hulme is running now, perhaps faster than he ever has in his life. His knees are high, and one arm is pumping like a sprinter's. But the other arm is holding his shirt. Later, he will feel a little self-conscious about that. Perhaps he should have worked out more, he'll think. He doesn't feel he is in the best shape to show off his upper body. He's not usually shy about such points of etiquette, but when he reflects on this moment that will be what he dwells on. He is running towards the metal gate which separates the changing rooms from the pitch. Seddon attempts to hold him back but Hulme pushes him away. He can see the fans there and he is running towards them. Just before he can reach the fans, though, Johnson, who has run 30 yards from the bench, reaches him and grabs him by the ears. Soon the rest of the team will be there too. The coaching staff, physio, subs as well. Some fans are attempting to embrace Hulme. He is becoming squashed between the throng behind him and the metal of the gate. Johnson is still pulling his ears. He's not sure why. 'It's because he's an idiot,' he decides later.

With 11 minutes of the game remaining, Salford had equalised. Billy Priestley, the defender they signed in March, headed in from a corner. With the game at 2-2, suddenly it feels as though the momentum has switched. However, there is a nearly calamitous moment just two minutes later. A Workington free-kick beats everyone in the box. Priestley stumbles on the ball as he attempts to clear and Workington's Kyle May attempts to scramble the ball in from four yards out. It only needs a strong nudge. But his shot loops up off Gumbs's out-stretched leg and Howson manages to clear it off the line. It's put straight back in to Workington's Matt Tymon, who is eight yards out. Goalkeeper Jay Lynch, who has come out to attempt to smother the cross, has left the goal wholly exposed, and even if Howson dutifully remains on the line, as does Priestley, it doesn't seem like much of a defence. Tymon sticks a leg out. Johnson and Morley crane their necks to see. Their view is obscured by a forest of players. Then they see the ball soaring out of the melee, clearing the crossbar and heading into the crowd behind the goal.

Salford have survived, but extra time now looks likely. Four minutes remain when Priestley comes to take a throw deep in the Workington half. Priestley has perfected the art of the long throw, hurling the ball into the opponents' penalty area from unfeasibly long distances. This one reaches Workington keeper Alex Mitchell, but he can only punch at it. It falls for Howson, who is up to win headers. He almost nods at the ball, but it rebounds off the post. Hulme, next to him, sticks out a foot but Mitchell parries it away. Only to Howson, however, who jabs at the ball. Mitchell is on the ground now. He desperately pushes it away, but with no power and the ball has no momentum. It drops in front of Hulme.

'The keeper flapped at it and Howson headed it on to the post,' says Hulme. 'But it was almost as if I knew it was going there as I had just stuck my foot out. It hit the post, Howson had another go and the keeper saved that, but the ball fell on the line. I just thought "I'm not taking any chances" and smashed it into the net.' Which is when he started running, sprinting away from his team-mates. All around, fans are shouting, yelling and bouncing with delight. The entire bench is running towards him, Johnson in the lead just ahead of Morley. His team-mates are chasing him. A huge explosion of celebration is about to ensue, while the referee, like a purse-lipped puritan, looks on disapprovingly and gestures the players back to their half for the restart. There are still three minutes of normal time to play and a few minutes of injury time. It is 3-2 to Salford.

***

The Salford players are fighting their way through the pitch invasion to the metal gate, now open, where Hulme had celebrated his goal, to get back to the dressing room. Gary Neville is there to greet them with embraces. He is beaming. 'They've got balls, this team,' he says. He is hugging almost anyone he sees. Butt has left. He has broken his ankle and is only just off crutches. A dressing room celebration is not what his recently mended bones need. Scholes has gone too. He is nursing a heavy cold and has decided not to inflict that on the dressing room. This is a moment for the team, not the owners, he feels. Soon everyone is bundled into the tight dressing room, including some additional members of the club. Barbara Gaskill is there, looking suddenly vulnerable with this group of young men towering over her. Karen Baird is there. Instinctively everyone knows what to do, including Gaskill and Baird. They gather themselves into a huddle of excited noise and start bouncing up and down. 'We are going up/Say, we are going up,' they chant rhythmically, again and again. Some are thumping the ceiling of the Portakabin in time to the chant. A panel is smashed; another threatens to fall on to the celebrating throng. Everyone is in there: Johnson, Morley, Rushton, McCarthy, Gaskill, Hulme, Stopforth, O'Halloran, Webber, Seddon. All the team, no outsiders. 'We are going up/Say, we are going up,' they chant. Again and again. The chanting doesn't stop.

There is an on-pitch presentation, a trophy to be lifted, photos to be taken. Many of the crowd are still milling around on the pitch, but most have retreated to the stands to acclaim the team. The cup is duly paraded and pictures are taken. On the PA a tune starts up. It's Will Sparks's 'Ah Yeah'. The thud of a drum machine interspersed with samples of eclectic sounds is building in to a crescendo. The team all point to Hulme. 'The dance!' they scream. 'The dance!' Hulme looks coy for a second and then thinks better of it. He springs up onto the roof of the dugout, a vantage point from which the entire stadium can see him. There are roars of approval. His top comes off, again. He starts to vogue, performing robot dance moves. And the climax comes. The team, the stadium seem to shout together, 'Ah Yeah!' And everyone is dancing for a moment.

***

The dressing room is almost empty. The Kit has been packed away but the floor is a muddy mess and it badly needs mopping up. The ceiling panels look precarious having taken a battering in the celebrations. At one end of the room are a couple of basic showers, which double up as urinals before the game; at the other end, the toilet. Grime mixed with the detritus of the game and spilt champagne means the mud on the floor sticks to the shoes.

Johnson is sat between John Johnston and Luke Clark, two of the younger players. The odd player drifts in but it is a sparse gathering. 'Best season of my life,' says Johnson, his grin irrepressible.

He is at his best in moments like this, with just a few players around after a win. And after this win there is an almost-tangible sense of relief and profound satisfaction in the now filthy Portakabin dressing room. They have just come from the bar area, where the The Pogues' version of 'Dirty Old Town' is playing on the PA. The bar is packed, people are singing and the party will go on for some time. But these three have chosen to sit here for a quiet moment.

Johnson looks at the mess on the floor and turns to JJ. 'You should be cleaning that up!'

'Fuck that!' says JJ.

'That's what wrong with football,' says Johnson. 'In my day, young player at Bury, that was my job: clean up the dressing room.'

'Fuck that,' repeats JJ. 'I'm a National League player!'

Johnson laughs. 'You don't know if we're keeping you on,' he replies, the manager's ultimate threat.

JJ laughs. Johnson is holding court. He turns to Clark, who is heading off to Thailand on holiday. 'When you back?' says

318

Johnson, worrying about pre-season training already. He'll be back in the middle of June.

Johnson is alarmed. 'You'll be a pudding by then, won't you?'

Clark nods, giggling.

'You'll be like a Buddha!' Johnson continues. Clark laughs. JJ laughs. Johnson is laughing.

Outside, the PA is now playing Bruce Springsteen's 'Dancing in the Dark.' Johnson sits back. No-one speaks. Johnson begins to join in, quietly, almost absent-mindedly. 'You can't start a fire ...' he sings to himself.

***

Paul:

We didn't play well in either of the play-off games really. But we won the games, which is the most important thing. It wasn't about performance really, it was just about going through, and we managed to do that in both games. The lads showed great character to stick in there while they weren't playing well and found a way to win. I just think we were mentally tougher. I always felt we'd win the game and didn't probably expect it to be as tough as it was really. But I think we're a mentally strong team. The two managers are like that and they demand that from the players, and that came through in the end. There do seem to be a lot of last-minute goals and dramatic wins. I don't think that comes from nowhere. I think it's solely down to the manager and players. The managers make high demands on the players and they make sure that they go right to the end. I don't think it's any fluke, like it was no fluke with us at Manchester United. They tell them to keep going and somehow they find a way of winning when, a lot of the time, they're not playing as well as they could.

We would have been disappointed if we hadn't gone up, but I don't think we would have been devastated. It still would have been a great season, getting as far as we did in the FA Cup and getting to the play-offs. But it's nice that it's happened twice in two years. We didn't expect it. We hoped for it and I think we gave a budget which was good enough to do it, but that doesn't always mean you're guaranteed to do it. Now we'll see what happens. Hopefully we can compete again. It's going to be a lot tougher, this league – I'm certain it's going to be a lot tougher. A lot of big teams have come down from the National League with big budgets and we have to try and compete with that. We know we're not going to go up every year. Next year might be a year we plateau, but it's not something we want to do. Our ambitions are still to go up and the managers' ambitions are still to go up.

We always have belief that we could get to the Football League. We're still a long way from it. The next two leagues, the National League and the National League North, are a different standard altogether. Getting out of these two leagues is going to be tough. There will be lots of clubs with budgets close to League One clubs which we're going to have to try to compete with.

* * *

Gary:

I was proud of them. Workington were by far the better team in the first half, but I always felt we are a more powerful, stronger team that keep going. I thought we would come stronger towards the end. What they've achieved in the last 18 months is just absolutely incredible. The spirit that they have. The togetherness. It's everything that you really want in a football team, whether you're a fan, a coach, an owner or a player. I have to say that I've not seen too many groups of players have a spirit like they have, and that's ultimately down to the managers and what they've created in the dressing room. It's not just Ramsbottom lads, as there's only five or six from there. It's the whole team that have bought into it all as well.

The question is: 'Do you need success to create that feeling in the dressing room? What would it be like if the team wasn't successful?' You saw it earlier on in the season, for instance, when it was a little bit more rocky and they lost a few games. Did it change then? The fact is they got through those critical moments and this team never give in, they always go to the end. Sir Alex Ferguson's teams are always renowned for that and we were lucky enough to be part of it for a long time, but Salford have a reputation of never giving in, a never say die spirit – they'll always score. That's been created by the managers in the dressing room. The results have been absolutely staggering. Not many clubs do two promotions on the bounce. Darlington have done it as well as us, so to have two teams do it in two years is really a rare achievement.

***

Nicky:

It was a strange feeling because I think in both the games we didn't play great in the first half and nothing was happening for us. People were mis-controlling it, the pitch was bobbly, we weren't getting the right crosses into the boxes. So you do start thinking, 'It's not going to be, this.' Then you get your goal back for 1-1 in the final and you think, 'Okay, we're going do it, we're going to kick on from here.' But they got the next goal, went 2-1 up. And probably in 15 minutes in the second half we became impatient and starting pumping the ball into the box and it wasn't working for us. It just wasn't working, and you start to think that this might not be our day.

But they sat back and invited us on, and with the forwards that we have and the players that we have, you do think we're going to get one or two chances – it's if we can take them.

It wasn't the way we played football that impressed; it was more of a hit-and-run kind of game, but I think that was nerves, tension, the way the game was going. We just started to get the ball in the box. It's not the way we play football, but fortunately we got chances and a couple of goalmouth scrambles and we got the goals.

I think all good teams at any level have the drive to win. I think obviously we did in 1999. Arsenal had it when they were dominant. Chelsea had it. Obviously the lower league teams have it at their level and Salford, hopefully, have it with the background of the managers. It all comes from the managers, it comes from the team spirit, and if you're a successful team you have to have that. You know when you're on a football pitch that no matter how long's left and you're 1-0 down, you know and the team that you're playing against know, that you will always come back. Successful teams don't give up. They always come back. They've got a fighting spirit. That never say die attitude. And when you put that fear into the opposition, it doesn't matter if they're 1-0 up, 2-0 up, they have that doubt in their mind and it plays against them. And you do create chances. After you've done it two, three or four times it's not a fluke, it becomes a habit. And it's part of your training; you train hard right to the end of your training session. It doesn't matter when you score the goal, if it's on 94 minutes or 95 minutes. You know you've still got a chance to score goals. And if you do that once, you do it twice, you do it three times, it builds your confidence. All successful clubs have that at any level of football or sport. If you're a dominant team and you have good team spirit and good leadership, then you have that.

***

Ryan:

During the final I had just finished training at Manchester United. I was in the analysts' room at the training ground in Carrington. There was some time between training and eating. We tried to get a live feed. We were desperately trying to get Radio Workington. We just couldn't, so we followed it on Twitter. I didn't expect it. I didn't expect promotion, and that's not being negative, it's just a realisation of how hard it is, how tough it is to get promoted and then promoted again. That's the way I think. I don't expect it next year as well, but I hope we do it. It's massive credit to the managers. To have back-to-back promotions. Obviously it's their fourth now in five years. It's huge respect to them and huge respect to the players, especially in the manner that they did it.

Winning with Salford is a different feeling from doing it as a player. When you're a player, you're caught up in it and you're quite selfish. You're trying to do it for yourself; but when you're an owner, you have more perspective and you can take in a lot more also. But also there's a massive sense of responsibility and that made the day more significant, because of everything that comes with it. You do feel that responsibility, so when you are successful, you're sharing it with so many people. As a player, you're sharing it with just your team-mates.

In many ways, it couldn't have gone any better in the last couple of years. People who may not have heard of us before or may not have had any interest in the club, even people who don't necessarily like football have been coming up to me and asking about the TV documentary and the FA Cup run. It's captured the imagination, and that's what we want to do whilst keeping the traditions as well. It is a responsibility to make sure we don't lose the spirit of the club, its roots. But we know what we're like. We know that that'll never happen, so we're quite relaxed about it, even though a lot of people will be worried about it. We want to grow the club but we want to keep its traditions.

What's next for the club? We're under no illusions. It's going to be tough. There's some big teams now in the National League North. It will be tough but we're ready for the fight. We're ambitious. We're starting to mix now with some non-league clubs with massive histories and big budgets. And it's going to be difficult. But also you have to be confident. You have to believe that you're going to do well because the club seems to be on the crest of a wave. We know we're coming up against some really good sides, but I think those clubs also know that they're coming up against a club who are really competitive, who are confident and, as we proved in the FA Cup, ready to mix it with the big boys in the league. We want to be in the Football League and we'll do everything we can to be in that.

***

Phil:

I was in Spain, following it on Twitter. I'd come home for the Ashton game and we'd gone to extra time, and we'd sneaked through. Everyone thought we were going to win it easy; we didn't. And I had a bad feeling about the final. I just thought we'd played extra time in the semi, we were tired and you think it can't always go our way. It can't. Everything seems to be going our way. I was preparing myself actually for the disappointment before the game, in case, because I wanted us to go up so badly. But I was preparing myself just in case, to have a balance about it and say, 'Look, actually, it's unrealistic to think we can get promotion after promotion, year after year.' So before the game and during the game when we went behind I was quite philosophical about it because I was preparing myself to speak to the managers after the game. I knew the players would be disappointed. And I knew it would feel like a disaster for them.

I was really calm during the game. I was at home with my brother-in-law and my sister-in-law and their kids, who'd come over to Valencia to see us for the weekend. We'd had training in the morning. My son had played football in the morning and I was really calm because I'd almost said to myself, 'Right, we're losing today, and tomorrow we're going to have to build again for next season.'

When the attendance came through and it was almost 2,000 people, I thought, 'Wow. People are getting us.' That actually gives me shivers because I think, 'We're doing something right. Something special is happening here. We're building something and it's growing, maybe faster than what we can probably handle.'

And when the goal went in, you could smell it. You would get that feeling with United sometimes. When it got to like February, March, you could smell it. In training there was an electricity about it. When we came back to 2-2, it was like the United days, honestly it was. We were losing 2-1 and you start to think, 'I know we're going to score.' The opposition know you're going to score. It just happens. I don't call it the spirit of '99. I call it Fergie time. Because it was Sir Alex Ferguson's drive which meant we kept fighting. When teams score late on I always think of Sir Alex straight away. It's special this. When you score in the last minute and you've come back twice and then you grab the winner and you win a title, that's special. And seeing all the players, the subs, the physios, the staff, all running down the touchline, all together, to celebrate, all of those that are not involved, I thought, 'Wow!' It sends your mind back to the moments in your career where you were successful and you think, what was the basis for that success? Spirit, togetherness. It all comes back. When Jordan scores the winning goal or Gareth scores the winning goal in extra time, that feeling is no different to being a child and seeing Norman Whiteside score the winning goal in the 1985 FA Cup final or Mark Hughes scoring an equaliser against Oldham in 1994. You celebrate the same and the feeling's the same.

***

Nicky:

I am confident about the future of Salford City because we have a vision. Any good project in any walk of life has to have a vision: a starting point and an end point and then an idea of how you get between those two points. How do you get to that final hurdle? What are your building blocks? And we have that in place. When we first took over I think there was just a shrug of the shoulders from most people, and they thought: 'It's just footballers with a little bit too much money who just want a bit of fun.'

But it's not. We've kept to our budgets. We've not been stupid. We've let the committee and accountants do their bit, do their work and do it well, which they do. We've done it like a business. We didn't want to get carried away with ourselves and throw stupid money at it. We have a plan. We're ahead of our schedule at the minute. We're going to the next league now. We know our budget to compete with the teams in there. So it's very much a strategic plan that we're keeping to. We want to be taken seriously, and hopefully after two promotions in two years we'll start to get taken seriously now. It's a big vision that we have for the club to go forward and really create something special for Salford. It's a place that's really close to our hearts. We keep saying it, and hopefully people will now start to realise that we mean business. We've still got a long way to go. We're going to make more mistakes along the way. It's not all going to be smooth running, but we have a plan that we think is going to work and we've got a time schedule that we think is realistic. Salford have the backing of the five of us and Peter Lim as well. We feel that every time you go, there are more and more people who are coming along to experience the ride with us. Bloody hell, we've gone from 80 people watching it to 800 already, and who knows where that can go next?

To get 2,000 people to come down and watch their local team in the play-off final felt special. We want to capture people's dreams. We want to help. We understand that most people will be Man. United fans or City fans or whatever they want to be, but we want to be their other team. We want to be the local team. We want youngsters to support us. We want to make it affordable for families. We want to make it a good day out with an environment that's value for money. We don't want to rip people off. We want to keep it at a nice level for people to go. You might go and watch

United whenever you can afford to do it. You might go and watch City whenever you can afford to do it. But you can come down and watch us every week and bring the family. You never know, they could be a league team within five or six years, and what a great journey that'd be for all the people who come along with us and who can say, 'We were there at the start.'

People probably did think it was a publicity stunt at the beginning and you can't blame them. We're five lads who own a non-league club and then start doing a documentary about it, and you think, 'Oh, it's just self-promotion.' But it's not. We've not taken out of the club. We've only put into it. No matter what we've done externally it's gone back into the club. We've brought better players, better contracts, better managers and better infrastructure. We're putting more facilities into the project. We're hoping to bring an academy out soon to give a chance to young people in the area. We want to bring jobs to the area. It's important to us. It's really important, and hopefully the more we can communicate that, then the more fans can go away and tell other people, because it's important to us to run the club right and not just be a bit of a flash in the pan story. We want it to be successful for years and years and years. I want to sit there with my grandkids and tell everybody how I helped us get to where we are.

***

Gary:

We were getting stronger and we were getting more powerful, and Workington had stopped attacking. I always think if teams stop attacking, they're in trouble. It's almost like the boxer who stops punching. They'd stopped counter-attacking. They were getting pushed back against the ropes and I wondered whether it would drop for us. I wondered whether it would go in. When it did, you almost knew what was going to happen. You knew it was inevitable that we were going to go and score again. It has been that type of club for two years. It has that little bit of something going for it, that spirit in the dressing room. You just knew there was going to be a late winner.

In fact, I was more confident in the second half against Workington than I was against Ashton United in the semis. I had very little faith against Ashton. I thought they were well organised, strong – I thought they'd sorted us out. They got stronger as the game went on and we got weaker, and then when we got to extra time we found a new lease of life. Seddon scored an unbelievable goal and that just sorted the game. But I had very little faith that night. Something didn't feel right. There wasn't a great atmosphere. There wasn't a great feeling in the ground. The crowd was a bit flat against Ashton, compared to Workington and the Cup tie against Notts County. That night, against Notts County, was absolutely unbelievable. That was one of the best moments I've had in football for I don't know how long. It really was a spine-tingling night.

We want to take this club as high as we possibly can from the eighth tier of football. We could have taken over a League One club and made it a lot easier for ourselves. We've gone right down to the bottom to come up, because we wanted a club that meant something to us, which we could mould in our style, in our way, in how we think. I generally believe at the moment that the club is representative of what we are. The managers are representative of what we are: they're fighters, they're tough; they want players to give their all, they want them to come off the pitch having given absolutely every last breath of energy. We want them to try to play the most aggressive, passionate football possible. We want them to love the club. All these things that we have and we want I think have been created at Salford: by the committee, the managers, everyone.

In the first 18 months we wanted to improve the team and raise awareness of the club and the city. I'd have to say that those goals have been achieved. I think now, the fact that we've accelerated the promotions quicker than we thought, we're now talking about spending significant money on Moor Lane, which was quicker than we expected. The budget, in the third year in the Conference North, is going to be a lot higher than we ever would have imagined. I think football does move. It does catch you by surprise. We always knew that there would have to be periods where some would be involved, some wouldn't be involved, and I feel at the moment the more attention the club gets from us, the more it has a chance of success. We're not responsible for the success in terms of delivery, but I do think we've set the tone of the club in terms of being there and generating excitement behind it. We always have to maintain our passion for this club or else other people will lose it. And ultimately the committee of the club have delivered for us in two years. The team and the management have delivered for us in two years. I might be wrong, but it seems like what could have been a difficult transition, has gone reasonably well. What might have been us coming in and jettisoning the committee, hasn't turned out like that. The heart of the committee is still with us. You still see Barbara, you still see Dave. A lot of the same principals you still see. And I'm proud of most of that really.

Me, Butty, Giggsy and Scholesy came here three years ago for a game and it was almost like watching a team on the park. There were 174 people in the ground and that defeat, 3-0 to Curzon Ashton, was a terrible standard. There was no sort of spirit in the ground really. In fact the day I went, when we'd agreed to take over and no-one else knew at the time, I did wonder, 'What the hell are we doing here? Are we doing the right thing?' It was always going to be a massive challenge. It was an uphill struggle but honestly what's been created in two years, with the committee, the managers and the players, is nothing short of a miracle. Honestly it is. People will sit there and say, 'Oh it's money.' But to go from 174 to 800 people, and at big games 2,000 people at the gate; to get to the second round of the FA Cup; to have two successive promotions. Of course money's been a factor, but actually it's more about the spirit which has been created.

It's funny, I was always a big celebrator of goals at United. And as a fan I would celebrate. But in this last couple of years, I can only really remember Anthony Martial's goal against Liverpool and Marcus Rashford's goal against West Ham, when he bent it in the corner. The most I've jumped up in the last two years is watching Salford. I think that moment when Jordan scored, we were cheering like fans. We were properly jumping up and down. We're fans of the club. We've come to love the club as fans of the club and we desperately want them to win.

***

Phil:

My son said to me the other day, you know your results go on *Sky Sports News* now? Salford, all of a sudden, are on *Football Manager*. You know what I mean? These are little things, but they're massive for me. Jeff Stelling on Sky is going to be reading out Salford City results. We're still a million miles away. I think the next two years will be our toughest. They always are. But like I said to you at the start, it's about the momentum. And it's building. It's building.

Gareth Seddon's contract wasn't renewed at the end of the 2015-16 season and he has since signed for Ramsbottom Town in the Evo-Stik First Division North.

Gary Stopforth turned down the chance to stay on at the end of 2015-16 season and joined Stockport County in National League North, the same division Salford are in.

Danny Webber retired at the end of the 2015-16 season and is now working as a player's agent with Platinum One.

Captain Chris Lynch moved to Australia in the summer of 2016 to join Murray United in the National Premier League, a semi-professional team in Victoria.

ACKNOWLEDGEMENTS

To Gary, Phil, Nicky, Ryan and Paul. Thank you for giving me the opportunity to write this book and for your help checking details, answering calls and generally being available above and beyond. Amidst all the hard work, it's been a genuine pleasure.

Everyone at Salford City has been generous in their welcome and with their time. But some have been exceptionally helpful: Dave Russell, for the guided tours of Salford and giving me a sense of the city's civic pride and history; Karen Baird, for talking me through the ups and downs of running the club; Frank McCauley, for reading drafts, correcting my history, and generally improving the words; and Babs and Terry Gaskill, for making the finest pie and mash north of Watford and for your hospitality.

Non-league football is meant to be a hard, tough world but the welcome I received from players and staff was incredibly warm. Thank you for allowing me in, even when games had gone badly and times were difficult.

James Poole, Steve Howson, Val McCarthy and Steve Phillips brought me into the group on that first coach journey and took an interest throughout. Your friendship and observations helped to make this book. Danny Webber, Gareth Seddon and Gary Stopforth were easy and enjoyable interviews. Good luck in your new clubs and ventures.

Jordan Hulme and Stephen O'Halloran: thank you for the music. And the dance.

And, of course, Bernard and Jonno. Your willingness to share the good and the bad brought this book to life. Thank you for your company, insights, lifts to and from games and for bringing me into the group.

Thanks also to Di Law, for assiduously smoothing over problems and keeping me amused with inadvertent text messages; to David Luxton and Rebecca Winfield, for doing the tricky stuff; to Lee Clayton, Alison Kervin and Mike Richards, for your support; to Charlotte Macdonald, for sitting through revisions of the text and making sense of it all; and to Albert DePetrillo, for nudging me gently in the right direction and somehow creating order from the chaos.

To Dad. Mum would be proud.

Lastly, to Helen, Oliver and Anna. For bearing with all the late nights, early mornings, missed play times and days away. You sustain me. This is for you.

INDEX